CLASSIC GERMAN BAKING

CLASSIC GERMAN BAKING

THE VERY BEST RECIPES FOR TRADITIONAL FAVORITES,
FROM PFEFFERNÜSSE TO STREUSELKUCHEN

Luisa Weiss

photographs by Aubrie Pick

TEN SPEED PRESS
Berkeley

For Hugo

Backe, backe Kuchen,
der Bäcker hat gerufen.
Wer will guten Kuchen machen,
der muss haben sieben Sachen,
Eier und Schmalz,
Zucker und Salz,
Milch und Mehl,
Safran macht den Kuchen gehl!
Schieb, schieb in den Ofen 'nein.
Hach, was wird das für ein leck'rer Kuchen sein!

—German children's song,
amended by Kerstin Beuchel

CONTENTS

ACKNOWLEDGMENTS

There is not enough gratitude in the world for the one person who truly helped bring this book into the world, Maja Welker. She showed up one day to help and had made herself completely indispensable by the next. Maja's dedication and hard work, creativity and skill, unflagging cheer and positivity, and humor and kindness are unparalleled. I couldn't have written this book without her. I'm also honored and grateful that she shared her family recipes with us.

At Ten Speed Press, many thanks to Aaron Wehner for being persistent and for believing in me. Thank you to Julie Bennett for her guidance, and to my sharp and sensitive editor, Lorena Jones. It was an honor to work with you. Thank you to designer Ashley Lima and to photographer Aubrie Pick, for the luminous photography and for capturing my Berlin so beautifully. Thanks, too, to illustrator Anna Ropalo.

A huge thank-you, as ever, to my intrepid and supportive agent, Brettne Bloom, at The Book Group. I am so grateful to know you and have you in my corner.

For lending me cookbooks, passing on recipes, giving me recipe advice, or simply being a source of inspiration, many thanks to Carmit Erez, Lutz Geissler, Stefanie Herberth, Elisabeth Hutzelmann-Hochreiter, Stephanie Levy, Cherie Millns, Deb Perelman, Meike Peters, Regine Schneider, Werner Schlötke, Katharina Seiser, Franziska Warkotz, Bertram Welker, Ann Wertheimer, and Meeta Khurana Wolff.

Thank you to Liana Krissoff for going above and beyond the call of duty as a recipe tester and a sounding board. I am so grateful.

Thank you to Maria Speck for believing in me and in this book from the start, and for your wise counsel.

Thank you to Shauna Sever Webb for your advice, assistance, and friendship. One day I'll get to hug you in person, and I can't wait.

Thank you to Diana Henry and David Lebovitz, whose enthusiasm and encouragement helped me get going at the beginning and kept me buoyed throughout.

Thank you to my army of testers: Sarah Abrams, Darlene Backer, Hilary Burke, Victoria Carr, Michelle Friedman, Maya Gonzales, Dervla Kelly, Giulia Pines Kersthold, Christina Kolb, Stacy Ladenburger, Tim Mazurek, Lily Morris, Adelaide Müller, Jennifer Murch, Karolina Palmer, Dave Pernal, Gemma Saylor, Kate Schirg, Gayle Squires, Kirsten Wandschneider, Erika Weiss, and Hillary Wexler.

To all my dear Berlin friends who came to pick up cakes, cookies, bread, and tortes; tell me what I needed to change; and cheer me on in the process: Katie Cantwell, Joanna Gröning and Julian Rönsch, Susanne Kaufhold and Kim Klakow, Sandy Chen Kluth, the Joly-Nelson family, Sylee Gore, Joe Diliberto and Adriano Vitale, Florian Duijsens, Anna Winger, Gisela Williams, and Susanne Opel, thank you.

Thank you to Jiffer Bourguignon and Ingo Zamperoni, my very own confectioners' sugar mules. Your help at the last minute was crucial and so appreciated.

Thank you to Heidi Swanson for the pep talk and brilliant advice at the eleventh hour.

An enormous debt of gratitude goes to my followers on Instagram, who came along for the #germanbakingbook ride, and who were amazing cheerleaders all throughout the eighteen-month testing phase. Some of you I know in person, most of you I don't, but I cannot overstate how much your support kept me going. You were the day-to-day wind beneath my baking wings.

Thank you to KitchenAid Europe for the loan of an artisan stand mixer, which I put to good use almost every day for eighteen months and which never wavered once, not even in the face of a ten-minute-beaten *Gugelhupf* batter.

Thank you to my family—Letizia Weiss, Richard Weiss, Susan Ernst, and Kerstin Beuchel—who tested recipes, tasted countless cakes and cookies, provided epigraph inspiration, and were excellent grandparents while I kept working.

Thank you to Joan Klakow for all the recipes, for all the stories, and for paving the road of my life with *Springerle*, *Leckerli*, and so much love.

Thank you to my husband, Max, who is always so supportive of my work; who toted countless leftover cakes, tortes, and batches of cookies to his office so that they wouldn't go to waste; and who happily took on solo weekends with our son so that I could keep on writing and baking.

And finally, thank you to my darling Hugo, my cake lover, my cookie eater, my sweet little monkey, who makes every day on this earth brighter and funnier. This book is for you. I hope it captures the flavors of your happiest childhood memories.

INTRODUCTION

I must confess that I used to worry, when contemplating the subject of German baking and the hefty book I planned to write, that you might consider me at first glance an improbable authority on the subject. After all, I'm half Italian, half American. I have no German grandmother who passed her recipes down to me. I grew up making *pollo ai peperoni* at my mother's knee and baked beans at my father's. And no one in my direct bloodline has ever liked to bake.

But I was born in Berlin—and even though our home there (and later, in Boston) was a little bubble of Italian and American culture and food, I did grow up eating warm, iced *Streuselschnecken* from the bakery on the way to school and always looked forward to slicing into the crisp white *Brötchen* in our Saturday morning bread basket and the fragrant, yeasty, fruit-topped *Kuchen* our friends would serve for afternoon tea. For me, Christmas isn't complete without chewy *Lebkuchen* coated in a thin layer of chocolate, and Easter can't be properly celebrated without a braided and burnished loaf of raisin-studded bread on the table.

I discovered at a very young age that I loved to bake. And I was encouraged by our dear family friend Joan whose Christmas cookies and yeasted celebration breads are still my gold standard, though in the meantime I also have German in-laws and other German and Austrian friends whose baking and dedication to the craft inspire me.

Six years ago, I moved back to Berlin after a decade in New York. I married into a family of talented bakers from Saxony, known across Germany as the source of some of its most famous and beloved pastries, such as *Stollen* and *Eierschecke*, a double-layered cheesecake baked on a thin yeasted crust. And I began to understand that German baking not only forms the foundation on which much of America's baking tradition is based, but also functions as a touchstone of quality around the world. From doughnuts to rye breads, Christmas cookies to cream-filled tortes, *Streusel*-topped coffee cakes to thin and crackling *Strudel*, so many of our favorites have their origins in Germany (and neighboring Austria, the birthplace of *Linzertorte*, *Gugelhupf*, and *Strudel*, among other important pastries).

I also discovered that recipes for those world-famous cakes, cookies, and sweet breads are still passed down from one generation to the next here to a degree that I haven't seen anywhere else. Most people I know still bake from old, tattered cookbooks with onionskin pages printed in *Fraktur* lettering because that's what their grandmothers swore by. Meanwhile, many of the baking books published in recent years in Germany have reflected a prevailing interest in French or American recipes—tarts, brownies, macaroons, and cupcakes—rather than the country's own baking traditions.

Cakes and other sweet treats are a hugely important part of German culture. My father-in-law, for example, still takes an afternoon break for coffee and cake *every single day* at his auto shop, in the time-honored German tradition. At 3:00 PM sharp he and his colleagues put down their tools, wipe off their grease-stained hands, and troop across the street to their local bakery, where they order fat slices of cake—plum *Streusel* on a yeasted crust, maybe, or cheesecake made with grainy *Quark*, or *Kranzkuchen*, a flaky braided pastry stuffed with almond paste and raisins—to eat as they sip their cups of coffee. And every single weekend, my mother-in-law, like *her* mother-in-law in Saxony, bakes one or two cakes (or more) for their weekend afternoon snack.

And they're not alone. Across the country people are still baking tray-size cakes for the Sunday afternoon *Kaffeezeit* (coffee time) with their friends and family, and many still begin to prepare elaborate cookie doughs and confections in mid-November, if not earlier, for the Advent season. These traditions are deeply entrenched here, which explains the annual outcry when mass-produced *Lebkuchen* and *Stollen* flood grocery stores in late August and early September.

I've always had a soft spot for German cakes and breads. But without a German grandmother's time-tested recipes to use, it can actually be challenging to find good recipes to re-create all those delicious *Kuchen*, *Brote*, and *Kekse*. With this book, I've not only collected the recipes I think are integral to the tradition, and all that I find deeply delicious or interesting or wonderful, but I've also tested them many times over, getting them just right for the home kitchen. There are recipes here for every skill set—from the baking challenged to the seasoned pro. And there are recipes here for any occasion—Christmas and Easter, birthdays, or just a happy Sunday afternoon.

Because I am a traditionalist, you won't find much newfangled stuff included. I adore old-fashioned and time-tested recipes. The majority of the treats in this book have been made the same way for many decades if not centuries.

Unlike American or English baking, German and Austrian recipes aren't always quick and easy. There is a heavy reliance on yeast, which scares some people, though I promise it shouldn't. I'll hold your hand all the way through until you agree with me. And while getting *Strudel* dough so thin that you can read a newspaper through it can be nerve-wracking at first, it's much easier than it seems. The Christmas chapter is partially an exercise in patience, as many of the cookies in it require ripening times of a few days or weeks in order to be really delicious, while old-fashioned *Lebkuchen* dough needs to rest for a couple months before being baked.

But your patience and rigor will be rewarded many times over, and I very much hope you also take away a broad education in what I like to call the original slow food. In any case, I've made sure to include many recipes that will provide almost instant gratification, too.

It is my hope that as you learn to bake German treats with this book, you will also incorporate some of my favorite German traditions into your life, like pausing for a gathering of friends and coffee on a weekend afternoon with at least two cakes to share, or creating your very own Advent *bunter Teller*, a jumble of different Christmas cookies offered to guests during the holiday season.

All of the recipes in the book were tested multiple times in my Berlin kitchen, and most were also tested in American kitchens by my recipe testers. I did my best to eliminate too much variation in the results, but always keep in mind that the calibration of temperature can vary from oven to oven, that your altitude affects the things you bake, and that even the moisture in the air on a cold or rainy day can make a yeast dough less puffy or a meringue weepy. Please take a minute to read through the Pantry Ingredients and Equipment sections for important notes on confectioners' sugar, the proper consistency of *Quark*, how to measure flour, what a poppy-seed grinder is for, and other essential information that you'll need to get your start in the German sweet kitchen.

Some of the cups and spoons measurements in this book may seem fussy. In the course of my recipe development and testing, I found that the common conversions from standard cup and spoon measurements to metric weight and volume measurements (and vice versa) were not as precise as I believe they must be to produce consistent and excellent results. As a result, I developed the recipes with precision as my standard. I hope that this precision will not only help you produce excellent baked goods, but that it will also make you feel confident as you embark on your German baking journey.

PANTRY INGREDIENTS

ALMOND PASTE AND MARZIPAN Almond paste is the English term for what Germans called *Marzipanrohmasse*, which is nothing more than almonds and sugar processed together so finely that they turn to paste. Marzipan, by contrast, is almond paste mixed with more sugar, rose water, and other flavorings. In this book, I exclusively call for almond paste, because it has fewer additives than marzipan. Good store-bought almond paste is widely available in the United States, but to make your own, see page 264.

APPLES The apples I like best for baking are compact and not too crisp, with a good balance of sweetness and tartness. Apples like this not only hold their shape during baking but also keep a fresh, puckery flavor even when baked with copious amounts of sugar and butter. In Germany, an easily found and reliable baking apple is the Golden Delicious variety, but in the United States, Golden Delicious apples can be cottony and soft. Choose apples that you also enjoy eating and that have a good, firm texture (soft apples like McIntosh have a hard time keeping their shape during baking). Heirloom apples are your best bet for both flavor and texture.

APRICOT JAM Apricot jam is often used as a glaze for yeasted sweet breads and delicate tortes. In German, it even has its own verb–*aprikotieren*, which means "to glaze with hot apricot jam." When used as a glaze or filling, apricot jam should be as smooth as possible, with no lumps of fruit. D'Arbo, the Austrian jam maker, sells a pureed apricot jam (the label should specify that it is *fein passiert*, or mesh sieved), but if you can't find that near you, use an immersion blender to puree your apricot preserves. Or you can push them through a fine-mesh sieve for a smooth, lump-free jam.

BAKER'S AMMONIA (AMMONIUM CARBONATE) Baker's ammonia is an old-fashioned leaven that reacts with heat to release strong-smelling gases whose propulsion leavens baked goods. Cookies made with baker's ammonia have a specific kind of airy texture that baking powder can't achieve, an especially even rise, and an almost honeycombed crumb; they are overall very light and crisp. Baker's ammonia also helps cookies keep their shape in the oven, so that instead of spreading, they propel upward. If you open the oven door to rotate a pan of cookies leavened with baker's ammonia halfway through baking, your eyes might sting from the gases. But don't worry; the gases evaporate as the baked goods cool, leaving behind no trace. Baker's ammonia, also known as ammonium carbonate, can be found online and at well-stocked specialty stores.

BUTTER The recipes in this book were developed exclusively with high-fat European-style butter. By law, American butter contains 80 percent butterfat, while European and European-style butters contain anywhere from 82 percent to 86 percent butterfat. Though this difference of a few percentage points may seem small, it makes a big difference in flavor, as well as the flakiness of pastry, the richness of cookie dough, and the moisture of cakes. If it is no hardship for you to buy that style of butter, then please use it for all the recipes in this book. Some of the recipes in the book will also work with regular American butter, but many must be made with high-fat butter to achieve the intended results. I have noted in the recipes when it is crucial to use high-fat butter.

I call for butter that is cold (straight from the refrigerator), softened (taken out of the refrigerator 1 hour before using), or at room temperature (butter that has been out for at least 6 hours and is quite soft). In my kitchen, I always have both room-temperature butter–stored in a butter keeper–which we use for toast and sandwiches, as well as for baking, and butter stored in the refrigerator, so that I never have to wait if I get the baking itch. I bake only with unsalted butter, which allows me to control the seasoning of each recipe.

CANDIED CITRON PEEL AND ORANGE PEEL Candied citrus peels are essential in many German, Austrian, and Swiss celebration breads and Christmas cookies. Their gently bittersweet flavor and chewy texture can be polarizing: some people really can't stand candied peel. Or more specifically, some people really can't stand the slightly medicinal flavor of citron, which is a thick-skinned citrus fruit also known as *cedro* in Italian and *cédrat* in French. In the recipes in this book, the candied peel is almost always chopped very finely, and I find it adds a nice complexity of flavor. If you don't like candied citron, replace it with extra candied orange peel. For information on where to buy candied citron peel and candied orange peel, see Sources (page 270).

CONFECTIONERS' SUGAR Confectioners' sugar can vary widely by weight, from 100 to 140 grams per cup, depending on which anti-caking agent was used and how much of it. I recommend reading the label on your confectioners' sugar carefully and measuring it by weight.

EGGS The recipes in this book were developed with European size M eggs, which are equivalent to large eggs in the United States.

FLOUR To avoid major discrepancies in flour quantities when using cup measurements, do not scoop flour from the canister with a measuring cup. Rather, aerate the flour with a spoon once or twice, and then spoon flour into your measuring cup, leveling it with a knife. This measuring method should be used for all the flours in this book, from all-purpose to whole wheat to rye to spelt.

FRESH YEAST Fresh yeast, also known as cake yeast, comes in foil-wrapped cubes and can be found in the refrigerated sections of some supermarkets. Fresh yeast can be hard to find in some parts of the United States, which is a shame because it is a truly excellent leaven and gives yeasted cakes and breads a wonderfully puffy texture and flavor. I urge you to seek it out where you live. It must be dissolved in lukewarm liquid before being used. "Lukewarm" means that you should be able to comfortably hold your finger in the slightly warmed liquid.

INSTANT YEAST As an alternative to fresh yeast, I suggest using instant yeast, which is also known as bread-machine yeast and is different from active dry yeast. Instant yeast has smaller granules than active dry yeast and is not dissolved in liquid (called "proofing") before using, so it can be added directly to the dry ingredients. I suggest buying a jar of instant yeast (Red Star and SAF are good brands) and storing it in your refrigerator. I do not recommend using active dry yeast; I find it unnecessarily fussy to use and not as reliable as fresh or instant yeast. Of course, if you are an experienced baker and very comfortable with substituting active dry yeast for instant or fresh yeast, you should feel free to use it. But for everyone else, I recommend sticking to instant or fresh yeast.

Each recipe that calls for fresh yeast also has the equivalent in instant yeast. The quantity differs slightly from recipe to recipe based on the other ingredients in the recipe. However, a rule of thumb is that 1/3 ounce/10g of fresh yeast equals 1/2 teaspoon of instant; 3/4 ounce/20g of fresh yeast equals 1 teaspoon of instant; and 1 1/2 ounces/42g of fresh yeast equals 2 teaspoons of instant. The more you learn to bake with fresh and instant yeast, the more you can start to fiddle with these numbers. I prefer baked goods with minimal amounts of yeast because I think they taste better, so I try to keep the amount I use in a recipe to a minimum wherever I can. But you may find that you like a yeastier flavor. Baking with yeast is all about practice.

LEMONS Grated lemon peel is an indispensable ingredient in this book. I call for organic lemons throughout, because it is less likely that they have been treated with chemicals or wax. If you have a source of untreated conventional lemons, by all means use those instead. No matter what kind of lemon you use, they should always be washed before the peel is used.

LINGONBERRY PRESERVES Lingonberries are called *Preiselbeeren* in Germany and are often confused with American cranberries there, though the two berries are quite different. Lingonberries are smaller and less aggressively sour than cranberries. They are required in the *Heidjertorte* (page 119) and can be found at well-stocked gourmet markets (where they are often sold as Swedish lingonberries), most IKEA stores, and online (see Sources, page 270).

NUTS German, Austrian, and Swiss baking rely heavily on nuts—usually almonds, hazelnuts, and walnuts—that are either ground, chopped, sliced, or blanched. Buy your nuts in bulk at a store with heavy turnover so that you can be guaranteed freshness, not rancidity.

To blanch whole almonds, place them in a heatproof bowl and cover with boiling water. Let sit for 10 minutes, and then drain off the water. The almond skin will be quite loose and can be either pushed or scraped off.

To skin hazelnuts, place them on a baking sheet in a single layer and roast for 10 to 15 minutes at 350°F/180°C. Spread out a clean kitchen towel and dump the roasted hazelnuts on top. Gather the towel up and rub vigorously, which will skin most of the nuts. (Don't worry about getting them perfectly skinned.) The benefit of the roasting method is that it gives hazelnuts a much richer, toastier flavor.

To grind any kind of nut, place room-temperature whole ones in a small food processor and pulse until they're mostly broken down, and then process until a fine powder emerges. If the nuts were soaked in hot water or roasted before being ground, they must be completely dried and cooled before processing or they risk turning to paste in the food processor. You can, however, buy preground almond meal or hazelnut meal for recipes in which ground almonds or hazelnuts are called for.

PEARL SUGAR Crunchy, snow-white, and able to withstand high oven temperatures without melting, pearl sugar is a gorgeous finishing sugar that is used regularly in European baking. In this book, the *Heidesand* (page 15) and *Nussstangen* (page 238) cookies are edged or topped with pearl sugar, and the *Rosinenzopf* (page 213) is spangled with it. It can't really be replaced by granulated sugar, which is too fine to keep from melting at high temperatures.

PFLAUMENMUS Dark, rich, and sticky, *Pflaumenmus* is a long-cooked plum butter subtly flavored with warm spices and only lightly sweetened. Also known as *Powidl* in Austria, it is an essential ingredient in the Austrian *Lebkuchen-Powidltatschkerln* (page 224) and the northern German *Friesentorte* (page 122). To make your own, see page 265. Otherwise, see Sources (page 270) for where to buy it.

POPPY SEEDS Poppy seeds, the tiny seeds of the opium poppy, are used in great quantities in central European baking. If your only exposure to poppy seeds has been as a light sprinkling on bagels, you may think they don't have much flavor at all. But in central Europe, poppy seeds are processed into thick and textured cake fillings, braided into sweet wreaths of bread, stuffed into dumplings, and baked up into light, flourless tortes. In such concentrated quantities, their flavor is unique and difficult to describe—slightly stony, a little dusty, faintly bitter, and hauntingly delicious. Poppy seeds have a high oil content, so they go rancid relatively quickly. Buy them at a store with high turnover and, if you don't use them up right away, refrigerate them or place them in the freezer at home. In this book, the poppy seeds must always be ground before using (except for when they are used as a topping, as with the *Mohnhörnchen* on page 175). This cracks their hard hulls and releases their essential oils, turning the dry seeds into a gravelly, fragrant mass. For maximum freshness and to guard against rancidity, it is best to grind your own poppy seeds. However, I do include two reliable sources for ground poppy seeds. For more information on grinding poppy seeds, see the Equipment section (page 11). For where to buy whole and ground poppy seeds, see Sources (page 270).

POTASSIUM CARBONATE OR POTASH Potash is an old-fashioned leaven that works by reacting with moisture to create carbon dioxide. Potash's use was far more widespread before baking powder was invented in the nineteenth century. It is particularly good at leavening stiff, heavy dough, like honey-based *Lebkuchen* dough (page 218). It also develops at a slow pace, which makes it an ideal candidate for leavening dough that must ripen for a long time at room temperature. Cookies made with potash have a particularly light and crisp texture. Unlike baker's ammonia, which helps cookies propel upward during baking, cookies made with potash spread a bit, so care must be given to leave enough space between them before baking. Potash is best dissolved in a small amount of liquid before being added to dough. Potash can be purchased at nuts.com and edelweissimports.com (where it is listed under its German name, *Pottasche*).

QUARK *Quark*, a sour, fresh cheese that is often compared—erroneously, in my opinion—to ricotta, is essential to the German kitchen. *Quark* is sourer than ricotta and lighter, too, unless you are lucky enough to find a source for *Sahnequark* (cream *Quark*), in which case you should simply drizzle it with a little honey or fold in fresh berries, and then dig in for a decadent treat.

In Germany, plain *Quark* is divided into four fat categories: 0 percent, 20 percent, 40 percent, and the aforementioned *Sahnequark*. *Quark* is used as a breakfast spread, either seasoned with chives or left plain and topped with a layer of jam; dolloped next to boiled potatoes with a drizzle of flaxseed oil for a simple dinner; whipped with eggs and sugar and baked into cheesecake; and kneaded into bread doughs and sweetened yeasted cake batters, among many other preparations. There's no way to overstate its importance in German baking.

Quark for baking should be relatively firm and creamy (it loosens considerably after whisking). When first dumped into a bowl, it should hold its shape. If your store-bought *Quark* is creamier than that and cannot hold its shape before whisking, scrape it into a fine-mesh sieve set over a bowl or pot and let it drain for a few hours. To make your own *Quark*, see page 264. To purchase *Quark* in the United States, see Sources (page 270).

REDCURRANT JELLY This sweet-tart jelly is essential in the *Mohntorte* (page 126). It can be difficult to find, but its sour profile holds its own against sweet and delicate pastry, which makes it worth seeking out. In a pinch, you can substitute raspberry or apricot jam.

SALT The recipes in this book were all tested with fine sea salt. If you use iodized salt, you should reduce the amount of salt called for in each recipe.

SOUR CHERRIES Canned or preserved whole sour cherries in sugar water are as common as applesauce in Germany and play a starring role in *Kirschstreuselkuchen* (page 61), *Schwarzwälder Kirschtorte* (page 123), and *Lottchen's Kirschkuchen* (page 57), among others. In the United States they can be more difficult to find, but Eastern European markets are a good place to start. For online sources, see page 270.

SPECK OR SCHINKENSPECK *Speck* is cured, cold-smoked bacon that is used widely in German cooking. It is usually sold in thick slabs, to be cut up into batons or cubes. *Schinkenspeck* is a very lean cured ham that is either dry-aged or smoked after curing. It has next to no visible fat. Cubed or diced American slab bacon can be substituted for *Speck*, but keep in mind that it has a different flavor because of the different wood used in smoking. To find *Speck* or *Schinkenspeck*, start by looking at local German or Italian delis in your area. Otherwise, see page 270 for online sources.

VANILLA As vanilla extract is largely unavailable in Europe, traditional German baking relies on *Vanillezucker* (vanilla sugar) when a vanilla flavor is desired. I've adapted almost all of the recipes to use pure vanilla extract instead, as that is the common vanilla flavoring agent in the United States, but a few recipes in the book require vanilla sugar, a recipe for which is on page 267.

EQUIPMENT

BAKING PANS I recommend having an assortment of 9- and 10-inch/23 and 25cm round pans for the recipes in this book. A 9-inch/23cm springform pan is an essential for most of the round cakes in this book (mine happens to be nonstick, though I don't think that's required), while a 10-inch/25cm round cake pan is required for some of the savory recipes and a few of the tortes. Most German sheet cakes are made to be baking sheet–size, which is great if you have a crowd to feed or if you like leftovers, but for practical everyday purposes, I found a 9 by 13-inch/23 by 33cm rectangular metal baking pan a more useful size and adapted the recipes accordingly.

BAKING SHEETS The baking sheets called for in this book are either for baking cookies or for making cakes like the sponge cakes on pages 63 and 66 or the *Marillenfleck* on page 69. So the baking sheets should be rimmed. Do not use a jelly-roll pan, which is too small. I recommend having at least two baking sheets when making cookies, so that you can alternate preparing cookies and baking them.

COOKIE CUTTERS AND MOLDS You'll need a small assortment of cookie cutters for the recipes in this book: a 1½-inch/4cm star cutter for the *Zimtsterne* (page 241), a 2-inch/5cm heart-shaped one for the *Basler Brunsli* (page 243), a 2-inch/5cm crescent-shaped cutter for the *Zedernbrot* (page 237), a 3-inch/8cm round or oval cutter for the *Lebkuchen-Powidltatschkerln* (page 224), and a rectangular one for the *Butterkekse* (page 14). I discuss carved *Spekulatius* and *Springerle* molds on pages 231 and 234. I find them essential for *Springerle*, less so for *Spekulatius*.

COTTON OR LINEN KITCHEN TOWELS OR DISHCLOTHS All yeasted dough must rest, covered, multiple times at room temperature in order to rise. I like to use cotton or linen kitchen towels rather than plastic wrap, because they let the dough breathe better and because they don't stick to the dough. A kitchen towel is also essential for rolling out *Strudel* dough and for rolling up sponge cake. I like to have an assortment of at least four or five clean towels in the kitchen at any time. Wash them with a fragrance-free detergent so that there is no danger of unwanted scents seeping into your baked goods.

ELECTRIC MIXER An electric mixer that includes a whisk attachment is essential for cake batters, meringues, and cookie doughs.

ELECTRIC SCALE A simple electric scale is an endlessly useful thing in the kitchen. These inexpensive and easy to use scales are very helpful when dividing dough into equal pieces for rolls or cookies, not to mention when using metric cookbooks. There are many different reliable brands to choose from these days.

FOOD PROCESSOR This appliance is indispensable for chopping or grinding nuts into meal, making *Vanillezucker* (page 267), and making *Marzipanrohmasse* (page 264). I also use it for chopping candied peel and grinding chocolate.

GUGELHUPF PAN A *Gugelhupf* pan is higher and narrower than a Bundt, which is more common in the United States. It is the signature pan of the Austrian yeasted *Gugelhupf* (page 95) but is also the cake pan I use for the *Marmorkuchen* (page 72) and *Marmorierter Mohnkuchen* (page 74). It is not essential—if you have a Bundt pan, it's fine to use it instead of the *Gugelhupf* pan, though keep in mind that the baking time will be affected (start checking about 15 minutes before the end of the given baking time) and that your finished cake will not be as high as it would be if baked in a *Gugelhupf* pan. But if you'd like to find one, Fox Run and Nordic Ware make them (called *Kugelhopf* pans).

MEASURING TAPE I keep a small, flexible measuring tape in my kitchen utensil drawer, which I use to measure everything from the size of pulled-out *Strudel* dough to the length of plaited sweet breads to the thickness of rolled-out cookie dough.

MICROPLANE GRATER The sharp files on these graters can't be beat for grating orange and lemon peels and nutmeg. I recommend having at least two—one with smaller files for citrus peels and nutmeg and one with larger files for chocolate or cheese.

MIXING BOWLS When a recipe has various elements, it is helpful to have enough vessels for everything. I recommend having at least 3 to 6 bowls of varying sizes. I like stainless steel bowls and ceramic bowls because they are nonreactive and easy to clean.

PARCHMENT PAPER AND SILICONE LINERS A reusable silicone baking sheet liner is a great item to have if you bake a lot of cookies, as it's more environmentally friendly than using a fresh sheet of parchment paper each time you bake. That said, I find parchment paper the only way to go for lining cake pans, not only to prevent sticking, but also so that I can use the paper as a sling to remove a cake from its pan after baking. A nice trick for getting a yeasted dough to fit a parchment paper–lined pan is to put the paper in the pan and then firmly run your fingers around the edges of the bottom, so that the paper takes on an imprint of the pan. Then remove the paper from the pan and place it on your workspace. The imprint of the pan will still be visible. Now you can set your dough in the middle of the paper and roll it out to fit the pan shape precisely before transferring the paper and dough to the pan.

PASTRY BAG WITH ASSORTED TIPS A pastry bag with an assortment of decorative tips is useful when finishing a cream-covered torte, like the *Schwarzwälder Kirschtorte* (page 123) or the *Heidjertorte* (page 119), but it's also a help when piping out cookie batter, like the *Löffelbiskuit* (page 27) or the *Russisch Brot* (page 26). A few different sizes of star tips and round tips will be enough.

PASTRY BRUSHES You'll need a couple—for brushing *Strudel* with butter or painting *Pfeffernüsse* with glaze, for example. I like brushes with natural bristles.

POPPY-SEED GRINDER Poppy seeds must be ground to crack their tiny little hulls and unfold their particular fragrance and flavor before they can be used in any of the recipes in this book, with the exception of the *Mohnhörnchen* (page 175), where the seeds are just a garnish. To grind poppy seeds, you must use a hand-cranked grinder, an electric coffee or spice grinder, or a high-powered blender like a Vitamix. A food processor, immersion blender, or regular blender will not be able to grind poppy seeds. Hand-cranked grinders can be expensive, but they can be used to grind nuts and grains as well, which may justify the cost. A very nice model is sold at hungariandeli.com. I own a Westmark grinder that can be purchased at edelweissimports.com. To grind the seeds in a coffee or spice grinder, run a handful of rice kernels through the grinder first to clean it thoroughly. Discard the ground rice, and you are set for the poppy seeds. To grind poppy seeds in a high-powered blender, place the seeds in the regular container and grind at medium speed for about 1 minute.

ROLLING PIN I long ago gave up my handled rolling pin in favor of a long, tapered pin (known as a French rolling pin), which I find handier to use, easier to clean, and better for rolling out things like *Strudel*.

SILICONE SPATULAS Scraping the last dregs of batter out of a bowl, getting to the nooks and crannies of a near-empty jam jar, and folding egg whites all require a good silicone spatula. I recommend having several different sizes.

STAND MIXER A stand mixer—which can have any number of beater attachments, such as a dough hook, a whisk, or a flat beater—is required for only a handful of recipes in this book, notably the *Gugelhupf* (page 95), the *Roggenbrötchen* (page 182), and the *Seelen* (page 177), which are all very wet yeast doughs that must be beaten for 5 to 10 minutes before being proofed. In all the other recipes, a large bowl paired with a hand mixer may of course be used if you don't have a stand mixer. But I find having a stand mixer in addition to a hand mixer very convenient because it allows me to make two elements of a recipe at once (cake batter and beaten egg whites, for example).

COOKIES

Traditionally, Germans call cookies *Plätzchen*, the diminutive of *Platz*, which means "round cake" in Old German, in reference to their flattish shape. They became popular several centuries ago among women of the upper classes, who wanted dainty treats to serve at their daily teatime. At the end of the nineteenth century, a German cookie maker named Bahlsen, who owned the Hannover Cakes-Fabrik, introduced a new type of crisp butter cookie to the German market, calling them Leibniz Cakes. But when pronounced in German, "cakes" sounds more like "keks." The cookies were so hugely popular that by the early twentieth century, the company had changed the name of the cookie to Leibniz-Keks. The company changed its name soon after, and then it was just a matter of time before *Keks* became an alternative name for any kind of cookie in Germany.

The majority of German cookies are eaten at Christmastime, and as a result, it can be difficult to find German cookie recipes that aren't Christmas cookies. In fact, I must warn that a few of the recipes in this chapter, such as the buttery-crisp *Heidesand* (page 15) and the snappy *Schwarz-Weiss Gebäck* (page 16), will alarm German traditionalists because they are supposed to be made only in December. In both cases, I beg forgiveness, as a foreign interloper into these traditions and because I find these cookies so good (and not so Christmas-like) that I don't want to deprive you of making them all year long.

I have also been slightly liberal with the term "cookie," including some recipes that in Germany would be more accurately categorized as *Teilchen*, or "little pieces," like the *Amerikaner* (page 36), whose overseas cousins you may recognize from the delis of New York City, *Mandelhörnchen* (page 20), *Nussecken* (page 28), and *Prasselkuchen mit Blätterteig* (page 33).

The recipes in this chapter that are made with butter must all be made with high-fat, European-style butter (see page 5).

BUTTERKEKSE
Simplest Butter Cookies

MAKES ABOUT 55 COOKIES

Butterkekse, "butter cookies," are to German children what animal crackers are to American kids—simple, wholesome cookies that have been a part of their treat landscape forever. (Despite their name, they aren't particularly buttery.) Leibniz Butterkekse, made famous by the Bahlsen cookie company, have perforated surfaces and little scalloped edges and have been in production for the past hundred years. They're the only cookies we buy from the store instead of making ourselves. Their familiarity and comfort are difficult to beat.

I'm not usually one for trying to replicate industrially produced cookies at home—I prefer to just buy the real thing. But this recipe produces its own kind of deliciousness: crisp, plain cookies that taste as good to children as they do to adults and that keep well in a tin for several weeks. The baker's ammonia gives them that trademark snappy texture and helps them keep their shape in the oven. Other than the fluted edges and the fork-tine decoration, the cookies are left unadorned. No egg wash, no glaze. Just a plain and simple cookie.

1⅔ cups, scooped and leveled, minus 1 tablespoon/ 200g all-purpose flour, plus more for rolling

⅓ cup plus 1 teaspoon/50g cornstarch

¾ cup/90g confectioners' sugar

⅛ teaspoon salt

⅛ teaspoon baking soda

¼ cup/60ml heavy cream

⅛ teaspoon baker's ammonia (see page 5)

¼ teaspoon vanilla extract

4 tablespoons plus 1 teaspoon/60g unsalted high-fat, European-style butter, at room temperature

1 Place the flour, cornstarch, sugar, salt, and baking soda in a mixing bowl and whisk together.

2 Measure the cream into a measuring cup and add the baker's ammonia. Stir to dissolve, and then stir in the vanilla extract. Pour the cream into the flour mixture and add the butter. Stir together by hand, and then knead in the bowl or on a lightly floured counter until smooth and well combined. Form the dough into a thick disk, wrap tightly in plastic wrap, and refrigerate for 1 hour.

3 Heat the oven to 350°F/180°C. Line a baking sheet with parchment paper. Take the chilled dough out of the refrigerator, unwrap it, and cut it into thirds. Rewrap 2 pieces and place back in the refrigerator. On a lightly floured surface, with a floured rolling pin, roll out the piece of dough until about ⅛ inch/3mm thick. Prick the dough evenly all over with a fork. Using a fluted rectangular cookie cutter (or any other cookie cutter), stamp out cookies and transfer them to the prepared baking sheet, leaving ¼ inch/6mm between them.

4 Place the baking sheet in the oven and bake for 10 to 12 minutes, or until the cookies are a toasty golden brown, rotating the baking sheet halfway through baking.

5 Using a spatula, transfer the cookies to a wire rack to cool. Repeat the rolling, cutting, and baking process with the remaining dough.

6 Let the cookies cool completely before storing them in an airtight container, where they will keep for up to 4 weeks.

HEIDESAND
Sandy Almond Sugar Cookies

MAKES ABOUT 50 COOKIES

Heidesand, which means "sand of the heath," is Germany's version of that most classic of cookies, the shortbread or *sablé*. Its sandy texture is supposed to be reminiscent of the sandy earth of the Lüneburg Heath in northern Germany. It can be considered a Christmas cookie, though I make *Heidesand* year-round.

This recipe is adapted from a recipe in one of Germany's most beloved cookbooks, *Backvergnügen Wie Noch Nie*. Unlike other *Heidesand* recipes, it includes almond paste, which you can't quite taste, but which adds a delicately nutty note and a buttery friability to the simple cookies.

Once the dough is made, it's shaped into rolls and coated in granulated sugar before being sliced for baking, just as French *sablés* are. But I prefer to coat the cookie logs in pearl sugar because it stays crunchy and white even after baking and is a wonderful textural contrast to the delicate, sandy cookie.

14 tablespoons/200g unsalted high-fat, European-style butter, at room temperature

¾ cup plus 1 tablespoon/100g confectioners' sugar

⅛ teaspoon salt

3 ounces/90g almond paste

¼ teaspoon vanilla extract

2 cups, scooped and leveled/250g all-purpose flour

1 egg yolk

½ to ⅔ cup/90 to 125g pearl sugar (see page 7), for coating

1 Place the butter in a bowl and add the confectioners' sugar and salt. Grate in the almond paste. If it is too soft to grate, pluck it into small pieces with your fingers. Add the vanilla extract. Work the ingredients together with your hands until well combined, rubbing any lumps of almond paste between your fingers until broken down. Add the flour and knead together until well combined.

2 Divide the dough in half, roll into 2 equal cylinders approximately 2 inches/5cm in diameter, wrap tightly in plastic wrap, and refrigerate for 2 hours, until firm, or up to 24 hours.

3 Preheat the oven to 375°F/190°C. Line a baking sheet with parchment paper. Whisk the egg yolk in a small bowl. Spread the pearl sugar on your work surface.

4 Take one log of cookie dough out of the refrigerator. Remove the plastic wrap. Brush the log evenly with the beaten egg yolk, and then roll the log in the pearl sugar, pressing down to make sure the grains of sugar stick to the log. Slice the log into ¼-inch-/6mm-thick slices and arrange them on the prepared baking sheet, leaving a bit of space between them.

5 Bake the cookies for 10 to 12 minutes, or until the edges are golden brown and the centers are still relatively pale. Remove from the oven and let the pan cool on a rack for a few minutes. Transfer the cookies to the rack to cool completely. Repeat with the remaining dough.

6 Let the cookies cool completely before storing them in an airtight container, where they will keep for at least 1 week.

SCHWARZ-WEISS GEBÄCK
Checkerboard Cookies

MAKES ABOUT 40 COOKIES

This is another cookie, like *Heidesand* (page 15), that many Germans associate with Christmas, but in my view it is far too delicious to be limited to just one month of the year. I mean, I could eat these cookies—crisp and buttery, satisfyingly chocolaty—*every* day, if given the chance.

Depending on your craft skills, you can create total works of art out of this dough—perfectly squared-off checkerboards, swirling pinwheels, or even striped squares. For checkerboards, form the dark and light doughs into an equal number of square logs of equal size and length (you need at least 4 logs—2 of each color—plus a portion of dough in either color to use as the "wrapping"). Using an egg wash, glue the 4 logs together into a checkerboard pattern. Then roll out the remaining piece of dough and encase the 4-log dough tightly in it, using more egg wash to glue the dough together. Refrigerate, and then slice and bake. For pinwheels, form 2 equal-size sheets of dough, one vanilla, one cocoa. Lay one piece over the other, using the egg wash to glue them together. Roll the dough up tightly. Refrigerate, and then slice and bake. For striped squares, roll out the 2 pieces of dough to equal size. Using a sharp knife, cut them into equally thick strips. Paint them with egg wash, and then glue 3 strips together in alternating colors (vanilla, cocoa, vanilla). Place alternating strips on top (cocoa, vanilla, cocoa). Then slice crosswise into squares.

If you are more of a lazy baker, as I am, you can make an easier version that resembles a four-leaf clover by following the instructions in the recipe. Luckily, no matter what your cookies look like, they will all be delicious. This recipe is easily doubled.

10½ tablespoons/150g unsalted high-fat, European-style butter, softened

9 tablespoons/75g confectioners' sugar

⅛ teaspoon salt

¼ teaspoon vanilla extract

1⅔ cups, scooped and leveled, minus 1 tablespoon/200g all-purpose flour

2½ tablespoons cocoa powder

1 egg yolk

2 tablespoons whole milk

1 Place the butter in the bowl of a stand mixer fitted with the flat beater attachment and beat for 1 minute, or until the butter starts getting creamy. Add the confectioners' sugar and salt and beat until light and fluffy. Beat in the vanilla extract. Sift in the flour and beat until just combined.

2 Scrape out half the dough, form into a disk, and wrap in plastic wrap. Beat the cocoa powder into the remaining dough until well combined. Form the cocoa dough into a disk and wrap in plastic wrap. Refrigerate both doughs for 1 hour.

3 Beat the egg yolk and milk together in a small bowl and set aside.

4 Preheat the oven to 350°F/180°C. Line a baking sheet with parchment paper.

5 Remove the dough from the refrigerator. Divide each piece into 2 equal portions (if you have a scale, use it to measure them precisely). Roll each piece until it is 13 inches/33cm long. Using a bench scraper or spatula, press the logs gently on all sides to create 4 sharp corners.

continued

6 Brush one side of each squared-off log with the egg wash, and then "glue" the pieces together into a square, alternating the plain and cocoa doughs. Press the pieces together firmly using the bench scraper or spatula. Cut the block of dough in half crosswise. Transfer the blocks of dough to a cutting board, cover loosely with plastic wrap, and refrigerate for at least 30 minutes.

7 Slice one block of dough into ⅓-inch-/8mm-thick slices and place the slices on the prepared baking sheet. If the individual checkerboard pieces fall apart during slicing, don't despair. Simply push them together closely on the baking sheet and they will fuse in the baking process. Bake the first batch of cookies for 12 to 15 minutes, or until the edges are just light golden. Remove the baking sheet from the oven and place on a rack to cool for a few minutes before transferring the cookies to the rack. Repeat with the remaining dough.

8 Let the cookies cool completely before storing them in an airtight container, where they will keep for at least 2 weeks.

BLITZKUCHEN
Almond-Sugar Cookies

MAKES ABOUT 45 COOKIES

Blitzkuchen is a tongue-in-cheek name for these thin, crisp sugar- and almond-spangled cookies that come together at lightning speed (*Blitz* means "lightning" in German). The recipe comes from my dear friend Joanie's East Prussian mother-in-law, Lottchen, and was her standard offering whenever anyone stopped by for an impromptu visit. (For sit-down teatime, in case you're wondering, Lottchen's standard was cheesecake.)

The simple cookie base is scented with lemon peel and rolled out on parchment paper. The lemon doesn't really flavor the cookies outright, but deepens the flavor and balances out the eggs and butter in the dough. The sheet of dough is then topped with a mixture of ground almonds and sugar. The dough bakes in the oven as one large sheet and then gets cut into quadrangles immediately after baking. Because they're so thin, the cookies cool off quickly. You could conceivably make a batch, let them cool, and serve them in less than an hour. In other words, lightning fast.

The almonds should be ground but not completely powdered.

COOKIE BASE

2 cups, scooped and leveled/250g all-purpose flour

½ cup plus 2 tablespoons/125g granulated sugar

Grated peel of 1 organic lemon

¼ teaspoon salt

10 tablespoons/140g unsalted high-fat, European-style butter, softened

2 egg yolks (reserve 1 egg white)

TOPPING

½ cup/70g almonds, ground

⅓ cup/70g granulated sugar

Big pinch of salt

1 egg white (reserved from the base), lightly beaten

1 Preheat the oven to 350°F/180°C. Cut a piece of parchment paper to fit a baking sheet and set aside.

2 To make the cookie base: Place the flour, sugar, grated lemon peel, and salt in a mixing bowl. Add the butter and egg yolks, setting aside a single egg white. Using your hands, knead together quickly until you have a smooth dough. Roll out the dough on the parchment paper until the entire sheet of paper is covered with an evenly thin layer of dough, just under ⅛ inch/3mm thick. Transfer the parchment paper and dough to the baking sheet.

3 To make the topping: Combine the almonds, sugar, and salt in a bowl and mix well. Brush the surface of the dough with the egg white. Immediately distribute the almond mixture evenly all over the dough. Using your hands, press the almond mixture gently into the dough.

4 Place the baking sheet in the oven and bake for 18 to 20 minutes, or until the dough is fragrant and turning golden brown. The cookie base might develop a few air pockets here and there, which is fine. Remove from the oven and, using a sharp knife, immediately cut into quadrangles by slicing 8 times diagonally in one direction, and then 8 times diagonally in the other direction.

5 Place the baking sheet on a rack. When completely cool, transfer the cookies to an airtight container, where they will keep for up to 1 week.

MANDELHÖRNCHEN
Chocolate-Dipped Almond Crescents

MAKES ABOUT 10 COOKIES

These gluten-free chocolate-dipped almond crescents are a beloved after-school snack in Germany. The cookie itself is chewy, like a macaroon, but gets a pleasing crunch from the sliced almonds embedded in the dough. The ends of *Mandelhörnchen* are usually dipped in chocolate. When developing the recipe, I realized that I preferred crescents that had a bit of chocolate in each bite, so I dip the bottom of each crescent in chocolate, instead of just the ends. Bakery-made specimens are often quite large, but I prefer to make a slightly smaller cookie, keeping the crescents no larger than palm-size.

In Germany, the ubiquity of *Mandelhörnchen* at every corner bakery means that hardly anyone makes them at home, but they are very simple to throw together. If you are a fan of almond paste, you will love these.

For maximum authenticity, *Mandelhörnchen* should be made with blanched sliced almonds.

7 ounces/200g almond paste

¼ cup/50g granulated sugar

1 egg white

1 cup/85g blanched sliced almonds

3½ ounces/100g bittersweet chocolate (minimum 50% cacao), chopped

1 Preheat the oven to 350°F/180°C. Line a baking sheet with parchment paper.

2 Cut or tear the almond paste into small pieces or grate it on a box grater's largest holes and place in the bowl of a stand mixer fitted with the flat beater attachment. Add the sugar and egg white. Beat together until creamy and uniform, 1 to 2 minutes.

3 Place the sliced almonds in a wide, shallow bowl. Place a bowl of cold water nearby. Dip your hands in the cold water, and then take a piece (about one-tenth) of the almond dough and roll out evenly to 4½ inches/11cm long. Place the log in the bowl of sliced almonds and turn to coat evenly all over. Place the log on the prepared baking sheet and form it into a crescent. Repeat with the remaining dough and almonds.

4 Place the baking sheet in the oven and bake for 15 minutes, or until the almonds are toasted and the cookie dough is golden brown and gently puffed. Place the baking sheet on a rack to cool.

5 When the crescents are completely cool, melt the chopped chocolate in a double boiler set over simmering water or in a microwave in short bursts, stirring after every few bursts. Brush the bottom of each cookie thinly with some of the melted chocolate and then dip the ends of each crescent about ¾ inch/2cm into the melted chocolate if you wish. Place the cookies on the lined baking sheet, chocolate-side down, to set the chocolate, about 1 hour.

6 When the chocolate is fully set, transfer the cookies to an airtight container, where they will keep for up to 1 week.

KNERKEN
Cardamom Snap Cookies

MAKES ABOUT 40 COOKIES

These cardamom-flavored cookies are a local specialty from the Halligen Islands, a group of small, undiked islands off the coast of Schleswig-Holstein. They also go by the names of *Hallignüsse* (Halligen nuts) and *Friesenkekse* (Frisian cookies). Historically, these cookies were taken on long sea voyages by sailors because they keep well for a very long time, unlike bread. Apparently, an old Frisian saying posits that *Knerken* made at Christmastime will still taste good at Easter. I've never had a batch last that long, but isn't it good to know they could?

Cardamom, while commonly used in Scandinavian baking, is nearly unheard of in of German baking, with the exception of the northern regions bordering the North and Baltic Seas, which, due to the Hanseatic League and spice trading, had more exposure to exotic ingredients than most other parts of Germany. These simple, slice-and-bake cookies are leavened with baker's ammonia, which gives them a wonderfully airy texture and long-lasting crispness.

8½ tablespoons/120g unsalted high-fat, European-style butter

½ cup minus 1 tablespoon/90g granulated sugar

2 teaspoons ground cardamom

1 egg

2 cups, scooped and leveled/250g all-purpose flour

½ teaspoon baker's ammonia (see page 5)

¼ teaspoon salt

Whole milk, for brushing

1 Place the butter in a small pot and melt over medium-high heat. Continue to cook until the butter browns and turns fragrant. Depending on your pot, once the butter has melted, this should take 4 or 5 minutes. Don't let the solids burn. Remove from the heat and let cool to room temperature.

2 Scrape the cooled browned butter into a mixing bowl or the bowl of a stand mixer and, using an electric mixer or the flat beater attachment, beat in the sugar, cardamom, and egg.

3 In a separate bowl, mix together the flour, baker's ammonia, and salt. Beat this mixture into the butter mixture until well combined.

4 Divide the dough into 2 equal pieces and roll out to 7-inch-/17cm-long rolls. Wrap the rolls tightly in plastic wrap and refrigerate for at least 2 hours and up to 1 day.

5 When ready to bake, preheat the oven to 350°F/ 180°C and line a baking sheet with parchment paper. Remove one roll from the refrigerator, unwrap, and cut into 20 equal slices (each piece will be about ⅓ inch/8mm thick). Place the slices, cut-side down, on the prepared baking sheet and lightly brush each slice with milk.

6 Place the first batch of cookies in the oven and bake for about 18 minutes, or until they are golden brown and fragrant. Transfer the cookies to a rack to cool and repeat with the remaining dough.

7 Let the cookies cool completely before storing them in an airtight container, where they will keep for at least 2 weeks.

ZIMTBREZELN
Cinnamon Pretzels

MAKES ABOUT 64 COOKIES

More than two hundred years ago, cinnamon pretzel cookies were the very first street food sold in Berlin—in Spandau, a far-western neighborhood of the city. It took another century for people to start selling *Würstchen* (sausages) at street stands (*Imbissbuden* in Berlin dialect). Nowadays, the humble cinnamon pretzel has faded from view, but the Spandau cinnamon pretzel was once so well-known that porcelain cups and plates hand-painted with gilded cinnamon pretzels, made by Berlin's Königliche Porzellan Manufaktur, can still be found at antiques stores.

I stumbled across a recipe for *Zimtbrezeln* in a small clothbound cookbook of old recipes from Berlin. Berlin has never been famous for its cuisine and claims precious few baked goods as its own, so I was intrigued by the recipe. As per usual with German cookbooks, there was little information about the cookies, except to say that they did indeed come from Spandau and were famously hawked by a woman named Jenny. I found that the recipe needed some tweaking, but after a few rounds of testing, I got what I was after—crisp, chubby, nicely spiced cookies, perfect with a cup of tea or pressed into the hands of a small child. So this one's in honor of Spandau Jenny and her legions of fans.

9 tablespoons plus 1 teaspoon/130g unsalted high-fat, European-style butter

1¼ cups/250g granulated sugar

1 tablespoon ground cinnamon

¼ teaspoon salt

4 eggs

4 cups, scooped and leveled/500g all-purpose flour

1 teaspoon baking powder

1 In a small saucepan over medium heat, melt the butter and then let it cook until it starts to brown and smell fragrantly nutty. The browning should take 4 to 5 minutes, depending on your pot or the level of heat. Don't let the solids burn. Pour the melted butter into a mixing bowl or the bowl of a stand mixer fitted with the flat beater attachment, taking care to scrape out as much of the solids as possible. Mix in the sugar, cinnamon, and salt. Beat in 3 of the eggs, one at a time, and then beat in the flour and baking powder. The dough will be soft but should not be too sticky. Scrape out of the bowl, wrap in plastic wrap, and refrigerate for at least 1 hour and up to 2 days.

2 Heat the oven to 350°F/180°C. Line two baking sheets with parchment paper.

3 Remove the dough from the refrigerator and unwrap. Break off walnut-size pieces of dough (about ½ ounce/15g each) and roll out to 10-inch/25cm lengths. No flour should be necessary. (The dough will be hard and slightly crumbly at first, but as it warms, it will become easy to roll and work with.) Form into pretzels directly on the prepared baking sheets, leaving about 1 inch/2.5cm between them. To form a pretzel, lay out the roll of dough horizontally. Curve the right and left ends upward to form a slightly relaxed U shape. Twist the ends around each other once, and then bring each end down on the opposite side, anchoring them at eight o'clock on the left side and four o'clock on the right side.

4 Beat the remaining egg in a small bowl and, using a pastry brush, brush the pretzels lightly with the beaten egg. Bake the first batch for 12 to 15 minutes, or until lightly browned. Remove from the oven and let the cookies cool on a rack while you bake the second sheet. Repeat with the remaining dough.

5 Let the cookies cool completely before storing them in an airtight container, where they will keep for up to 3 weeks.

WALNUSS-ZWIEBACK
Twice-Baked Walnut Crisps

MAKES ABOUT 38 COOKIES

I have a soft spot in my heart for dowdy cookies and cakes. You know the ones: old-fashioned, unassuming, and not too sweet—the kind of thing your grandmother probably grew up eating or the sort of cookie you'd feel good giving to your toothless baby to gum on. You'd barely even register them if they showed up next to a towering, sexy, fudge-frosted layer cake. But what they lack in looks they more than make up for in flavor.

These *Zwieback* (which means "twice-baked") are the quintessential plain-Jane cookie. Their base is a simple sponge loaf with walnuts folded in. Once baked and cooled, the loaf is thinly sliced, and then the slices are baked until they turn faintly golden. Out of the oven, the cookies—subtly fragrant with toasted walnuts—get more and more crisp as they cool. They're addictive in their own quiet way. The *Zwieback* keep for a good long while and are excellent either at teatime or served with fruit sorbet for a very chic dessert.

You can swap out the walnuts for other nuts, such as almonds or hazelnuts (which should be skinned and toasted before being coarsely chopped; see page 7), add tiny dried currants (as in the photograph), or, for a cookie with Austrian flair, use pumpkin seeds.

4 egg whites

⅛ teaspoon salt

½ cup/100g granulated sugar

1 cup, scooped and leveled, plus 1 tablespoon/135g all-purpose flour

1⅓ cups/135g shelled walnuts, coarsely chopped

1 Preheat the oven to 350°F/180°C. Line a loaf pan with parchment paper, letting the sides hang over the edge to function as a sling after baking.

2 Place the egg whites in the bowl of a stand mixer fitted with the whisk attachment. Add the salt. Whisk at medium speed until the eggs are starting to bubble. Increase the speed and whip, adding the sugar slowly by the spoonful, until the egg whites are stiff and glossy and the sugar has completely dissolved. (Rub a bit of the egg mixture between your thumb and forefinger to test for undissolved granules.)

3 Sift the flour over the beaten egg whites and fold in, taking care not to deflate the mixture much. Fold in the chopped walnuts. Very gently scrape the batter into the prepared pan and smooth the top.

4 Place the pan in the oven and bake for 25 to 30 minutes, or until the loaf is only very faintly browned. Remove the pan from the oven and let cool completely on a rack before using the parchment paper as a sling to remove the loaf from the pan. Wrap up the loaf in the parchment paper and let sit at room temperature overnight or for at least 8 hours.

5 The next day, preheat the oven to 350°F/180°C. Line two baking sheets with parchment paper.

6 Unwrap the loaf, which will feel sticky or tacky. Slice the loaf into scant ⅛-inch-/3mm-thick pieces and place as many slices on each prepared baking sheet as will fit. Place one baking sheet in the oven and bake for 12 to 15 minutes, or until the cookies are firm to the touch and only faintly toasted. They will crisp up as they cool. Remove from the oven and let cool briefly before transferring the cookies from the pan to a rack to cool completely. Repeat with the second baking sheet.

7 Let the crisps cool completely before storing them in an airtight container, where they will keep for at least 2 weeks.

RUSSISCH BROT

Cocoa-Meringue Alphabet Cookies

MAKES ABOUT 70 COOKIES

It's not entirely clear where these alphabet meringue cookies came from. The two companies that produce *Russisch Brot* differ in their accounts: According to one, they came from Russia and were imported to Germany in the nineteenth century via a Saxonian baker. According to the other, the name is directly descended from Old German words that mean "crunchy bread" and have nothing to do with Russia.

Russisch Brot is most commonly store-bought and not homemade. I tried the store-bought kind but found them underwhelming—a cookie you had to grow up with to love. But Nicole Stich, the blogger emeritus behind one of the longest-running German food blogs, *Delicious Days*, discovered a recipe for *Russisch Brot* that is crave worthy. The cookies are lightly flavored with cocoa and cinnamon, and as they cool they become delectably crunchy. They're only slightly sweet, which makes them perfect for small children.

A bag of *Russisch Brot* is considered de rigueur for the celebratory cone-shaped *Schultüte* (a bag stuffed with special treats and supplies for the school year) that is presented to children on their first day of school. That day is a big deal for German families—everyone gets dressed up, and the whole family accompanies the child to a ceremony at school. A bag of these excellent *Russisch Brot* tucked into the *Schultüte* would make for a very special first day.

4 egg whites

⅛ teaspoon salt

½ cup plus 2 tablespoons/125g granulated sugar

¼ teaspoon vanilla extract

1¼ cups, scooped and leveled, minus 1 tablespoon/150g all-purpose flour

2 tablespoons cocoa powder

½ teaspoon ground cinnamon

1 Place the egg whites and salt in the bowl of a stand mixer fitted with the whisk attachment. Beat on high speed for 1 minute. Then, with the motor still running, add the sugar one spoonful at a time. When all the sugar has been added, add the vanilla extract. Beat until the sugar has fully dissolved, about 5 minutes.

2 In a separate bowl, mix together the flour, cocoa, and cinnamon and sift over the egg whites. Using a spatula or the whisk attachment, gently fold the flour mixture into the egg whites until well combined.

3 Preheat oven to 350°F/180°C. Line two baking sheets with parchment paper. Scrape the batter into a pastry bag fitted with a ¼-inch/6mm round tip and pipe out 2¼-inch-/5.5cm-high alphabet letters onto one prepared baking sheet, leaving ½ inch/12mm between the letters.

4 Bake for 15 to 18 minutes, piping out the next batch of cookies while frequently checking the batch in the oven. The baking cookies will puff slightly; remove them from the oven before they darken at the edges. To test whether the cookies are done, remove a cookie from the oven and let it cool for 1 minute before snapping it in half (or eating it). The cookie should be dry and crunchy, with no soft or chewy spots. (The letter *I* will be done before *Q* or *R*.) If the cookie is not quite done, bake the remaining cookies for 1 to 2 minutes longer.

5 Place the baking sheet on a rack to cool while you slide the next baking sheet of cookies into the oven. Repeat with any remaining batter. When completely cool, gently tug the cookies off the parchment paper and place in an airtight container, where they will keep for at least 2 weeks.

LÖFFELBISKUIT

Ladyfingers

MAKES ABOUT 50 COOKIES

Germany is just one of several European countries that count ladyfingers as an essential part of their baking canon. You may know these as *savoiardi* or *langues de chat* from Italian or French baking books, but, yes, *Löffelbiskuit* (*Löffel* means "spoon" and *Biskuit* is the German term for "sponge cake") are also a German favorite. Hardly anyone makes them at home anymore, but they're actually a lovely little treat and so different from store-bought ones—delicately cakey and airy on the inside, faintly crunchy with sugar on the outside. Their simplicity and shape make them ideal cookies for small children. They fit perfectly into small fists.

To shape the ladyfingers, a pastry bag will give the best and most even results. If you don't have a pastry bag, scrape the batter into a resealable plastic bag and snip off one corner to improvise one. Even if you are as clumsy as I am with a pastry bag (which is unlikely, as I am the reigning queen of clumsiness), it's hard to mess these up. They may end up looking more like dog bones than ladyfingers on your first tries, but they'll of course taste good no matter what they look like. They will stay crisp in an airtight container for about a week but will get slightly softer and cakier during the second week of storage.

4 eggs

½ cup plus 2 tablespoons/125g granulated sugar

⅛ teaspoon salt

¾ cup, scooped and leveled, plus 1 tablespoon/100g all-purpose flour

⅓ cup plus 1 teaspoon/50g cornstarch

Confectioners' sugar, for dusting (optional)

1 Preheat the oven to 350°F/180°C. Line two baking sheets with parchment paper.

2 Separate the eggs. Place the egg yolks in a bowl and add ¼ cup/50g of the sugar. Beat with an electric mixer for 3 minutes, or until thick and fluffy.

3 Place the egg whites in the bowl of a stand mixer fitted with the whisk attachment, or in a large metal bowl if using an electric mixer (with clean, dry beaters). Beat at high speed until small bubbles start to form. Add the salt and continue beating the egg whites at high speed. When large bubbles start to form, slowly pour the remaining 6 tablespoons/75g sugar by spoonful into the egg whites, beating continuously. When all the sugar has been incorporated, beat for another minute, until the egg whites hold stiff peaks.

4 Fold the egg yolk mixture into the beaten egg whites. Then sift the flour and cornstarch over the egg mixture and fold together until well combined.

5 Spoon the batter into a pastry bag fitted with a ½-inch/12mm round tip. Pipe out 3-inch-/8cm-long cookies, exerting a little pressure at the beginning and the end to create the trademark ladyfinger shape. Alternatively, you can simply pipe out even lengths. Space the cookies about 1 inch/2.5cm apart on the prepared baking sheets.

6 Place the first baking sheet in the oven and bake for 15 to 17 minutes, or until the cookies are faintly golden brown and dry to the touch. Remove the first baking sheet from the oven and place on a rack before sliding the next baking sheet into the oven.

7 When the cookies are completely cool, store them in an airtight container, where they will keep for up to 2 weeks.

NUSSECKEN
Chocolate-Hazelnut Cookie Bars

MAKES 24 WEDGES

Nussecken, chocolate-dipped nut bars beloved all over Germany, are one of those standard treats, like *Mandelhörnchen* (page 20), that are for sale at almost every bakery in the land. As a result, I spent most of my life in Germany ignoring them until I made them myself for this book. What a revelation! Imagine a buttery shortbread base, topped first with a thin layer of jam and then with a mixture of ground and chopped toasted hazelnuts. The mixture is baked until crisp-edged and toasty before being cut into triangles and dipped in chocolate. What results is a rich, caramelized wedge that is crisp at the edges and chewy within, with a thin slick of chocolate to nudge it into obsession territory. Now I understand why *Nussecken* are so adored.

The classic recipe calls for hazelnuts, which pair wonderfully with chocolate, but you can replace them with an equal amount of almonds or walnuts or a mixture of any of those nuts if you like. The jam should be something relatively tart, such as apricot or redcurrant; you don't end up tasting the jam, but it gives the bars a bit of juicy, bright contrast.

COOKIE BASE

1¼ cups, scooped and leveled, minus 1 tablespoon/150g all-purpose flour

¼ cup/50g granulated sugar

½ teaspoon baking powder

¼ teaspoon salt

4 tablespoons plus 2 teaspoons/65g unsalted high-fat, European-style butter, softened

1 egg

⅓ cup/100g apricot jam or redcurrant jelly

NUT TOPPING

10½ tablespoons/150g unsalted high-fat, European-style butter

1¼ cups/150g toasted, skinned, chopped hazelnuts (see page 7)

¾ cup/150g granulated sugar

2 tablespoons water

½ teaspoon vanilla extract

¼ teaspoon salt

1½ cups/150g toasted, skinned, finely ground hazelnuts (see page 7)

10½ ounces/300g bittersweet chocolate (between 50% and 70% cacao), chopped

1   Preheat the oven to 350°F/180°C. Line a 9 by 13-inch/23 by 33cm metal baking pan with parchment paper, letting the sides hang over the edge to function as a sling after baking.

2   To make the cookie base: In a large bowl, whisk together the flour, sugar, baking powder, and salt. Cut the butter into cubes and add with the egg. Using your hands, quickly knead the ingredients together until you have a smooth dough. It will be on the sticky side. Quickly press the dough evenly into the prepared pan or roll it out between two pieces of plastic wrap and then transfer to the prepared pan. Do not make a rim—the dough should be one even plane. Poke the dough all over with a fork. Cover with a piece of aluminum foil and fill the pan with pie weights or dried beans. Bake for 15 to 20 minutes, or until the base is just starting to color. Take the pan out of the oven and remove the aluminum foil and pie weights; maintain the oven temperature. Spread the apricot jam evenly over the hot base. Set aside.

3 To make the nut topping: Place the butter in a saucepan over medium heat to melt. Add the chopped hazelnuts and cook until toasted, 5 to 7 minutes, stirring occasionally. Add the sugar, water, vanilla extract, and salt and stir. As soon as the mixture comes to a boil, remove from the heat and stir in the ground hazelnuts until well combined. Spread this mixture evenly over the jam.

4 Return the pan to the oven and bake for 20 to 25 minutes, or until the top is a deep golden brown and the edges are caramelizing. Take the pan out of the oven and let cool on a rack for 15 minutes. Then cut the mass in the pan into thirds lengthwise, and then into quarters crosswise, and finally cut each piece in half diagonally, forming triangles. Leave in the pan to cool.

5 When the bars have fully cooled, remove from the pan using the parchment paper as a sling, and cut through the slice marks again to separate the bars fully. Return the parchment paper to the baking sheet.

6 Melt the chocolate in the top of a double boiler over simmering water or in a microwave in short bursts, stirring after every few bursts. Dip two sides of each triangle into the chocolate about ½ inch/12mm deep. Return the bars to the baking sheet; allow the chocolate to set, 2 to 3 hours.

7 When the chocolate is fully set, transfer the cookies to an airtight container, where they will keep for up to 1 week.

EISENBAHNSCHNITTEN

Almond Cream Jam Bars

MAKES ABOUT 50 BARS

I first discovered *Eisenbahnschnitten* ("railroad track bars") when my husband, Max, was working in Kassel, a small town in Hessen. World War II left Kassel in ruins, and its reconstruction in the postwar years was, to put it gently, not inspired. But Max had the good fortune of finding a little apartment in the only remaining picturesque part of Kassel, Bad Wilhelmshöhe. Right next to his apartment was an enormous park, filled with horses, ponies, and fields of rapeseed that bloomed yellow in spring.

Max came back to Berlin most weekends, and I occasionally took the train to visit him. The more I got to know Kassel, the more I came to like it. I think it might have been helped by the fact that for such a small place, Kassel boasts a large percentage of fantastic family-run bakeries. Close to Max's apartment was my very favorite, Streiter, which sold wonderful *Müsli* rolls, seedy and raisiny, as well as delicious cakes and tortes.

One day, on the hunt for a snack with my afternoon tea, I saw in the glass display case at Streiter a sheet pan full of a pastry crust topped with alternating stripes of redcurrant and apricot jam and piped, golden-brown ridges of almond cream. I'd never seen anything like it in the bakeries of Berlin. Intrigued, I bought a fat slice and went home, intending to eat only half and save the other half for Max when he got home from work. Well, let's just say that with one bite, any hope Max might have had of tasting that *Eisenbahnschnitte* went straight out the window. The crisp and buttery cookie crust, the tangy jam filling, and the chewy, bronzed frangipane topping all sandwiched together were just too irresistible. I ate the entire slice and immediately went on the hunt for a recipe.

The recipe here is slightly simplified for the home cook. I've given instructions to make both apricot and redcurrant bars because I can't decide which one I like best, but you can, of course, make just one or the other. It's important to use a tart enough jam to counterbalance the sweet topping and the short-crust base.

After two years in Kassel, Max got a job closer to Berlin and moved back home again. But whenever I make these little bars for us back in Berlin, we reminisce about our Kassel years, feeling nostalgic for the gorgeous park next door, and all those great bakeries. Those Kassel years turned out to have been rather special after all.

CRUST

4 cups, scooped and leveled/500g all-purpose flour

1¼ cups/150g confectioners' sugar

½ teaspoon salt

21 tablespoons/300g unsalted high-fat, European-style butter, softened, cubed

1 egg

Grated peel of 1 organic lemon

2 teaspoons cold water

½ cup plus 1 tablespoon/175g apricot jam

½ cup plus 1 tablespoon/175g redcurrant jelly

TOPPING

12½ ounces/360g almond paste

2 tablespoons honey

3 tablespoons confectioners' sugar

1 tablespoon unsalted high-fat, European-style butter, softened

¼ teaspoon salt

2 egg whites

continued

1 To make the crust: Place the flour, confectioners' sugar, and salt in a large bowl. Add the butter to the bowl. Using your fingers, work the butter into the dry ingredients. As you go, add the egg, grated lemon peel, and water. Continue kneading just until a relatively smooth dough forms. Divide into 2 equal pieces (if you have a scale, use it to measure them precisely). Wrap each piece of dough in plastic wrap and refrigerate for at least 1 hour and up to 1 day.

2 When ready to bake, preheat the oven to 350°F/180°C. Line a 9 by 13-inch/23 by 33cm metal baking pan with parchment paper, letting the sides hang over the edge to function as a sling after baking.

3 Remove one piece of dough from the refrigerator and roll it out to fit the pan. Prick the dough all over with a fork, and then, using a sharp knife, score it lightly into 4 strips lengthwise. Do not cut all the way through.

4 Bake for 18 to 20 minutes, or until the dough is a toasty golden brown. Remove from the oven and immediately cut through the base at the score marks. Let the crust cool for another 10 minutes on a rack before using the parchment paper as a sling to remove the crust from the pan. Set aside.

5 Repeat, lining the pan and rolling, scoring, baking, and cooling the second piece of dough. You should now have 8 equal strips of cooled short crust. Place the parchment paper on a baking sheet. Place the cooled crust strips on the paper.

6 Warm ½ cup/75g of the apricot jam in a small pot over medium heat until loose. Brush the hot jam evenly over 2 of the crust strips. Place 2 crust strips neatly over the jam-topped ones. Repeat with ½ cup/75g of the redcurrant jelly (heating it in a

separate pot) and with the remaining crust strips. Set aside the pots used to warm the jams for use again in a few minutes. You should have 4 jam bars in total, 2 apricot and 2 redcurrant.

7 To make the topping: Grate the almond paste on the large holes of a box grater and combine with the honey, confectioners' sugar, butter, salt, and egg whites. Using a hand mixer or a stand mixer fitted with the flat beater attachment, beat the ingredients together until smooth and well combined. This may take a little time—even fresh, soft almond paste can be quite stubborn about breaking down. When the mixture is smooth and creamy but thick enough to hold its shape after piping, spoon it into a pastry bag fitted with a small star tip. Starting at the edge of one of the stacked jam bars, pipe the almond cream topping all the way around the bar, leaving the center empty. Repeat with the remaining 3 stacked jam bars.

8 Heat both remaining jams separately until smooth, and then spoon them into the crevices between the piped lines of almond cream topping. (The apricot jam should go on the apricot jam bars, the redcurrant jelly on the redcurrant jelly bars.)

9 Preheat the broiler. Place the baking sheet under the broiler to brown (not burn) the ridges of the almond cream topping. Watch carefully; this should take only a few minutes. Let the bars cool on a rack. Any remaining almond cream can be piped on a baking sheet in rounds and baked at 350°F/180°C until pale golden and chewy for a baker's treat.

10 When the bars are completely cool, slice each one crosswise into 1-inch/2.5cm pieces and transfer to an airtight container in a single layer, where they will keep for at least 1 week and up to 2 weeks.

PRASSELKUCHEN MIT BLÄTTERTEIG
Saxonian Glazed Streusel Slices

MAKES 12 BARS

The cakes and sweet desserts of Saxony, an eastern German state that borders Poland and the Czech Republic, are legendary throughout Germany. *Prasselkuchen* is among Saxony's simpler creations—crisp puff pastry topped with a layer of *Streusel* (and often a layer of jam between the two), drizzled with a lemon glaze, and cut into snack-size pieces. The textural interplay of shatteringly flaky pastry and crumbly, buttery *Streusel* is fantastic, even if these are definitely treats that must be eaten over a plate. Many of my contemporaries who grew up in the German Democratic Republic remember this treat in particular as something they loved intensely as children. Fans also include the great German writer Erich Kästner, who seems to have had quite a sweet tooth.

I file *Prasselkuchen* along with *Blitzkuchen* (page 19) under the category of last-minute cookies that are good enough for guests because they are so easy to throw together, especially with good-quality frozen puff pastry available at many grocery stores. All you need to do is knead together some *Streusel* and prepare a baking sheet. The lemon glaze is essential, not only because it helps anchor the *Streusel* to the base, but also because it gives the slices an extra sugary slick that helps them go down even faster. I like the buttery purity of these *Prasselkuchen* without jam, but if you like, you can spread 1 cup/300g of apricot jam over the puff pastry before topping with the *Streusel*.

1⅓ cups, scooped and leveled, plus 1 tablespoon/175g all-purpose flour

½ cup/100g granulated sugar

Large pinch of salt

7 tablespoons/100g unsalted high-fat, European-style butter, softened

1 sheet store-bought puff pastry, defrosted

13 tablespoons/90g confectioners' sugar

1 to 2 tablespoons freshly squeezed lemon juice

1 In a large bowl, mix together the flour, granulated sugar, and salt. Cut the butter into cubes and add to the flour mixture. Using your fingertips, rub the butter into the flour mixture until bean-size pieces develop. The *Streusel* should not be entirely uniform; a good mixture of smaller and larger pieces is desirable. Cover and refrigerate the *Streusel* until ready to use.

2 Preheat the oven to 425°F/220°C. Line a baking sheet with parchment paper. Place the puff pastry on the parchment paper and brush with water. Scatter the *Streusel* evenly all over the pastry sheet. Place in the oven and bake for 15 to 20 minutes, or until the *Streusel* is lightly browned and the pastry is crisp and fragrant. Remove from the oven and place the baking sheet on a rack to cool.

3 Place the confectioners' sugar in a small bowl and add the lemon juice. Stir until smooth and creamy, taking care to break up all the lumps. Drizzle the glaze in squiggles all over the still-warm sheet of pastry. Let cool completely.

4 Slice the pastry sheet lengthwise into 3 equal strips, and then crosswise into 4 equal strips. When the glaze is fully set, transfer the bars to an airtight container, where they will keep for up to 1 week.

SCHWÄBISCHER PRASSELKUCHEN
Swabian Streusel-Jam Slices

MAKES ABOUT 30 BARS

While the Saxonians may hold *Prasselkuchen* dear, it turns out that Swabians—also famed across Germany for their cuisine and baked goods—make a similar bar cookie, using short-crust pastry instead of puff pastry. And, no surprise, it's delicious. The cookie base is flavored with lemon peel to keep the cookies from tasting too rich, and the *Streusel* has chopped almonds in it for a pleasing crunch. I've added a small amount of cinnamon to the *Streusel*, too, just to give it a slightly more rounded flavor.

The jam layer is essential here—we liked apricot best, but you could try redcurrant or raspberry jam instead. It's important that the jam be on the tart side, so as not to drag these cookie slices down into saccharine territory.

CRUST
2 cups, scooped and leveled/250g all-purpose flour

¼ cup plus 2 tablespoons/75g granulated sugar

¼ teaspoon salt

10½ tablespoons/150g unsalted high-fat, European-style butter, softened

1 egg yolk

Grated peel of ½ organic lemon

1 teaspoon water

STREUSEL
½ cup/75g blanched almonds

1¼ cups, scooped and leveled, minus 1 tablespoon/150g all-purpose flour

¼ cup/50g granulated sugar

¼ teaspoon ground cinnamon

¼ teaspoon salt

7 tablespoons/100g unsalted high-fat, European-style butter, softened

1 cup/300g apricot jam

1 To make the crust: Place the flour, sugar, and salt in a large bowl. Cut the butter into cubes and add to the bowl. Using your fingers, start working the butter into the dough. As you go, add the egg yolk, grated lemon peel, and water. Continue mixing until a relatively smooth dough forms. Don't overwork it. Wrap the dough in plastic wrap and refrigerate for 1 hour.

2 Meanwhile, make the *Streusel*: Place the almonds in a small pan and toast over medium to high heat until fragrant and lightly toasted, but not browned. Remove from the heat, let cool slightly, and then chop coarsely.

3 In a bowl, mix together the flour, sugar, cinnamon, salt, and chopped almonds. Cut the butter into cubes and add to the *Streusel* mixture. Using your fingertips, rub the butter into the flour mixture until lima bean– and pea-size pieces develop. The *Streusel* should not be entirely uniform; a good mixture of smaller and larger pieces is desirable. Cover and refrigerate the *Streusel* until ready to use.

4 Preheat the oven to 375°F/190°C. Line a 9 by 13-inch/23 by 33cm metal baking pan with parchment paper, letting the sides hang over the edge to function as a sling after baking.

5 Remove the dough from the refrigerator and roll out to fit the baking pan, forming ¼-inch-/6mm-high raised edges. Prick the crust all over with a fork. Bake the crust for 10 minutes. Remove from the oven; maintain the oven temperature.

6 Spread the apricot jam filling evenly over the crust. Sprinkle the almond *Streusel* evenly over the jam. Place the pan back in the hot oven and bake for 20 minutes, or until the *Streusel* is lightly colored and the jam is bubbling. Remove the pan from the oven and let cool completely on a rack before using the parchment paper as a sling to lift the *Prasselkuchen* onto a cutting board. Slice crosswise into 3 equal strips, and then lengthwise into 1-inch/2.5cm bars.

7 When the bars are completely cool, transfer to an airtight container, where they will keep for up to 1 week.

AMERIKANER
Lemon-Glazed Cakelets

MAKES 10 LARGE CAKELETS

There's quite a lot of confusion when it comes to the genesis of *Amerikaner*, those sugar-glazed cakelets that are known, at least in the greater New York area, as black-and-white cookies. At first glance, you might think it obvious that the black-and-white cookie was the progenitor that migrated to Germany, where it was henceforth known as *Amerikaner*. Seems reasonable enough.

But according to culinary historians in Germany, the name *Amerikaner* is actually a distortion of the cookie's original name: *Ammoniakaner*, which comes from the cakelets being traditionally leavened with ammonium carbonate. So it seems likely, or at least possible, that these little cakes were born in Germany and made their way to the States with one of the many waves of German immigrants over the past couple of centuries.

No matter where these cookies came from originally, most people can agree that a truly well-made *Amerikaner* is a real pleasure. In Germany, they are often considered a children's treat and crop up frequently at birthday parties, usually topped with a cheerful, lemony glaze. In fact, two young friends of mine who came to visit the day I tested the last version of this recipe managed to eat four whole *Amerikaner* in the time it took me to make a cup of tea.

Plenty of contemporary recipes for *Amerikaner* call for baking powder, but I urge you to seek out baker's ammonia (see page 5) before you make these—besides giving the cakelets better flavor, it helps produce a wonderfully light and porous texture, deliciously crunchy edges, and a smooth, fine crumb. Baking powder will work to leaven the cakelets, too, but won't give the same fine-crumbed and smoothly domed results.

I like the simplicity of using just a lemon-juice glaze on *Amerikaner*, but you can ice them with a thin film of melted chocolate instead. To make black-and-white cookies, replace the lemon juice in the glaze with an equal amount of water. Brush half of each cakelet with the plain glaze, and then add a spoonful or two of sifted cocoa powder to the remaining glaze to make a chocolate glaze for the remaining halves. You can also make smaller cakelets by simply reducing the amount of batter you dollop on the baking sheet.

7 tablespoons/100g unsalted high-fat, European-style butter, softened

½ cup/100g granulated sugar

½ teaspoon vanilla extract

2 eggs

2 cups, scooped and leveled/250g all-purpose flour

¼ cup plus 1 teaspoon/40g cornstarch

¼ teaspoon salt

1 teaspoon baker's ammonia (see page 5)

6 tablespoons/90ml whole milk

2 cups/200g confectioners' sugar

2½ tablespoons freshly squeezed lemon juice

1 Preheat the oven to 350°F/180°C. Line two baking sheets with parchment paper.

2 Place the butter and granulated sugar in the bowl of a stand mixer fitted with the whisk attachment; beat until light and fluffy. Beat in the vanilla extract and the eggs, one at a time.

3 In a separate bowl, whisk together the flour, cornstarch, and salt. In a separate, small bowl, dissolve the baker's ammonia in the milk.

4 Beat the flour mixture into the butter mixture until mostly combined. Scrape down the sides of the bowl, and then beat in the milk mixture until the batter is creamy and smooth.

5 Dollop 8 equal portions of the batter on the first prepared baking sheet and 2 equal portions on the second baking sheet. Using the spoon or your index finger, shape the portions into roughly circular shapes.

6 Place the first baking sheet in the oven and bake for 20 minutes, or until the cakelets are domed and just lightly browned. Remove from the oven and gently tug the parchment paper with the cakelets onto a rack to cool. Bake the remaining cakelets in the same way.

7 When all the cakelets have fully cooled, make the glaze. Place the confectioners' sugar in a small bowl and whisk in the lemon juice until the glaze is smooth and lump-free. Turn the cakelets upside down and spread the flat sides of the cakelets evenly with the glaze. Return the cakelets to the rack, flat side up, to let the glaze set.

8 When the glaze is fully set, transfer the cakelets to an airtight container, with the layers separated by parchment paper, where they will keep for up to 3 days.

CAKES

Cakes are a huge part of everyday German social life. For Germans, the next step to getting to know others isn't getting together at home for cocktails, like in France, or for dinner, like in the United States, but inviting them over for cake and coffee on a weekend afternoon. Birthdays are also a very big deal in Germany. They aren't just for children; grown-ups, too, take their own birthdays very seriously, and tradition dictates that on your birthday you have to make or buy cake to share with other people. Each year on my husband's birthday, in fact, I bake two separate batches of cake—one for the friends and family we celebrate with, and the other for him to take to work for his colleagues. At cafés and *Gasthäuser* (taverns) all over the country, if you're celebrating any happy occasion with a larger group, it's perfectly acceptable to bring your own homemade cakes, while the restaurant serves coffee and tea.

The cakes in this chapter are leavened with baking powder or the impressive power of beaten egg whites. They run the gamut from simple batter cakes topped with fruit and old-fashioned sponge cream rolls to German cheesecakes and a few others in between. Many of them are also considered celebration cakes, like the *Marmorkuchen* (page 72), which is a standard at children's birthday parties all over the country, or the cream-filled sponge rolls, which look so much more impressive and complicated than their simple preparation would have you believe. In fact, the cakes in this chapter are well suited to today's busy lifestyles; they are easy enough to throw together in an hour or two, after work in the evening, for example. Some of the simpler cakes in this chapter are what a lot of people in my generation grew up with.

People have less time for recreational baking these days, but traditions like birthday baking and the almost-holy Sunday afternoon *Kaffeezeit* with family or friends still hold strong, so the German baker needs to have a sizable repertoire of cakes to draw from. With this chapter and the next one devoted to yeasted cakes, you should have something for everyone.

ANISBROT
Aniseed Sponge Cake

MAKES 1 (9 BY 5-INCH/23 BY 12CM) CAKE

While Germany's towering cream-filled tortes are total lookers, it was this homely loaf cake, delicately flavored and light as air, that stole my heart. A classic sponge cake, despite its name (*Anisbrot* translates as "anise bread"), it is made by whipping together eggs and sugar until the mixture more than triples in size before folding in flour and whole aniseed. This thick, glossy batter is piled into a loaf pan and rises beautifully as it bakes, the beaten eggs helping to push it up until it towers impressively over the edge of the pan.

Because the cake's only fat comes from the eggs, it is quite light and on the dryish side. This is not a defect; it's just the way the cake is—old-fashioned and very much its own thing. In Germany, you rarely see this kind of cake in bakeries; it is firmly in the category of "grandmother cakes" that are baked at home, with recipes that have been passed down from generation to generation. These cakes may not win any style awards, but they will fill you with nostalgia and comfort every time you make them.

When *Anisbrot* is freshly baked, I like to slice it thickly and eat the fragrant slices with a cup of green tea. You could, however, dress it up as a light dessert by plating slices of it next to a puddle of stewed or poached fruit, the syrup soaking into the anise-flavored crumb. But the cake can be transformed, too, into cookie form, by cutting a cooled loaf into ¼-inch/6mm slices, arranging them on a baking sheet, and toasting them in a 350°F/180°C oven for 15 minutes. The cookies, known as *Aniszwieback*, will crisp up as they cool and keep for ages in a tin.

If aniseed is not your thing, you can flavor this cake instead with organic lavender buds, crushed cardamom, or—in the spirit of old English seed cakes—caraway seeds.

5 eggs

1½ cups/300g granulated sugar

¼ teaspoon salt

2⅓ cups, scooped and leveled, plus 1 tablespoon/300g cake flour

2 teaspoons whole aniseed

1 Preheat the oven to 350°F/180°C. Line a 9 by 5-inch/23 by 12cm loaf pan with a piece of parchment paper, letting the sides hang over the edge to function as a sling after baking.

2 Place the eggs, sugar, and salt in the bowl of a stand mixer fitted with the whisk attachment. Turn the motor to the highest setting and beat for 5 to 7 minutes (set a timer!), until the mixture is thick, pale, and glossy and has tripled in size. The grains of sugar should have dissolved fully.

3 Remove the whisk attachment and sift in the flour. Add the aniseed. Then, using a spatula, gently fold the flour and aniseed into the egg mixture until well combined. Take care not to deflate the batter, which should be light and airy.

4 Gently pour the batter into the prepared pan and smooth the top. Place in the oven and bake for 55 to 60 minutes; after 30 minutes of baking, rotate the pan and cover with a piece of aluminum foil to keep the top from browning too much. The cake is done when it is a pale golden brown and a toothpick or cake tester inserted into the center comes out clean.

5 Place the pan on a rack to cool for 30 minutes. Using the parchment paper as a sling, remove the cake from the pan and return it to the rack to cool completely before serving. Tightly wrapped in plastic wrap, the cake will keep for at least 2 days at room temperature.

NUSSKUCHEN
Toasted Hazelnut Loaf Cake

MAKES 1 (9 BY 5-INCH/23 BY 12CM) CAKE

In the United States, loaf cakes and quick breads are quite moist and rich affairs. In Germany, they tend to be drier and lighter; in sum, a little more restrained. In this classic *Nusskuchen*, hazelnuts are toasted until fragrant, and then pulsed finely before being folded into a simple cake batter plumped up with a bit of milk or brandy. You can take the basic recipe further by folding in chopped chocolate or grated lemon peel. The chocolate gives the cake more heft and makes for a great autumn weekend cake, while the lemon pairs nicely with the roasted hazelnuts for a more delicately flavored cake. Either way, slices of *Nusskuchen* are wonderful eaten with a hot cup of coffee or tea.

The cake keeps well for a few days wrapped tightly in plastic wrap. But if it does get stale, you may be interested to know that an acquaintance of my assistant on this book, Maja Welker, once told her that her family used to repurpose stale loaf cakes like this one by placing slices of them on buttered rye bread at snack time. Ever curious, Maja tried this unusual snack and reported back that it is indeed delicious, if a little unorthodox. What we still haven't figured out is whether this is a regional oddity or simply a familial one. In any case, it speaks to the resourcefulness of most Germans, who are loath to waste any food.

18 tablespoons/250g unsalted butter, softened, plus more for the pan

2 cups/200g whole hazelnuts, toasted, skinned, and finely ground (see page 7)

1 cup/200g granulated sugar

1 teaspoon vanilla extract

4 eggs

1⅔ cups, scooped and leveled, minus 1 tablespoon/200g all-purpose flour

2 teaspoons baking powder

2 tablespoons whole milk or brandy

5¼ ounces/150g bittersweet chocolate (minimum 50% cacao), chopped (optional)

Grated peel of 1 organic lemon (optional)

Confectioners' sugar (optional), for dusting

1 Preheat the oven to 350°F/180°C. Butter a 9 by 5-inch/23 by 12cm loaf pan. Spread the hazelnuts on a baking sheet in a single layer and toast in the oven, until the nuts are toasted and fragrant. Remove the pan from the oven and let the nuts cool completely before rubbing them gently with a clean dishcloth (this will remove most of their skins). Place the cooled hazelnuts in the bowl of a food processor and pulse until the nuts are ground to a very fine meal. Take care not to overprocess by pulsing after they are finely ground, or you will end up with hazelnut paste.

2 Place the butter and sugar in the bowl of a stand mixer fitted with the flat beater attachment and beat until creamy and fluffy; beat in the vanilla extract. Add the eggs, one at a time, and beat until each one is incorporated into the batter. Slowly add the ground hazelnuts and beat until combined.

3 Sift the flour and baking powder together, and then, with the mixer running at medium speed, gradually add the flour to the butter and sugar. Finally, beat in the milk or brandy and fold in the chocolate or grated lemon peel. Scrape the batter evenly into the prepared pan. Bake for 1 hour and 15 minutes, or until the cake is golden brown and a tester inserted into the center comes out clean.

4 Place the pan on a rack to cool for a few minutes before unmolding. Let the cake cool completely. Dust lightly with confectioners' sugar before slicing and serving. Wrapped tightly in plastic wrap, the cake will keep at room temperature for at least 3 days and up to 5.

VERSUNKENER APFELKUCHEN
Sunken Apple Cake

MAKES 1 (9-INCH/23CM) CAKE

There are countless apple cakes in Germany, but this one, in which a rather plain batter rises up and bakes around sliced apples, has to be one of the most popular. Cakes like these are often called *Mittwochskuchen* (Wednesday cakes) because they can easily be made during the week when time is short.

Various regions of Germany try to lay claim to the cake by changing its name to reflect their geography, but it's pretty clear that it's a countrywide favorite. And no wonder: it's great for baking newbies or for people baking with small children. It's also relatively wholesome, with a high apple-to-cake ratio. Slicing the apple quarters almost all the way through guarantees that they'll cook through in the same amount of time that the relatively thin batter takes. A light sprinkling of raw sugar on top gives each piece a pleasing crunch. It is practically mandatory in Germany to serve this type of cake with a dollop of *Schlagsahne*, lightly sweetened whipped cream.

3 apples

½ organic lemon

½ cup plus 2 tablespoons/125g granulated sugar

9 tablespoons plus 1 teaspoon/130g unsalted butter, softened

½ teaspoon pure vanilla extract

3 eggs

1½ cups, scooped and leveled/190g all-purpose flour

2 teaspoons baking powder

¼ teaspoon salt

1 to 2 tablespoons demerara (raw) sugar

Schlagsahne (page 267), for serving (optional)

1 Peel, core, and quarter the apples. Thinly slice each quarter lengthwise without cutting all the way through to the core side, leaving the quarter hinged together. Grate the peel of the lemon into the bowl of a stand mixer and set aside; save the lemon half.

2 Preheat oven to 350°F/180°C. Line the bottom of a 9-inch/23cm springform pan with parchment paper.

3 Place the sugar and butter in the bowl with the lemon peel and, using the stand mixer fitted with the flat beater attachment, cream until light and fluffy. Stop the machine and scrape down the sides; add the vanilla extract and one of the eggs. Beat until combined before adding the second egg. Beat until combined and then add the third egg. Scrape down the sides. Beat until combined.

4 In a separate bowl, whisk together the flour, baking powder, and salt. With the mixer on low speed, beat in the flour mixture until just combined, squeezing in the juice from the reserved lemon half. Scrape down the sides with a spatula and give the batter one last mix by hand.

5 Scrape the batter into the prepared pan and smooth the top. Gently press the apple quarters into the batter, core side down, leaving only a bit of space between each quarter. If you have any apple left over, break off slices and insert them into any open space available. Sprinkle the top evenly with the demerara sugar. Bake for 35 to 40 minutes, rotating the pan halfway through baking, until the cake is golden brown and a tester inserted into the cake (not apple) comes out clean.

6 Place the pan on a rack to cool for 5 minutes before running a knife around the edge and removing the springform ring. Serve at room temperature with a spoonful of *Schlagsahne*. The cake will keep at room temperature, wrapped lightly in plastic wrap, for 2 days.

APFEL-MARZIPAN-KUCHEN
Apple-Almond Cake

MAKES 1 (9-INCH/23CM) CAKE

I sourced recipes for this book from everywhere, and I mean *everywhere*: friends, mothers-in-law, abandoned magazines in hotels, strangers, newspapers, antique cookbooks, stained handwritten notebooks, the Internet, and even from the back of a generic brand of almond paste sold at the grocery store around the corner from my house.

I can explain: My assistant, Maja, and I had tried a couple of apple–almond paste cakes earlier in our testing, but they were nothing special. In fact, after the most recent lackluster one, I'd decided to omit this cake, even though I love the combination of almond paste and apples and I was sort of surprised we hadn't cracked that particular code. Three days before the manuscript was due, I was looking on the back of a packet of almond paste and out of the corner of my eye I saw a little recipe. I mean *really* little; it was printed on the short side of the 4-inch-/10cm-wide rectangular packet. It was less than a knuckle's length of printed information, but as soon as I saw it, I knew we'd have to try it.

We had almond paste. We had apples. We had an hour between one loaf rising and another cake baking. So we made a few tweaks (more apples, for one, and adding almond extract and salt for better flavor plus brushing a hot apricot glaze on top to give the cake a special sheen) and an hour later we had the world's best apple-almond cake in front of us. No joke. This cake is epic.

The crumb is so incredibly tender, it's almost creamy (don't skip the cornstarch!), and tastes of both sweet cream and faintly boozy almonds. You can't taste the almond paste outright, but it gives the crumb an ineffable richness. The apples add lovely little punches of juicy tartness here and there, since they're both cubed and folded into the batter and also sliced and laid out attractively on top. Baked in a 9-inch/23cm pan, the cake is a satisfyingly full 2 inches/5cm tall. The apricot glaze gives it a gorgeous, company-ready finish. And it keeps well, if wrapped in plastic, for a couple days on the counter. So in every way, this cake was worth the wait.

6 small apples (1¾ pounds/800g)

Juice of 1 lemon

7 ounces/200g almond paste

¼ teaspoon salt

14 tablespoons/200g unsalted butter, melted and cooled, plus more for the pan

¾ cup/150g granulated sugar

1 teaspoon almond extract

4 eggs

1¼ cups, scooped and leveled, minus 1 tablespoon/150g all-purpose flour

9½ tablespoons/85g cornstarch

2 teaspoons baking powder

¼ cup/75g apricot jam

1 Preheat the oven to 350°F/180°C. Line the bottom of a 9-inch/23cm springform pan with parchment paper and butter the sides of the pan.

2 Peel, halve, and core 3 of the apples, and cut each half into 6 even slices. Toss the apple slices with half of the lemon juice and set aside.

3 Peel, halve, and core the remaining apples, and then cut into ⅓-inch/8mm dice. Toss with the remaining lemon juice and set aside.

4 Grate the almond paste and place it in the bowl of a stand mixer fitted with the flat beater attachment. Add the salt and melted butter; beat for 1 to 2 minutes, until smooth. Then beat in the sugar and almond extract. Beat in the eggs, one at a time, beating for 30 seconds after each addition. Scrape down the sides of the bowl.

5 In a separate bowl, whisk together the flour, cornstarch, and baking powder. Beat into the almond batter, and then fold in the diced apples. Scrape the batter into the prepared pan and smooth the top. Distribute the sliced apples decoratively in concentric rings on the top of the cake. Then, using the flat of your hand, gently push the apples into the batter; they should not be submerged, but rather lightly anchored.

6 Place the pan in the oven and bake for 1 hour and 10 minutes, or until the top is golden brown and a tester inserted into the middle of the cake comes out clean. Remove the pan from the oven and place on a rack to cool.

7 Immediately heat the apricot jam over medium-high heat until just bubbling. Brush a thin layer of the hot jam over the still-hot cake. Let cool completely before removing the springform ring. The cake will keep at room temperature, lightly wrapped in plastic wrap, for several days.

GEDECKTER APFELKUCHEN
Glazed Apple Cake

MAKES 1 (9-INCH/23CM) CAKE

Gedeckter Apfelkuchen (covered apple cake) is one of the cakes you're sure to find in almost every single bakery across Germany. To make it, you line a springform pan with a sweet short pastry, fill the crust with a chunky cooked apple filling studded with raisins and flavored with cinnamon and lemon, and then use the same crust dough to make a lid for the cake. I sometimes wonder if it isn't the precursor to America's apple pie, though in this cake, even after baking, the pastry remains soft and cakey thanks to the moist, cooked apple filling and a lemon glaze that is brushed on the top crust after baking.

Gedeckter Apfelkuchen from industrial bakeries tends to be unbearably sweet. In fact, I always thought I didn't much care for it until I tried making it at home, and now I'm smitten. I like to use apples that have a good balance of sweetness and acidity for the filling and I leave them unsweetened, which gives a nicely tart contrast to the sweet, glazed crust.

2⅓ cups, scooped and leveled, plus 1 tablespoon/300g all-purpose flour

¾ cup/150g granulated sugar

1 teaspoon baking powder

Pinch of salt

10½ tablespoons/150g unsalted high-fat, European-style butter, softened

1 egg, at room temperature

6 large apples (2 pounds 10 ounces/1.2kg)

Juice of 1 lemon plus 2 teaspoons freshly squeezed lemon juice

1 teaspoon ground cinnamon

½ cup/75g raisins

¼ cup/60ml plus 2 teaspoons water

¾ cup/75g confectioners' sugar

1 Mix the flour, granulated sugar, baking powder, and salt together in a large bowl. Cut the butter into cubes and add to the flour mixture. Using a pastry cutter or your hands, work the butter into the flour until it's no longer visible. Add the egg and knead until the dough is smooth. Wrap tightly in plastic wrap and refrigerate for at least 1 hour and up to 24 hours.

2 Peel, core, and quarter the apples. Cut them into slices ⅛ to ¼ inch/3 to 6mm thick and put the slices in a large pot. Add the juice of 1 lemon along with the cinnamon, raisins, and the ¼ cup/60ml of water. Cover the pot and bring to a simmer over medium heat, stirring occasionally. Cook the apples for 15 to 20 minutes, or until silky and relatively broken down. The apples should not turn completely to mush but still retain some shape. Take the pot off the heat.

3 Preheat the oven to 350°F/180°C. Line the bottom of a 9-inch/23cm springform pan with parchment paper. Take two-thirds of the dough and pat it evenly into the springform pan, forming a 1-inch-/2.5cm-high rim at the edges. Refrigerate the remaining dough. Prick the dough in the pan evenly all over with a fork. Line the dough with a sheet of aluminum foil and fill the pan with pie weights or dried beans. Bake for 20 minutes, or until the crust is starting to firm up but is not yet browning. Remove from the oven and carefully remove the aluminum foil and pie weights; maintain the oven temperature.

4 Scrape the apple mixture evenly into the par-baked shell and smooth the top. The apple filling should precisely fill the crust. Roll out the remaining one-third of the dough between two

pieces of plastic wrap until just slightly larger than the circumference of the pan. Trim the edges of the circle and then gently transfer the circle to the top of the cake, laying it over the apple filling. Tuck in the top crust and cut off any excess. Cut 3 small slits in the top of the dough. Put the pan back in the oven and bake for 35 to 40 minutes, or until the top is golden brown and slightly puffed.

5 Remove the pan from the oven and let cool for 10 minutes while you prepare the glaze. Sieve the confectioners' sugar into a small bowl and whisk in the 2 teaspoons of lemon juice and the 2 teaspoons of water until smooth. Brush the glaze over the still-hot cake and then let the cake cool completely before serving. The cake will keep at room temperature, covered lightly with plastic wrap, for 2 to 3 days.

KÄSEKUCHEN
Classic Quark Cheesecake

MAKES 1 (9-INCH/23CM) CAKE

Quark, a fresh, sour cheese that has been a staple in eastern and central Europe (*twaróg* in Polish, *tvorog* in Russian) since the fourteenth century, is essential to the German sweet kitchen. *Quark* is more sour and grainy than ricotta, to which it is often erroneously compared. It can be eaten as is or used in baking. In its natural state, regardless of its fat content, which can range from 0 percent all the way up to 50 percent and higher, it is quite firm. When combined with other ingredients like eggs and sugar, it becomes quite loose and creamy, almost like sour cream.

If you've ever been to Germany, it's likely you've come across the very best use of *Quark*: *Käsekuchen*. Popular from north to south and east to west, *Käsekuchen* may well be Germany's national cake. There are too many versions of *Käsekuchen* to count (this book alone has four), but the one thing they all have in common is the use of *Quark*.

Thick, creamy, and imposing, this classic crusted *Käsekuchen* is one for the ages. Faintly sour from the *Quark*, not too rich or sweet despite its height, and only lightly flavored with vanilla, a fat wedge of this cheesecake can be put away without any deleterious effects. I adapted the recipe from one that I found in an issue of *Die Zeit*, a serious national weekly newspaper with a wonderful food section. The accompanying article was all about how difficult it was, even for Germans, to crack the code of perfect *Käsekuchen*, and the author lamented the miserable state of contemporary store-bought *Käsekuchen*. Several bakers, as well as the head of a pastry school in Berlin, were interviewed, and strong feelings about regional differences in cheesecake were aired. The article featured four different recipes, but this one clearly stole the show.

The filling calls for almost an entire kilo of *Quark*, which is lightened with beaten egg whites and enriched with a bit of whipped cream. Poured into a par-baked short crust, the filling puffs up impressively in the oven. Since this enormous amount of filling is still only baked in a 9-inch/23cm pan, the cake comes out gorgeously thick, which makes for truly satisfying wedges. And trust me, you're not going to be happy with just a thin sliver of this stuff.

If possible, the cake should be made and refrigerated at least a day before serving. Before refrigeration, the cake has an airy, fluffy quality that is just fine, but once refrigerated it settles into something thicker and creamier and so much more satisfying.

CRUST

1²/₃ cups, scooped and leveled, minus 1 tablespoon/200g all-purpose flour

½ cup/100g granulated sugar

Pinch of salt

1 egg

7 tablespoons/100g unsalted high-fat, European-style butter, softened, cut into cubes

FILLING

3²/₃ cups/900g *Quark* (page 264), drained if necessary (see page 8)

6 tablespoons/90ml whole milk

1 cup minus 1 tablespoon/190g granulated sugar

⅓ cup/45g cornstarch

½ teaspoon vanilla extract

6 eggs, separated

¼ teaspoon salt

6 tablespoons/90ml whipping cream

1 To make the crust: Mix together the flour, sugar, and salt in a large bowl, and then knead in the egg and butter until a dough forms. Wrap in plastic wrap and refrigerate for 30 minutes.

2 Meanwhile, preheat the oven to 400°F/200°C. Line a 9-inch/23cm springform pan with a piece of parchment paper, letting the sides hang over the edge to function as a sling after baking.

3 Press the dough evenly into the pan, creating a 2-inch-/5cm-high rim. Line the crust with aluminum foil and fill with pie weights or dried beans. Bake for 25 minutes.

4 While the crust is baking, make the filling: Place the *Quark*, milk, sugar, cornstarch, vanilla extract, and egg yolks in a large mixing bowl and whisk together until smooth. In a separate bowl, whip the egg whites and salt together until the egg whites hold stiff peaks. Fold into the *Quark* mixture. In another bowl, whip the cream until thick. Fold into the *Quark* mixture.

5 When the crust has finished baking, remove the pan from the oven and immediately remove the aluminum foil and weights; maintain the oven temperature. If the crust has slumped down in the pan and thickened, use the back of a large spoon to press the crust back up the sides of the pan and even it out.

6 Pour the *Quark* mixture into the crust (the filling will come up over the crust almost to the edge of the pan, but don't worry). Gently place the pan back in the oven and bake for 30 minutes. Remove from the oven and insert the tip (1 inch/2.5cm) of a sharp knife horizontally into the portion of the cake that has risen up over the edge of the pan. Holding the knife steady, run it all the way around the cake. This will keep the cake from cracking later. Maintain the oven temperature.

7 Place the pan back in the oven and bake for an additional 20 minutes. After 10 minutes, you may need to cover the top of the cake with a piece of aluminum foil if it's getting too dark. When it's done, the cake should be golden brown and wobble gently in the center when carefully jiggled. Remove the cake from the oven and let it cool completely on a rack before loosening and removing the springform ring. The cake can be served the day it is made, but it improves with a few days' rest in the refrigerator. The cake will keep for up to 5 days in the refrigerator.

KÄSEKUCHEN OHNE BODEN
Crustless Quark Cheesecake

MAKES 1 (9-INCH/23CM) CAKE

There are two camps of cheesecake eaters in Germany—those who insist on a cheesecake in a crust (see *Käsekuchen*, page 48) and those who prefer crustless cheesecakes.

Quark is a pretty stable cheese to begin with, and when it's baked with eggs and the key ingredient here, semolina, it doesn't actually need a crust to corset it into place. You don't have to whip egg whites or do any kind of folding. You just need to whisk all the ingredients together and pile the batter into a pan. The cake shoots up during baking, towering over the edge of the pan, but it slumps back down on itself as it cools, creating an appealingly wavy, lumpy top. It's rustic all right, but it's beautiful. Don't worry if it cracks; that's part of its appeal. I keep the sugar quantity relatively low because I like letting *Quark*'s natural flavor shine and because the raisins also contribute some sweetness to the cake.

Ah, yes, the raisins: You see, the other point on which people differ passionately here in Germany is the inclusion of rum-soaked raisins in cheesecake. If you are a raisin hater, you will be pleased to know that you can simply leave out the raisins. (Just add the juice of the second lemon half instead.) If you are a raisin lover, well, then, you're welcome. The winey pops of sweetness scattered throughout are a lovely contrast to the lemony, creamy cake. The rum is undetectable in the finished cake, but if you'd like to leave it out, substitute an equal amount of freshly squeezed orange juice when soaking the raisins.

This cheesecake can be eaten the day it is made, but it improves greatly with a night in the refrigerator. The crumb, for lack of a better word, dries out slightly and becomes thicker, more compact.

½ cup/75g raisins

2 tablespoons dark rum

⅓ cup/60g semolina, plus more for the pan

2 teaspoons baking powder

10½ tablespoons/150g unsalted butter, melted and cooled, plus more for the pan

¾ cup/150g granulated sugar

4 eggs

1 teaspoon vanilla extract

4 cups/1kg *Quark* (page 264), drained if necessary (see page 8)

1 organic lemon

1 Several hours before you make the cake, place the raisins in a small bowl with the rum and set aside, covered, to macerate.

2 When you are ready to bake, preheat the oven to 400°F/200°C. Butter a 9-inch/23cm springform pan and sprinkle with a few spoonsful of semolina to coat the bottom and sides thinly. In a small bowl, whisk together the ⅓ cup/60g of semolina and the baking powder. Set aside.

3 Place the cooled, melted butter in a large bowl. Whisk in the sugar, eggs, vanilla extract, *Quark*, the grated peel of the entire lemon, and the juice of half of it. Then whisk in the semolina mixture. Finally, whisk in the macerated raisins and any remaining rum in the bowl. Whisk until you have a smooth, creamy, well-combined batter.

4 Scrape the batter into the prepared pan and smooth the top. Place in the oven and bake for 45 minutes. The top will get quite dark but should not burn. The center will still jiggle slightly when you remove the pan from the oven.

5 Place the pan on a rack to cool completely before removing the springform ring. Serve at room temperature or chilled. The cake will keep for at least 3 days and up to 1 week in the refrigerator.

QUARKKUCHEN MIT MANDARINEN
Mandarin Orange Cheesecake

MAKES 1 (9-INCH/23CM) CAKE

My husband would usually rather eat a bag of salted nuts than a piece of cake, but he makes exceptions for a few beloved favorites, including the almond-paste-stuffed *Kranzkuchen* on page 104 and this *Quarkkuchen* topped with mandarin oranges. Several years before this book was a glimmer in my eye, he came home from a visit to his mother's house bearing a small newspaper clipping of a recipe for cheesecake with mandarin oranges. It was the first and only time he has come to me with an actual baking request.

At first I was skeptical about the inclusion of canned mandarins, which have always seemed a bit dubious to me. I associated them more with things like the massive, saccharine Chinese chicken salads at that mainstay of my college years, the Cheesecake Factory, than I did with delicious baked goods. Why would I want to sully the purity of a delicate, sour *Quark* filling with something as pedestrian as canned fruit?

Well, the joke was on me. There's a reason this variation on *Käsekuchen* is so hugely popular in Germany (as is subbing wedges of canned apricots for the orange segments): it's delicious. The citrusy mandarin orange segments work really nicely with the sour *Quark*, which won't surprise a single fan of the Creamsicle. And the mandarin oranges manage to stay juicy even after baking, which mystifies me a little but makes for a wonderful eating experience: as you eat, the little segments sort of burst in your mouth and flood it with juice, along with the lovely, creamy *Quark*.

In this recipe, I place the mandarin orange segments on top of the cheesecake before baking. But an alternative is to hide them, so to speak, in the cake by pouring half of the batter into the prepared pan, distributing the mandarin oranges across the batter, and then topping with the remaining batter.

This one's for you, *Herzchen*.

CRUST

1½ cups, scooped and leveled/190g all-purpose flour

1 teaspoon baking powder

¼ cup/50g granulated sugar

Pinch of salt

1 egg

7 tablespoons/100g unsalted high-fat, European-style butter, at room temperature, cubed

FILLING

1 cup/200g granulated sugar

4 eggs

⅓ cup plus 1 teaspoon/50g cornstarch

⅛ teaspoon salt

4 cups/1kg *Quark* (page 264), drained if necessary (see page 8)

½ cup/120g sour cream

1¼ teaspoons vanilla extract

½ cup/120ml neutral vegetable oil

½ cup/120ml milk

2 (11-ounce/310g) cans mandarin oranges, drained

1 To make the crust: In a mixing bowl, mix together the flour, baking powder, sugar, and salt. Stir in the egg and then add the butter. Knead together by hand until smooth. The dough will be quite soft. Shape into a disk, wrap in plastic, and refrigerate for 1 hour.

2 Preheat the oven to 350°F/180°C. Remove the dough from the refrigerator and unwrap. Sandwich the dough between two pieces of plastic wrap and, using a rolling pin, roll it out to make a circle 11 inches/28cm in diameter. Carefully transfer to a 9-inch/23cm springform pan, pressing the excess dough against the sides of the pan to form

a 1-inch/2.5cm edge. You may need to patch the crust here and there due to the dough's softness. Don't worry about overworking the dough. Line the crust with aluminum foil and fill with pie weights or dried beans. Place in the oven and bake for 20 minutes.

3 While the crust is baking, make the filling: Place the sugar and eggs in the bowl of a stand mixer fitted with the whisk attachment and whip together until thick and pale, about 1 minute. Add the cornstarch and salt and mix at medium-low speed until the cornstarch has been absorbed. Add the *Quark* and sour cream and mix until well combined. Add the vanilla extract, vegetable oil, and milk and mix until well combined.

4 Remove the pan from the oven and remove the pie weights and aluminum foil. If the dough has shrunk down from the sides, use the back of a large metal spoon or measuring cup to push it back up again. Scrape the *Quark* mixture into the hot crust and smooth the top. In all likelihood, the Quark

mixture will be higher than the crust you've made. Arrange the mandarin oranges decoratively (in concentric circles, for example) on top of the *Quark*. Alternatively, scrape half the *Quark* mixture into the hot crust and smooth. Arrange the drained mandarin oranges on top of the filling and then top with the remaining filling and smooth the top. Return the pan to the oven and bake for 65 to 70 minutes, or until the cake is set and the rim of the cake is slightly browned. The cake will still jiggle, but should be dry to the touch.

5 Place the pan on a rack to cool for 30 minutes. Remove the springform ring and let cool completely. Refrigerate it overnight before serving because the cake settles into itself slightly and will take on a denser, creamier quality. (The cake can also be eaten the day it is made, in which case it will have a very light and airy consistency.) The cake will keep for at least 3 days and up to 1 week in the refrigerator. Before serving, let the refrigerated cake sit at room temperature for 30 minutes.

RUSSISCHER ZUPFKUCHEN
Chocolate Quark Cheesecake

MAKES 1 (9-INCH/23CM) CAKE

Ask Germans between the ages of twenty-five and forty-five what their favorite cake is and they will probably tell you it is *Russischer Zupfkuchen*, a *Quark* cheesecake baked in a chocolate crust with pieces of chocolate *Streusel* on top. (*Zupfen* means "to pluck," which is what you do with the *Streusel* topping.) I confess, though, that I was well into my thirties before I even tried it. I knew *Russischer Zupfkuchen* only from bakery cases, where I could never really figure out what I was looking at. Was it chocolate cake? Was it cheesecake? And what did Russia have to do with it? It didn't help that it always looked a little sweaty and lumpy under the bright bakery lights. When the time came to order, I'd end up picking something else.

Its origins are mysterious. Some say the cake was invented by the Dr. Oetker company (which brought out its *Russischer Zupfkuchen* cake mix in the early 1990s). Others swear their grandmothers have been baking it since at least the early 1960s. All say that no one in Russia has ever heard of the cake. But it continues to endure as one of Germany's most beloved cakes.

Once I got around to making it myself, I discovered that it is indeed a cake to love. You line a pan with cocoa-flavored dough, setting aside some of it, and fill the crust with a vanilla-flavored *Quark* filling. Then you take the remaining cocoa dough and pluck off pieces of it, which you scatter over the top of the filling. The *Quark* filling is substantial enough that the dough pieces don't sink into it, but float rather plushly on the thick, creamy cheese. As the cake bakes, the filling rises up and browns slightly, while the cocoa *Streusel* pieces puff and spread. Once cooled and sliced, the crust and *Streusel* are like a thick chocolate cookie, while the vanilla-flavored *Quark* filling is cool, dense, and slightly sour. It's no wonder that it's a

modern classic at *Kaffeezeit* all year long. So while it may have taken me three decades to get to know it, I'm happy to say that I'm making up for lost time now.

Russischer Zupfkuchen is best if left to rest for a day before eating and it keeps well, which makes it an ideal make-ahead treat.

CRUST

7 tablespoons/100g unsalted high-fat, European-style butter, softened

½ cup/100g granulated sugar

1 egg

1½ cups, scooped and leveled, minus 1 tablespoon/180g all-purpose flour

¼ cup/30g cocoa powder

¾ teaspoon baking powder

⅛ teaspoon salt

FILLING

8½ tablespoons/120g unsalted butter

2 cups/500g *Quark* (page 264), drained if necessary (see page 8)

½ cup plus 2 tablespoons/125g granulated sugar

2 eggs

2 teaspoons vanilla extract

1 tablespoon cornstarch

1 To make the crust: In the bowl of a stand mixer fitted with the flat beater attachment, cream together the butter and sugar until fluffy. Beat in the egg and scrape down the sides.

2 In a separate bowl, combine the flour, cocoa powder, baking powder, and salt. With the motor of the mixer running, beat the flour mixture into the

butter mixture until well combined. Scrape out the dough onto a piece of plastic wrap and form into a disk. It should be soft but not sticky. Wrap it up and refrigerate for 30 minutes.

3 Divide the dough in half and form each piece into a disk. Wrap one disk in the plastic wrap and return it to the refrigerator. Roll out the second disk between two pieces of plastic wrap until it is approximately 11 inches/28cm in diameter. Peel off the top piece of plastic wrap, and then invert the dough over a 9-inch/23cm springform pan and fit it gently into the pan, removing the plastic wrap as you go. The dough should come up the sides by about 1 inch/2.5cm. Trim any excess and use it to patch any imperfections or set it aside to combine with the remaining dough for the topping. Refrigerate the lined pan while you make the filling.

4 To make the filling: Heat the oven to 350°F/180°C. Melt the butter. Set aside to cool slightly. Place the *Quark* in a mixing bowl and whisk in the sugar, either by hand or with an electric mixer. Beat in the eggs, one at a time, and then the cooled butter, vanilla extract, and cornstarch.

5 When the mixture is creamy and well combined, remove the crust from the refrigerator and pour the filling into the crust. Smooth the top. If necessary, using a knife, trim the sides of the cocoa crust so that it is even all the way around and about ¼ inch/6mm higher than the *Quark* filling. Reserve any trimmings.

6 Remove the reserved dough from the refrigerator and briefly knead together with any reserved trimmings. Pluck off ½-inch/12mm pieces of the dough and scatter them evenly over the surface of the *Quark* filling. The pieces of cocoa dough won't sink, but rather will rest on top of the raw filling. When all the dough has been used up, place the pan in the oven and bake for 45 to 50 minutes. The *Quark* filling will be golden brown and puffed up. The crust should be dry to the touch, but should not be burned.

7 Remove the pan from the oven and let cool on a rack for 20 minutes. After 20 minutes, run a thin knife around the edge of the pan, loosening the cake. Let the cake cool completely before removing the ring. The cake is best if served a day after baking. After it has fully cooled, it can be lightly wrapped in plastic wrap and refrigerated. Serve at room temperature or chilled. The cake will keep well for at least 3 days and up to 1 week in the refrigerator.

LOTTCHEN'S KIRSCHKUCHEN
Sunken Lemon-Cherry Cake

MAKES 1 (9-INCH/23CM) CAKE

I sometimes think there are as many recipes for this simple cherry cake as there are German grandmothers. This particular recipe comes from my beloved friend Joanie's German mother-in-law, Lottchen, and has a fine, tender crumb heavily scented with lemon peel, which underlines the sour punch of the cherries. Lottchen faithfully made it every time sour cherry season rolled around, and it became the favorite cake of at least one of her grandsons.

Lottchen, who was from East Prussia (now part of Poland), had a childhood classmate whose family were local landowners. Her family's kitchen *Mamsell* (the name for the family cook, derived from the French *mademoiselle*) provided the recipe that became the family standard. In fact, decades later, when Lottchen passed the recipe on to Joanie, it still used the weight of an egg as the measuring standard. You were supposed to weigh an egg and then use "two egg weights" of butter and "three egg weights" of flour. I updated the measurements for us contemporary bakers but kept the large quantity of lemon peel, which is one of the elements that sets this cake apart.

The cake may be made with pitted fresh sour cherries or canned ones in sugar water, which are a pantry staple in Germany but may be more challenging to find in the United States (if you have a Russian or Polish market near you, look there). Canned sour cherries must be drained before using.

I like to fold the cherries into the batter before baking so that they are well distributed throughout the crumb. If you prefer a mostly plain crumb with cherries sunk into the top, then don't fold them into the batter. Instead, scrape the batter into the pan and top with the cherries, pressing them down ever so slightly before placing the pan in the oven.

In Germany, this cake would almost always be served with *Schlagsahne* (lightly sweetened whipped cream; page 267).

9 tablespoons plus 1 teaspoon/130g unsalted butter, at room temperature

1 cup minus 1½ tablespoons/180g granulated sugar

3 eggs

Grated peel of 1 organic lemon

1½ cups, scooped and leveled, minus 1 tablespoon/180g all-purpose flour

½ teaspoon baking powder

¼ teaspoon salt

2 cups/500g pitted sour cherries, drained if canned

Confectioners' sugar, for dusting (optional)

1 Preheat the oven to 350°F/180°C. Line the bottom of a 9-inch/23cm springform pan with parchment paper.

2 Place the butter and granulated sugar in a bowl and beat together until light and fluffy, scraping down the sides a few times. Beat in the eggs, one at a time. Beat in the grated lemon peel.

3 In a separate bowl, stir together the flour, baking powder, and salt. Beat into the butter mixture just until combined. Scrape down the sides. Fold the cherries into the batter using a spatula.

4 Scrape the batter into the prepared pan and smooth the top. Place in the oven and bake for 55 to 60 minutes, or until the cake is golden brown and starting to pull away from the sides of the pan.

5 Remove the pan from the oven and let cool on a rack for 20 minutes before removing the springform ring. When completely cool, dust with a small amount of confectioners' sugar, if desired, and serve.

DUNKLER KIRSCHKUCHEN
Spiced Chocolate-Cherry Cake

MAKES 1 (9-INCH/23CM) CAKE

Sour cherries preserved in sugar water are a staple in Germany, ladled onto rice pudding, stirred into *Quark*, thickened and used as a filling in cream puffs and tortes, or folded into cake batter. The cake batter can be simple or more complex, like this dark, rich spiced cake made with ground nuts and grated chocolate and shot through with pockets of fruit.

Spiced chocolate-cherry cake has firmly established itself as one of the country's favorites and is a recipe that is often made at home. The combination of warm spices such as cinnamon and allspice with ground nuts and sour fruit might remind you of the *Linzertorte* (page 134), which is considered a Christmas-only recipe in Germany. In fact, this cake is usually made in autumn or winter here. But when you find a good source of canned or jarred sour cherries, nothing will stop you from making it year-round.

The cake batter is relatively simple to make and bakes up nicely, with a tender crumb that is just ever so nubby from the ground almonds. Using both dark chocolate and cocoa in the recipe gives the cake moisture and richness, and the cake keeps well for days. My assistant, Maja, and I adapted the recipe from a cookbook by Anne-Katrin Weber, punching up the spices a bit, subbing lemon peel for orange peel, and using ground almonds instead of hazelnuts for their subtler flavor. Germans would serve this with a dollop of *Schlagsahne* (lightly sweetened whipped cream), but you can forgo it if you prefer.

10½ tablespoons/150g unsalted butter, softened, plus more for the pan

⅔ cup/100g whole, raw almonds

2⅓ cups/585g canned pitted sour cherries in sugar water

3½ ounces/100g bittersweet chocolate (minimum 50% cacao)

¾ cup/150g granulated sugar

4 eggs, separated

¾ cup, scooped and leveled, plus 1 tablespoon/100g all-purpose flour

2 tablespoons cocoa powder

1 teaspoon baking powder

½ teaspoon ground cinnamon

¼ teaspoon ground allspice

1 pinch grated nutmeg

Grated peel of ½ organic lemon

¼ teaspoon salt

Schlagsahne (page 267), for serving (optional)

1 Preheat the oven to 350°F/180°C. Butter a 9-inch/23cm springform pan and set aside. Toast the almonds on a baking sheet in the oven until golden brown and fragrant, about 8 minutes. Set aside to cool.

2 Place the sour cherries in a sieve to drain completely.

3 Melt the chocolate in the top of a double boiler over simmering water or in a microwave in short bursts, stirring after every few bursts. Set aside.

4 When the almonds are completely cool, grind them in a food processor until fine but not reduced to a paste.

5 Place the butter and sugar in the bowl of a stand mixer fitted with the flat beater attachment and beat until light and fluffy. Beat in the egg yolks one at a time.

6 In a separate bowl, combine the ground almonds, flour, cocoa powder, baking powder, cinnamon, allspice, nutmeg, and grated lemon peel; mix well. Beat into the butter mixture just until combined. Scrape in the melted chocolate and mix until combined.

7 Beat the egg whites with the salt in a clean bowl until they hold firm peaks. Gently stir one-third of the egg whites into the batter to lighten it. Then fold in the remaining egg whites until no streaks remain.

8 Scrape the batter into the prepared pan evenly. Scatter the drained cherries over the batter and very gently press into the batter with your hands or the back of a spoon. They shouldn't be submerged into the batter, but rather lightly anchored. Place the cake in the oven and bake for 45 to 50 minutes, or until the cake has risen up around the cherries and a tester inserted into the middle comes out clean. Place the pan on a rack to cool for 10 minutes before removing the springform ring.

9 When the cake is completely cool, cut into wedges and serve with the *Schlagsahne*, if desired. The cake will keep, wrapped in plastic wrap, for at least 3 days and up to 5.

KIRSCHSTREUSELKUCHEN
Sour Cherry Streusel Cake

MAKES 1 (9 BY 13-INCH/23 BY 33CM) CAKE

In the verdant countryside surrounding Berlin, there are many U-pick farms where we pick our own strawberries in late spring, apples in early fall, and blueberries in summer. The blueberry fields are in the middle of a pine forest, and when we have finished filling our pails with kilos and kilos of blueberries, enough to see us through the winter, we head to a snack area at the edge of the clearing. There is a hut where coffee and treats are sold—like freshly made waffles topped with whipped cream and hot blueberry sauce, and a thick yellow cake with blueberries baked into the top. The cake has a wavy, bumpy top and a vanilla-scented, close-crumbed structure. Eating a chunk of it under the pine tree canopy, with a cup of steaming coffee in hand, after an afternoon of blueberry picking with family and friends, is one of the nicest small pleasures of my summer.

While many fruit- and *Streusel*-topped cakes in Germany are made with yeasted doughs (such as the *Pflaumenstreuselkuchen*, page 88, or the *Apfelkuchen*, page 86), this one is made with a regular cake batter, which is richer and sweeter than a puffy yeasted dough. It pairs particularly well with fruit that's on the tart side, like freshly picked blueberries. But as I discovered when developing the recipe, it is even better when made with sour cherries. I like to use jarred or canned sour cherries in sugar water, but instead of discarding the liquid, I thicken it with a bit of cornstarch, just enough so that it holds its shape somewhat, and then spread that mixture all over the thick and creamy batter. On top goes a mess of *Streusel* that has been seasoned ever so slightly with cinnamon, which brings a bit of warmth and depth to the sweet-tart topping.

In the oven, the cherry juice thickens further and bubbles, while the cake rises high and the *Streusel* becomes crunchy and crisp. Warm from the oven,

the cake is incredibly good, but what I might love even more is how good it is on day two, day three, and even day four. The *Streusel* solidify slightly, getting pleasingly chewy, and the cherry topping keeps the cake moist. I can't guarantee that you'll ever be able to keep the cake around for 4 days, but should it happen, you'll be happy to know that it tastes just as good then, too.

Look for canned or jarred sour cherries at Eastern European markets. This cake is also delicious made with fresh or frozen blueberries, quartered Italian prune plums, or sugared rhubarb. If you're using fresh fruit, leave out the cornstarch and skip Step 3. Simply cover the cake with the fruit (cut into bite-size pieces and sprinkled with sugar if need be), and then top with the *Streusel* and bake.

STREUSEL

7 tablespoons/100g unsalted high-fat, European-style butter, softened

½ cup/100g granulated sugar

1 cup, scooped and leveled, plus 1 tablespoon/135g all-purpose flour

¼ teaspoon salt

Pinch of ground cinnamon

CHERRY TOPPING

1 (24-ounce/680g) jar or can pitted sour cherries in sugar water

2 tablespoons cornstarch

BATTER

15½ tablespoons/220g unsalted high-fat, European-style butter, softened

¾ cup plus 2 tablespoons/175g granulated sugar

continued

3 eggs

¾ teaspoon vanilla extract

2⅓ cups, scooped and leveled,
plus 1 tablespoon/300g all-purpose flour

2 teaspoons baking powder

¼ teaspoon salt

3 tablespoons whole milk

1 Preheat the oven to 350°F/180°C. Line a 9 by 13-inch/23 by 33cm metal baking pan with parchment paper, letting the sides hang over the edges to function as a sling after baking.

2 To make the *Streusel*: Cut the butter into cubes and place in a large bowl. Add the sugar, flour, salt, and cinnamon. Work together with your fingertips until the mixture is well combined and crumbly, with both lima bean– and pea-size clumps. Place in the refrigerator until ready to use.

3 To make the cherry topping: Drain all of the liquid from the cherries into a small saucepan, reserving the cherries. Place 3 tablespoons of the liquid in a small bowl. Bring the remaining liquid in the saucepan to a boil over medium-high heat. While you're bringing the liquid to a boil, whisk the cornstarch into the bowl of reserved juice until no lumps remain. When the cherry juice in the pot starts boiling, whisk the cornstarch slurry into the pot. The juice will almost immediately start to thicken and gel. Remove the pot from the heat and continue to whisk until the mixture is smooth. Fold the reserved cherries into the hot, thickened juice and set aside to cool.

4 To make the batter: In the bowl of a stand mixer fitted with the flat beater attachment, cream together the butter and sugar until light and fluffy. Beat in the eggs, one at a time. Then beat in the vanilla extract. In a separate bowl, whisk together the flour, baking powder, and salt. Beat the flour mixture into the butter mixture, scrape down the sides, and then beat in the milk. Scrape the batter into the prepared pan.

5 Distribute the cherries and thickened juice evenly all over the cake batter. Remove the bowl of *Streusel* from the refrigerator, work through it with your fingers to break up any large clumps, and distribute the *Streusel* evenly over the cherries. Place the pan in the oven and bake for 45 to 50 minutes, or until the *Streusel* is light golden.

6 Remove the pan from the oven and let cool on a rack. The cake can be served slightly warm or at room temperature. The cake will keep at room temperature, loosely wrapped in plastic wrap, for several days.

ERDBEER-SAHNE BISKUITROLLE
Strawberry Cream Roll

MAKES 1 (13-INCH-/33CM-LONG) ROLL

The combination of fruit and sponge cake is a classic throughout Germany. In fact, sponge cake is considered an important cake to master for home bakers, since it is such an integral part of so many different tortes and cakes. Luckily, it's easy to master and fun too—you whip egg whites with sugar and a bit of water until they are thick and more than tripled in size. Then you stir in the egg yolks. You add flour and cornstarch, to make the crumb as fine and velvety as possible, as well as a bit of baking powder to help leaven the batter. This gossamer-light mixture is spread onto a baking sheet and then briefly baked until golden brown. Sponge cake is tender and airy, ideal for summer desserts.

To transform a sponge base into a rolled cake, a beloved if old-fashioned fixture at *Kaffeezeit* all over the country, the cake must be immediately inverted and removed from the pan and then rolled up while still hot, so that it doesn't crack and break. The technique here has you invert the cake onto a sugar-strewn dishcloth. You then roll up the cake and dishcloth together and let the cake cool. When you unroll the cooled cake later to fill it, the sugar keeps the surface of the cake from sticking to the cloth and leaves a lovely crystalline spangling all over the cake. The supple cake can then be filled, rolled up again, and served.

The classic filling for a rolled sponge cake is strawberries folded into slightly sweetened whipped cream. You could, of course, exchange the strawberries for another soft fruit, like raspberries or blackberries, or you could chop up a couple of nice ripe peaches to mix with the whipped cream instead. I found that if the fruit is ripe, it doesn't require any additional sugar as long as the whipped cream is sweetened. Not sugaring the fruit also means less juice leakage into the cream.

Once the cake is assembled, you can serve it right away, but a few hours of mellowing in the refrigerator won't do it any harm. Keep this recipe in your back pocket for when you have unexpected guests dropping in.

SPONGE CAKE

4 eggs, separated

Pinch of salt

3 tablespoons hot water

½ cup plus 1½ tablespoons/120g granulated sugar, plus 2 tablespoons for the dishtowel

½ cup, scooped and leveled, plus 2 tablespoons/90g cake flour

3 tablespoons/30g cornstarch

1 teaspoon baking powder

FILLING

1 pound/455g fresh strawberries

2 cups/480ml whipping cream

3 tablespoons granulated sugar

1 Preheat the oven to 400°F/200°C. Line a 13 by 18 by 1-inch/33 by 46 by 2.5cm rimmed baking sheet with parchment paper.

2 To make the sponge cake: Place the egg whites in the bowl of a stand mixer fitted with the whisk attachment. With the motor running, add the salt and water. Whip, adding the ½ cup plus 1½ tablespoons/120g sugar very slowly, until the egg whites are stiff and glossy.

3 Turn off the motor and remove the whisk attachment from the machine. Using the whisk attachment by hand, stir in the egg yolks one at a time, taking care not to deflate the eggs.

continued

4 In a separate bowl, mix together the flour, cornstarch, and baking powder. Sift over the top of the egg mixture. With the whisk attachment in hand, carefully stir in the flour mixture until well combined.

5 Scrape the batter gently onto the prepared pan. Using a bench scraper or offset spatula, smooth out the batter evenly to create a 13 by 16-inch/33 by 40cm rectangle. Place the pan in the oven and bake for 15 minutes, or until the cake is golden brown and dry to the touch.

6 While the cake is baking, spread a clean linen dishcloth (preferably one that has been laundered with unscented soap) on your work surface. Scatter the 2 tablespoons of sugar evenly over the dishcloth.

7 When the cake is done, remove the pan from the oven; if any spots of cake have fused onto the sides of the pan instead of the parchment paper, immediately run a thin knife around them to loosen them. Then turn the pan upside down to unmold the cake onto the sugar-strewn dishcloth. Remove the pan. Brush the parchment paper with cold water to loosen it, and gently but firmly tug off the parchment paper and discard. Fold the bottom edge of the dishcloth over the edge of the cake and roll the cake up in the dishcloth. Set aside to cool completely. (Note: For a shorter, thicker roll, roll from the shorter side.)

8 When you are ready to serve, make the filling: Hull and quarter the strawberries. Whip the cream and sugar together until thick. Fold in the strawberries. Unroll the cake and spread with the whipped cream mixture, leaving a small border on all sides. Roll the cake back up again, using some pressure to squeeze the filling to the edges of the roll.

9 Transfer the cake to a serving platter, slice, and serve. The cake can be made up to 6 hours before serving, but be sure to refrigerate it once it is assembled. The cake will keep, wrapped and refrigerated, for 1 additional day.

ZITRONENBISKUITROLLE
Lemon Cream Roll

The fruit-and-cream-filled sponge cake is archetypal for summer, but for the seasons in which fresh berries aren't available, or if you like puckery-sour lemon desserts, this lemon-flavored creamy filling is just as refreshing. Sweetened *Quark* cheese is mixed with both lemon peel and lemon juice and then folded together with stabilized whipped cream before being rolled up in the sponge cake.

Despite the cream, the cake remains quite light because of *Quark*'s leanness—and if you can let the cake sit for at least a few hours before serving, the sponge cake will soak up a bit of moisture and the whole thing will become a wondrously creamy affair. Between the lightly fluffy sponge and the whipped filling, the cake will almost dissolve in your mouth. It's perfect for an elegant afternoon tea—though perhaps not one in which you are serving hungry teenagers, who will surely demolish it in the blink of an eye.

The cake's length and shape make it challenging for serving platters, which are usually round. To serve on a round platter, cut the roll in half and place the pieces alongside each other. But if you have a long oval or rectangular platter, the full roll will look lovely on that, too.

SPONGE CAKE

4 eggs, separated

Pinch of salt

3 tablespoons hot water

½ cup plus 1½ tablespoons/120g granulated sugar, plus 1 to 2 tablespoons for the dishcloth

11 tablespoons, scooped and leveled/90g cake flour

3 tablespoons/30g cornstarch

1 teaspoon baking powder

FILLING

1 organic lemon

2 cups/500g *Quark* (page 264), drained if necessary (see page 8)

½ cup plus 1½ tablespoons/120g granulated sugar

1 cup/240ml whipping cream

¼ teaspoon cornstarch, sifted

1 Preheat the oven to 400°F/200°C. Line a 13 by 18 by 1-inch/33 by 46 by 2.5cm rimmed baking sheet with parchment paper.

2 To make the sponge cake: Place the egg whites in the bowl of a stand mixer fitted with the whisk attachment. With the motor running, add the salt and hot water. Whip, adding the ½ cup plus 1½ tablespoons/120g sugar very slowly, until the egg whites are stiff and glossy.

3 Turn off the motor and remove the whisk attachment from the machine. With the whisk attachment in hand, stir in the egg yolks one at a time, taking care not to deflate the eggs.

4 In a separate bowl, mix together the flour, cornstarch, and baking powder. Sift over the top of the egg mixture. Again, with the whisk attachment in hand, carefully stir in the flour mixture until well combined.

5 Scrape the batter gently onto the prepared pan. Using a bench scrapper or offset spatula, smooth out the batter evenly to create a 13 by 16-inch/33 by 40cm rectangle. Place the pan in the oven and bake for 15 minutes, or until the cake is golden brown and dry to the touch.

6 While the cake is baking, spread a clean linen dishcloth (preferably one that has been laundered with unscented soap) on your work surface. Scatter the 1 to 2 tablespoons of sugar evenly over the dishcloth.

7 When the cake is done, remove the pan from the oven. If any spots of cake have fused onto the sides of the pan instead of the parchment paper, immediately run a thin knife around them to loosen them. Then turn the pan upside down to unmold the cake onto the sugar-strewn dishcloth. Remove the pan. Brush the parchment paper with cold water to loosen it, and then gently but firmly tug off the parchment paper and discard. Fold the bottom edge of the dishcloth over the edge of the cake and roll the cake up in the dishcloth. Set aside to cool completely. (Note: For a shorter, thicker roll, roll from the shorter side.)

8 To make the filling: Grate the peel of the lemon into a large bowl. Cut the lemon in half and squeeze the juice into the bowl. Add the *Quark* and whisk together until smooth. Whisk in the sugar. Set aside.

9 Place the whipping cream in a large bowl and beat until stiff, adding the sifted cornstarch toward the end of the beating. Fold the whipped cream into the *Quark* mixture until well combined.

10 Unroll the sponge cake and spread with the *Quark* mixture, leaving a small border on all sides. Roll the cake back up again, using some pressure to squeeze the filling to the edges of the roll.

11 Place on a serving plate and refrigerate for at least 2 hours and up to 12 hours and then slice and serve. The cake will keep, wrapped and refrigerated, for 1 additional day.

MARILLENFLECK
Austrian Apricot Sheet Cake

MAKES 1 (13 BY 18-INCH/33 BY 46CM) CAKE

In this simple and traditional Austrian summer cake—which I first discovered on Austrian food writer Katharina Seiser's beautifully written blog *Esskultur* (esskultur.at)—a delicate yellow batter is scraped onto a rimmed baking sheet and dimpled with halved raw apricots. During baking, the cake rises up around the apricot halves, which sink down into the batter. Once the cake has cooled and has been dusted with confectioners' sugar, the apricot halves shine out like little suns. It becomes the most cheerful cake I've ever seen. The combination of cream of tartar and baking soda makes for a very light and airy crumb.

I first made this for my dear friend Joanie's birthday picnic in early summer. Fresh apricots weren't available then, so—encouraged by veteran cookbook author Rick Rodgers's version of this cake—I did the unthinkable and used canned apricots instead. The cake was a huge hit. Since then, I've made the cake with both fresh and canned apricots, and while fresh ones are of course preferable, it's good to know that canned can be used as well. After all, this is the kind of crowd-pleasing cake you'll want to make year-round.

The cake batter is so simple that it lends itself well to experimentation with other fruits. Try scattering a few handfuls of blueberries or halved, pitted sweet or sour cherries onto the batter before baking.

3¼ pounds/1.5kg ripe apricots or 3 (15¼-ounce/432g) cans apricot halves, drained

14 tablespoons/200g unsalted butter

1⅔ cups, scooped and leveled, minus 1 tablespoon/200g all-purpose flour

¾ teaspoon baking soda

¼ teaspoon cream of tartar

⅛ teaspoon salt

1½ cups plus 2 tablespoons/200g confectioners' sugar, plus more for garnish

4 eggs, at room temperature

1 teaspoon vanilla extract

Grated peel of ½ organic lemon

1 tablespoon freshly squeezed lemon juice

1 Preheat the oven to 350°F/180°C. Line a 13 by 18 by 1-inch/33 by 46 by 2.5cm rimmed baking sheet with parchment paper. Wash, dry, halve, and pit the apricots, and set aside.

2 Melt the butter and remove from the heat as soon as it has melted. While the butter is melting, whisk together the flour, baking soda, cream of tartar, and salt in a medium bowl.

3 Pour the melted butter into a large mixing bowl or the bowl of a stand mixer. Add the confectioners' sugar and beat with a whisk or with the whisk attachment just until no lumps remain. Add half of the flour mixture and mix until well combined. Beat in the eggs one at a time. Beat in the vanilla extract, grated lemon peel, and lemon juice just until combined. Beat in the remaining flour mixture and scrape down the sides of the bowl with a spatula.

4 Scrape the batter onto the prepared pan, spreading it out into the corners. Place the apricot halves, cut-side up, on the cake batter, distributing them evenly and leaving only a little bit of space between them.

5 Bake for 25 to 30 minutes, or until the cake is golden brown and a cake tester inserted into the cake (not an apricot) comes out clean.

6 Remove the pan from the oven and cool on a rack. When the cake is completely cool, dust evenly with more confectioners' sugar, cut into squares, and serve.

RHABARBERKUCHEN
Simple Rhubarb Cake

MAKES 1 (10-INCH/25CM) CAKE

After the long, dark German winter, spring always feels like a miracle. The tender green shoots pushing up through the frozen soil, the tentative fingers of light that the sun casts through the spidery trees, the blessed sound of the first returning birds early in the morning—it feels impossible to ever take any of that for granted after surviving the previous months, no matter how many spicy, comforting Christmas cookies you squirreled away. Rhubarb is the first tangible marker of spring in the markets and is used to make countless sheets of cake when the air is still on the chilly side but the days are steadily growing longer.

Rhubarb is a very common plant in Germany. Anyone with a garden will likely have a couple of leafy bushes of rhubarb growing in it. Because it's so sour, it's traditionally paired with delicate cake batters, sugary *Streusel*, sweet custard, or even meringue. And most people here feel that any rhubarb cake *must* be accompanied by *Schlagsahne*—sweetened whipped cream. This tastes delicious but also makes sense from a nutritional standpoint: pairing calcium-rich foods with food high in oxalic acid (such as rhubarb) is said to help reduce the supposed harmful effects that oxalic acid can have.

This particular rhubarb cake is one of the simplest. It's perfect for those teatimes when you don't have time or energy to make anything fancy but still want something sweet and satisfying. The batter, flavored with a bit of lemon peel and vanilla, is simple and easy—and lets the fruit on top steal the show. A lot of chopped rhubarb is piled on a relatively thin layer of batter, but in the oven, the fruit slumps down and the cake puffs up around it. In the end, you have a balanced ratio. The tender, delicate cake batter also pairs really nicely with sour cherries or chopped plums.

If you like, you can top the cake with *Mandelstreusel* (page 266) to make a simple *Rhabarberstreuselkuchen*. If so, use just 2 tablespoons of sugar to toss with the rhubarb, and bake for an additional 5 to 10 minutes, or until the *Streusel* is golden brown. Many Germans think rhubarb paired with yeasted sweet dough is a particularly delicious treat, so another alternative is to make a batch of the yeasted dough on page 86 (*Apfelkuchen*) and top it with 1 pound/500g chopped rhubarb mixed with 3 to 4 tablespoons/40 to 50g of sugar, and a batch of plain *Streusel* (page 266). Serve with whipped cream, always.

1 pound 2 ounces/500g rhubarb, trimmed

¾ cup plus 1 tablespoon/160g granulated sugar

7 tablespoons/100g unsalted high-fat, European-style butter, softened

2 eggs

½ teaspoon vanilla extract

Grated peel of ½ organic lemon

1½ cups, scooped and leveled/190g all-purpose flour

2 teaspoons baking powder

¼ teaspoon salt

¼ cup/60ml whole milk

Confectioners' sugar, for serving (optional)

Schlagsahne (page 267), for serving

1 Preheat the oven to 350°F/180°C. Line a 10-inch/25cm cake pan with a piece of parchment paper, letting the sides hang over the edge to function as a sling after baking.

2 Chop the rhubarb into ½-inch/12mm pieces and toss with 3 tablespoons of the sugar. Set aside.

3 In a mixing bowl, cream together the butter and remaining ½ cup plus 2 tablespoons/125g sugar until light and fluffy. Beat in the eggs one at a time. Then beat in the vanilla extract and grated lemon peel.

4 In a separate bowl, sift together the flour, baking powder, and salt. Beat half of this mixture into the butter mixture, and then beat in the milk. Beat in the remaining flour mixture just until combined.

5 Scrape the batter into the prepared pan, distributing it evenly. Scatter the rhubarb over the batter and press it lightly into the batter. It will seem like a lot of rhubarb, but this is just right. Place the pan in the oven and bake for 1 hour, or until the batter has puffed up slightly around the rhubarb and is golden brown.

6 Remove the pan from the oven and place on a rack to cool completely before removing the cake and peeling off the parchment paper. The cake can be eaten the day it is made but is even better after a night's rest. Dust with confectioners' sugar before serving, if desired. Cut into wedges and serve with the *Schlagsahne*. The cake will keep at room temperature, loosely wrapped in plastic wrap, for 1 additional day.

MARMORKUCHEN
Marble Cake

MAKES 1 (9-INCH/23CM) CAKE

You may not think you need another recipe for marble cake, but I am here to tell you that you absolutely do. This one, a family recipe from my assistant Maja, is the best one I've ever tasted. It was *the* birthday cake of her childhood. (Marble cakes often show up as children's birthday cakes in Germany—at my son's day care, almost all the children request it when their birthday rolls around.) But it's definitely not just for kids—it has a richness and intensity that adults fall in love with, too. Just the other day, Maja's uncle requested this cake for his eightieth birthday party.

Maja's secret is stirring melted white chocolate into the plain batter. Don't worry; this doesn't make the batter taste of white chocolate. When the cake is baked, the white parts simply taste richer, toastier, and more complex. Instead of quickly munching through them to get to the chocolate cake, you'll actually want to savor the white cake as well—a first, at least in my marble cake experience.

Baked in a *Gugelhupf* pan, the cake rises up to great heights, making for satisfyingly big slices. You can, of course, make this in a Bundt pan instead (reduce the baking time by 10 to 15 minutes). Surprisingly, the cake actually gets better with age, so if you can, try to bake it a day before you plan to serve it. And to make the marble cake look just a bit more special, dust it with confectioners' sugar before serving.

3½ ounces/100g bittersweet chocolate (minimum 50% cacao), chopped

3½ ounces/100g white chocolate, chopped

18 tablespoons/250g unsalted high-fat, European-style butter, softened, plus more for the pan

1¼ cups/250g granulated sugar

¼ teaspoon salt

1 teaspoon vanilla extract

4 eggs

2 cups, scooped and leveled/250g all-purpose flour, plus more for the pan

1 tablespoon baking powder

2 tablespoons cocoa powder

3 tablespoons whole milk

Confectioners' sugar, for dusting (optional)

1 Preheat the oven to 350°F/180°C, placing the rack in the bottom third of the oven. Liberally butter and flour a *Gugelhupf* or Bundt pan.

2 Put the bittersweet and white chocolates into two separate small stainless steel bowls that can be set over a small saucepan of simmering water, or in microwave-safe bowls. Melt the chocolates, one bowl at a time, over the saucepan of simmering water or in the microwave in small bursts, stirring after every few bursts. Set aside to cool.

3 Place the butter in the bowl of a stand mixer fitted with the flat beater attachment. Add the sugar and salt and beat until light and fluffy. Beat in the vanilla extract and then the eggs, one at a time, scraping down the bowl after each addition, until the mixture is well combined.

4 In a separate bowl, whisk together the flour and baking powder. Beat the flour into the butter mixture. Then scrape out two-thirds of the batter into a medium bowl and stir all of the melted white chocolate into the larger batch of batter until no streaks remain.

5 Add the melted bittersweet chocolate, cocoa powder, and milk to the remaining one-third of the batter and beat until fully combined and no streaks remain.

6 Scrape half of the white batter into the prepared cake pan. Top with the bittersweet batter. Then scrape the remaining white batter on top. Using swooping motions, drag the blade of a knife through the batter to create a marbled cake. Place the pan in the oven and bake for 60 minutes, or until the white part of the cake is golden brown and a tester comes out clean. (If using a Bundt pan, start testing after 45 minutes.)

7 Place the pan on a rack to cool for 10 minutes before unmolding it onto the rack and letting it cool upside down. When the cake has cooled completely, dust with confectioners' sugar, if desired, and serve. The cake can be made a day ahead. Any leftovers will keep, wrapped in plastic wrap, for 3 days at room temperature.

MARMORIERTER MOHNKUCHEN
Marbleized Poppy-Seed Cake

MAKES 1 (9-INCH/23CM) CAKE

What I have come to understand from my time in Germany is that you either love poppy seeds or hate them. I happen to love their haunting, stony flavor, and how it reminds me so strongly of childhood afternoons spent at my friend Joanie's apartment, where there was always something delicious baking in the oven. To use poppy seeds in cakes, you must grind them to crack their tiny little hulls, which releases their oils and delicate fragrance. Left whole, they just won't have the same flavor and creamy-nubby texture. To grind poppy seeds, use a hand-cranked poppy-seed grinder, an electric coffee grinder, or a high-powered blender. A food processor won't do, as the seeds are too tiny to be caught in the big blades. (For more information, see page 11.)

This marbleized cake is made by swirling a creamy vanilla batter together with a sturdy poppy-seed batter flavored with vanilla and almond extracts to give the ground poppy seeds extra ballast. In the finished cake, the poppy seed crumb is textured and a lovely bluish gray, contrasting with the tender and buttery yellow crumb. It is an excellent candidate for afternoon teatime, pairing well with both tea or coffee.

In Germany, this kind of cake would be baked in a *Gugelhupf* pan, which is more compact and taller than a Bundt pan. I'm not big on spending money on specialty baking pans, but it's worth seeking out one for the satisfying wedges you can cut out of a *Gugelhupf*-shaped cake. Of course, the cake will taste equally good if made in a Bundt pan. Just remember that it won't need to bake as long. A dusting of confectioners' sugar will give the cake a nice finish at serving time, no matter which pan you use.

I call for cake flour in the recipe to achieve a delicate crumb. This cake can, however, also be made with all-purpose flour if that is all you have. It will result in a sturdier, denser crumb.

POPPY-SEED FILLING

½ cup/120ml whole milk

¾ cup plus 2 tablespoons/125g poppy seeds, ground (see page 7)

½ cup/100g granulated sugar

½ teaspoon vanilla extract

⅛ teaspoon almond extract

CAKE BATTER

18 tablespoons/250g unsalted high-fat, European-style butter, softened, plus more for the pan

1 cup/200g granulated sugar

4 eggs

1 teaspoon vanilla extract

3⅔ cups, scooped and leveled, minus 1 tablespoon/450g cake flour, plus more for the pan

¼ cup plus 1 teaspoon/40g cornstarch

1 tablespoon baking powder

¼ teaspoon salt

⅔ cup/160ml whole milk

Confectioners' sugar, for dusting (optional)

1 Preheat the oven to 350°F/180°C. Liberally butter a *Gugelhupf* pan or Bundt pan and dust it lightly with flour.

continued

2 To make the poppy-seed filling: Heat the milk over medium-high heat until just boiling. Place the ground poppy seeds in a medium bowl and pour in the milk. Stir in the sugar and the vanilla and almond extracts until well combined. Set aside to cool; the poppy seeds will swell.

3 To make the cake batter: Place the butter and sugar in the bowl of a stand mixer fitted with the flat beater attachment. Beat together for several minutes, until the mixture is light and fluffy. Scrape down the sides. Beat in the eggs, one at a time, until well combined. Scrape down the sides. Beat in the vanilla extract.

4 In a separate bowl, whisk together the flour, cornstarch, baking powder, and salt. With the motor running on low speed, mix one-third of the flour mixture into the batter, and then one-third of the milk. Mix in another one-third of the flour mixture and one-third of the milk. Finally, mix in the remaining one-third of the flour mixture and end with the milk. Scrape down the sides and give the mixture another quick mix by hand. Scrape one-third of this mixture into the bowl with the poppy-seed filling and stir well, until no streaks remain.

5 Dollop half of the plain cake batter on the bottom of the prepared pan. Top with the poppy-seed batter and then distribute the remaining plain cake batter on top. Drag a knife in swooping motions through the batters to create a marbled effect. Place in the oven and bake for 1 hour, or until a tester inserted into the center of the cake comes out clean. (If using a Bundt pan, start testing after 45 minutes).

6 Place the pan on a rack to cool for 30 minutes before turning it upside down and removing the pan. Let the cake cool completely. Dust with confectioners' sugar before serving, if desired. The cake will keep for 3 days at room temperature, wrapped in plastic wrap.

YEASTED CAKES

For Americans, the concept of a sweet yeasted cake can be strange. Yeast is, after all, far more associated with bread than with cake in the United States. But sweetened yeasted doughs topped with everything from fresh fruit to creamy poppy-seed puddings or even just a simple scattering of butter and sugar are actually the backbone of the German sweet kitchen.

The traditional meals of a regular German day are a little different from those elsewhere. The day starts with an early breakfast. Then, sometime around ten or eleven in the morning, a second breakfast is taken (called *zweites Frühstück*). In modern times, this has been supplanted by the *Pausenbrot* (two slices of grainy dark bread spread with butter and a slice of cheese or ham, which every child takes to school for snack time), which is by no means restricted just to schoolchildren. My husband takes a couple *Pausenbrote* to work every day. In the middle of the day comes *Mittagessen* (lunch), of course, which is almost always a hot meal, as opposed to *Abendbrot* (dinner), which is usually cold. Between lunch and dinner comes the all-important *Kaffeezeit*, or coffee time, when cake is eaten.

This tradition reaches back to Germany's agricultural times, when people who worked the land would have been ravenous in the afternoon and in need of sustenance that wasn't too sweet or rich. Yeasted cakes fill this need perfectly, since they are relatively wholesome, low in sugar and fat when compared to batter cakes, and often laden with fresh fruit. Traditionally, these cakes are baked in sheet pans so that many mouths can be fed at the same time.

Yeasted sweet cakes are found all over eastern and central Europe. The most famous specimen would probably be the turban-shaped *Gugelhupf* (page 95), which both France and Austria have claimed as their own. But Germany's fruit-topped yeasted cakes, like *Pflaumenkuchen* (page 88)—prune plum cake, made with or without *Streusel*—or the sticky almond- and caramel-topped *Bienenstich* (page 90), also deserve accolades.

In my experience, baking with yeast is satisfying and fun. I love the satiny, pliable texture that yeasted sweet doughs have, and their inimitable scent and flavor when baked. But for many, baking with yeast can seem intimidating or difficult. If you are frightened

of baking with yeast, I promise that it is much easier than it seems—the key is to use either fresh yeast or instant yeast (also known as bread-machine yeast; see page 6), both of which are more user-friendly and reliable than active dry yeast.

Some more tips: The ingredients for the yeasted doughs should be at room temperature when possible, unless cold butter is specifically called for. Your kitchen or work space should be relatively warm, without any drafts. Identify a good spot for proofing the dough (letting it rise): either a warm corner near a radiator, or in the oven (turned off), for example. Kneading is a forceful job that should feel like an upper-arm workout, with most of the power coming from the heels of your palms. Resist adding too much flour to the dough as you knead, or it can become tough. Yeasted cake doughs are usually heavy with

eggs and butter, so the traditional rule of thumb when working with yeasted dough, that a dough should double in size during proofing, will not always apply here. After proofing, the dough should feel light and slightly puffy, even if it has not doubled in bulk. One last word: practice, practice, practice. The more yeasted doughs you make, the more comfortable you will get at working with this type of dough and identifying the floppy and soft sweet spot that a well-made yeasted dough should have when it's ready to proof.

This chapter includes recipes for yeasted cakes as well as sweet yeasted braids, which may look more breadlike than cakelike but are so rich and delectable that one bite will leave you with no question about which category they belong in.

HOW LONG IS NOW

ZUCKERKUCHEN

Sugar Cake

MAKES 1 (9 BY 13-INCH/23 BY 33CM) CAKE

Zuckerkuchen is nothing more than a sheet of buttery, yeasted dough covered with a thick spangling of sugar before being baked, but it is pure comfort in a pan. The smell of *Zuckerkuchen* is intoxicating—that special amalgam of sweet yeastiness, caramelizing sugar, and nutty, toasting butter is irresistible. Using a good cultured or imported butter here is imperative.

Traditionally, *Zuckerkuchen*, like *Butterkuchen* (page 82) and *Streuselkuchen* (page 84), was baked in great big slabs at a communal bakery. My friend Dietrich, whose parents lived in the German Democratic Republic, still remembers the lines that would form down the block when the local bakers in Brieselang, near where his parents lived, would take freshly made *Zuckerkuchen* out of their ovens and slice it up for sale. At some greenmarkets in Berlin, you can still find *Zuckerkuchen* being baked in huge slabs and sliced up for shoppers to take home, or to eat right there on the spot, much like *pizza al taglio* in Italy.

Zuckerkuchen is excellent for picnics—easily transported and easily eaten with your hands. I also love it for very young children's birthdays as it is quite wholesome compared to lavishly frosted birthday cakes. I don't think I've ever met a child who didn't like *Zuckerkuchen*. Or an adult either, for that matter.

2 cups, scooped and leveled/250g all-purpose flour, plus more for kneading

1 teaspoon instant yeast

½ cup/120ml whole milk

½ cup plus 2 tablespoons/125g granulated sugar

1 egg yolk

3 tablespoons/40g unsalted high-fat, European-style butter, melted and cooled

⅛ teaspoon salt

4 tablespoons plus 1 teaspoon/60g unsalted high-fat, European-style butter, cold, cut into small cubes

1 Line a 9 by 13-inch/23 by 33cm pan with parchment paper, letting the sides hang over the edge to function as a sling after baking.

2 Place the flour and yeast in a mixing bowl. Add the milk in a thin stream, mixing with a wooden spoon as you pour. Add ¼ cup plus 2 tablespoons/75g of the sugar and the egg yolk to the bowl and mix. The dough will start to come together shaggily. Add the melted butter and the salt. Mix until a rough ball starts to form. Scrape this mixture onto a floured surface and knead for a few minutes, until smooth. You may need to add a little flour to keep the dough from sticking, but don't add too much; you want the dough to be soft and slightly floppy. Form the dough into a ball and place it in the prepared pan. Cover with a clean dishcloth and put in a warm, draft-free place for 1 hour.

3 Preheat the oven to 350°F/180°C. Remove the paper from the pan, lay it on your work surface, and roll out the dough until it fits the indentations of the pan on the paper, and then transfer the paper and dough back to the pan. Using your fingers, make dimples all over the dough.

4 Distribute the cold butter evenly all over the dough. Then sprinkle the entire cake with the remaining ¼ cup/50g sugar. Cover the pan with the dishcloth again and let sit for 20 minutes.

5 Bake for 20 to 25 minutes, or until the cake is golden brown and bubbling.

6 Let cool on a rack for 15 minutes. Using the parchment paper as a sling, lift the cake out of the pan and place it on a cutting board. Cut into squares and serve warm. This cake is best eaten the day it is made.

BUTTERKUCHEN
Butter-Almond Cake

MAKES 1 (9 BY 13-INCH/23 BY 33CM) CAKE

Zuckerkuchen (page 81), *Streuselkuchen* (page 84), and *Butterkuchen* make up the sisterhood of Germany's most understated cakes. They are simple yeasted affairs, always baked in a sheet pan and topped with nothing but hefty portions of butter, sugar, or *Streusel*, sometimes with sliced almonds tossed in for good measure. Their plain-Jane looks belie their popularity, though. They'll never win an award for beauty, but these are cakes with rock-star status.

Butterkuchen is made by dimpling the surface of a rich yeast dough (it has more butter and eggs than others in the book) and dropping what seems like an enormous quantity of butter into all of those little dimples, along with sprinklings of sugar and sliced almonds. When the cake bakes, the dough puffs up slightly and then slumps down a bit under the melting butter, creating a light yet chewy cake, while the almonds turn crisp and toasty. When you slice a freshly baked *Butterkuchen*, it will crackle faintly under the knife. Much like the sound of the first pour of wine coming out of a freshly opened bottle, that crackle is addictive.

If ever there was a time to seek out high-fat, European-style butter, this is it, both for better flavor and for a toothsome texture. Remember, too, that this is not the time to skimp on quantity—*Butterkuchen* only turns out as deliciously juicy and tasty as it's supposed to be if you go whole hog (pardon the expression) on the called-for quantities of butter. A dry *Butterkuchen* is a sad thing indeed.

In some regions of Germany, *Butterkuchen* is the traditional cake served at christenings and funerals, which makes sense when you consider its crowd-pleasing simplicity, ease of preparation, and yield. (Here, as elsewhere, for modernity's sake, I've developed the recipe to fit a 9 by 13-inch/23 by 33cm metal baking pan instead of a sheet pan, but the recipe is easily doubled if you'd like to feed a crowd.) There is some regional disagreement about whether *Butterkuchen* and *Zuckerkuchen* are two distinct cakes or the same cake with different names. I have two different recipes and love them both.

CAKE

1 teaspoon instant yeast

2 tablespoons granulated sugar

2 cups, scooped and leveled/250g all-purpose flour, plus more for kneading

Grated peel of ½ organic lemon

2 pinches of salt

9 tablespoons plus 1 teaspoon/130g unsalted high-fat European-style butter, at room temperature

2 eggs, at room temperature

TOPPING

10 tablespoons/140g unsalted high-fat, European-style butter, cold

1 cup/85g blanched sliced almonds

½ cup/100g granulated sugar

¼ teaspoon salt

⅛ teaspoon ground cinnamon

1 Line a 9 by 13-inch/23 by 33cm metal baking pan with parchment paper, letting the sides hang over the edge to function as a sling after baking.

2 To make the cake: Place the yeast, sugar, flour, grated lemon peel, salt, butter, and eggs in the bowl of a stand mixer fitted with the flat beater attachment. Beat together for several minutes, until the dough is shiny and starts flapping around the bowl and beaters in larger chunks. The dough will be quite soft but should no longer be sticky to the touch. Alternatively, you can make the dough by hand. Mix the yeast, sugar, flour, grated lemon peel, and salt together in a large bowl. Make a well in the middle of the flour and crack in the eggs. Stir the eggs into the flour with one hand and start adding the soft butter, having cut it into chunks. Knead the dough together in the bowl until it comes together, then scrape it out onto a lightly floured work surface and knead until smooth and no longer sticky. Resist adding too much flour; you want the dough to remain soft and slightly floppy.

3 Scrape the dough together and form into a smooth ball using your hands. Place the dough in the middle of the prepared pan and cover the pan with a clean dishcloth. Set aside in a warm, draft-free spot for 1 to 2 hours. The dough will not necessarily double in size, but it should be quite puffy and soft to the touch.

4 Preheat the oven to 375°F/190°C. Using the tips of your fingers, push the dough down gently into the pan so that it lines the entire pan evenly, or remove the paper from the pan, lay it on your work surface, and roll out the dough until it fits the indentations of the pan on the paper, and then transfer the paper and dough back to the pan. The dough will be very thin. Using your fingers, dimple the surface of the dough all over.

5 To make the topping: Cube the cold butter into ¼-inch/6mm pieces and drop the cubes evenly all over the cake. It will seem like a very large amount of butter. Scatter the almonds evenly all over the cake. Mix the sugar, salt, and cinnamon together and scatter evenly all over the cake.

6 Place in the oven and bake for 25 to 30 minutes, or until the topping is golden brown.

7 Remove the pan from the oven and let cool on a rack for 10 minutes. Using the parchment paper as a sling, lift the cake out of the pan and place it on a cutting board. Cut into squares and serve warm. This cake is best eaten the day it is made.

STREUSELKUCHEN
Yeasted Streusel Cake

MAKES 1 (9 BY 13-INCH/23 BY 33CM) CAKE

Streuselkuchen, a simple yeasted cake topped with nothing but great handfuls of *Streusel*, and then baked until puffy, fragrant, and a pale gold color, is beloved around the country. Considered a typical *Sonntagskuchen* (Sunday cake), something you'd make on Sundays for the cozy afternoon *Kaffeezeit*, it can be thrown together in very little time, despite what you might think about working with yeast.

A sweet yeasted dough comes together very quickly, especially when you're working with a stand mixer. And making *Streusel* is child's play. Once the dough is patted out into a pan and the *Streusel* is distributed evenly on top, all your work is done. During baking, the cake fills the house with the appetizing, wholesome smell of yeast, and of sugar and butter caramelizing. Because there is not much here to adorn this cake—no lemon peel or vanilla extract or other distractions—try to use the very best quality butter you can find. Any European or high-fat butter will do nicely.

I like to say that I'm on a one-woman crusade to get Americans to stop saying "strew-sel" and learn to say "stroy-sel." In fact, *streuen* ("stroy-yen") is the German verb for "to scatter," which is how *Streusel* got its name. It's hard to think of something more emblematic of German baking than *Streusel*, which adorns countless cakes and breakfast rolls across the country. And every baker I know has a slightly different recipe for the best *Streusel* ever. (The winner, in my unscientific opinion, has to be my husband's Saxonian grandmother, whose *Streusel* cakes are unparalleled.)

The cake can be tweaked by layering fruit between the cake and the *Streusel*, but the basic cake is divine in its own right, especially when served still warm from the oven. The *Streusel* crackles slightly under your teeth as they sink down into the sweet, soft,

pillowy base. Keeping the sugar amounts relatively restrained means you'll find yourself eating far more pieces of *Streuselkuchen* than you ever thought possible. Note that this recipe makes a relatively thick base cake; if you'd like a thinner cake, with a higher *Streusel*-to-cake ratio, halve the recipe for the cake base, but bake it in the same pan (to halve the egg, simply beat it in a small bowl, pour half of it into the dough, and discard the rest).

Streuselschnecken, flat disks of yeasted dough topped with *Streusel* and thickly iced, are a beloved afternoon snack in Germany. To make them, follow Steps 1 and 2. Then divide the dough into 8 equal portions. Roll each portion of dough to a ball and place on a parchment-lined baking sheet. Cover with a dishcloth and let proof for 45 minutes. Make the *Streusel* as directed in Step 4. When the dough has finished proofing, preheat the oven to 350°F/180°C. Remove the dishcloth and, using a rolling pin, gently roll out each ball to ¼-inch/6mm thickness. Cover each disk liberally with a generous handful of *Streusel*, pressing it down gently onto the dough. Place the baking sheet in the oven and bake until golden brown, 20 to 25 minutes. Remove the pan from the oven and let the *Schnecken* cool completely. Make a thick but pourable glaze by mixing 1½ cups/150g confectioners' sugar with 1 tablespoon of lemon juice and 1 tablespoon of water. If necessary, thin with a few more drops of water or lemon juice. Drizzle the glaze liberally all over the *Schnecken*. Let the icing set before serving. *Streuselschnecken* are best the day they are made.

CAKE

2 cups, scooped and leveled/250g all-purpose flour, plus more for kneading

1 teaspoon instant yeast

¼ cup plus 1 tablespoon/60g granulated sugar

¼ teaspoon salt

½ cup/120ml whole milk

1 egg, at room temperature

3½ tablespoons/50g unsalted high-fat, European-style butter, at room temperature

STREUSEL

1⅔ cups, scooped and leveled, minus 1 tablespoon/200g all-purpose flour

¼ teaspoon salt

⅔ cup plus 1 teaspoon/140 granulated sugar

10 tablespoons/140g unsalted high-fat, European-style butter, softened, cut into chunks

1 To make the cake: Place the flour, yeast, sugar, and salt in the bowl of a stand mixer fitted with the flat beater attachment. Turn the motor on low and pour in the milk and then add the egg. Cut the butter into 3 pieces. Turn the motor up and beat in the butter 1 piece at a time, until the dough is well mixed. Continue to beat for 1 to 2 minutes. Turn off the mixer.

2 Scatter a generous handful of flour on your work surface. Using a dough scraper or spatula, scrape out the dough, which will be sticky, onto the work surface and knead it lightly by hand until it is smooth and supple but still relatively loose. You may need to add more flour if the dough sticks to your hands or the counter too much, but try to resist adding too much flour. You don't want this to be a stiff dough; you want it to feel soft and yielding after kneading.

3 When the dough is no longer sticky, form it into a ball and place back in the mixing bowl. Cover with a clean dishcloth and place somewhere warm and draft-free to proof for 1 hour. In the meantime, line a 9 by 13-inch/23 by 33cm metal baking pan with parchment paper, letting the sides hang over the edge to function as a sling after baking, and prepare the *Streusel*.

4 To make the *Streusel*: Place the flour, salt, sugar, and butter in a bowl. Using your fingers, work all the ingredients together until well combined, with both lima bean- and pea-size clumps. Place the *Streusel* in the refrigerator until you're ready to bake.

5 Heat the oven to 350°F/180°C. Take the risen dough, which will be slightly puffy to the touch, and place it in the baking pan. Using your fingers, gently push it out to the edges of the pan, leveling it all around, or remove the paper from the pan, lay it on your work surface, and roll out the dough until it fits the indentations of the pan on the paper, and then transfer the paper and dough back to the pan. Cover the pan with the dishcloth and let sit for 20 minutes.

6 Remove the dishcloth and scatter the *Streusel* evenly all over the yeasted dough, pressing down very lightly with your hands. Place the pan in the oven and bake for 30 to 35 minutes, or until the *Streusel* is faintly golden and the cake has puffed and risen.

7 Remove the pan from the oven and place it on a rack to cool for 20 minutes. Then, using the parchment paper as a sling, remove the cake from the pan, cut into squares or rectangles, and serve. *Streuselkuchen* is best eaten still warm or cool on the day it is made. If you must keep it an additional day, wrap it in plastic wrap, and then freshen it up in a warm oven for a few minutes before serving.

APFELKUCHEN
Yeasted Apple Cake

MAKES 1 (9 BY 13-INCH/23 BY 33CM) CAKE

In American baking, we tend to think of cake as being something rich and sinful—an occasional indulgence rather than a daily treat. But in Germany, cake has a more benign reputation. Of course, this has to do with the German coffee culture, in which most of society still honors the afternoon snack with a cup of coffee and a bite of something sweet. But I think it also has to do with the kinds of cakes available in Germany.

An everyday cake in Germany is more likely to be made with a yeasted base, which is a far lighter affair than a buttery cake batter, and it is often topped with generous amounts of fruit. These yeasted fruit-topped cakes are chewy and juicy and not anywhere as sweet as what you may be accustomed to, though they definitely still qualify as cake and not bread. To gild the lily, they are often served with *Schlagsahne*, lightly sweetened whipped cream. (In fact, many informally polled German friends consider this accompaniment almost mandatory.)

This apple cake is wonderfully simple, consisting of just a yeasted base scented with lemon peel and topped with chunked apples and sugar. I like it best that way, plain and simple (and I eschew whipped cream, because I usually end up eating squares of *Apfelkuchen* out of hand while standing at the counter). But it can be tweaked in a few different directions, for example by adding rum-soaked raisins (soak ½ cup/80g of raisins in 2 tablespoons of dark rum for 3 hours and scatter across the risen dough before adding the apples) or sliced blanched almonds (scatter ½ cup/40g of almonds evenly across the apples before baking) or both. To make *Apfelstreuselkuchen*, you can top the apples with a batch of plain or almond *Streusel* (both on page 266) before baking.

I like the moisture and flavor that fresh yeast brings to the cake, but instant yeast can easily be substituted. The lemon peel in the dough and the lemon juice in the apples are important, because together they give the cake a delicately floral note that works well with the sweet-sour apples and the sweet, chewy base. The apples give off quite a bit of moisture, which can be nerve-wracking during baking because you might think that all that juice will keep the dough from baking through. But don't worry; the long baking time takes that into consideration. The apple juice mixes with the sugar and caramelizes the edges of the cake, something you discover only once you unmold it.

Apfelkuchen is, as with all yeasted cakes, best the day it's made, but if you have leftovers that you wrap in aluminum foil, I can attest that it makes for an excellent breakfast with a cup of hot coffee.

¾ ounce/20g fresh yeast, or 1 teaspoon instant yeast

2 cups, scooped and leveled/250g all-purpose flour, plus more for kneading

¼ cup plus 2 tablespoons/75g granulated sugar, plus 3 to 4 tablespoons/40 to 50g for sprinkling on the fruit

½ cup/120ml whole milk, lukewarm

1 egg yolk

3 tablespoons/40g unsalted high-fat, European-style butter, at room temperature

Grated peel and juice of ½ organic lemon

¼ teaspoon salt

6 apples

1 Line a 9 by 13-inch/23 by 33cm pan with parchment paper, letting the sides hang over the edge to function as a sling after baking.

2 If using fresh yeast, lace the flour in a mixing bowl and make a well in the middle. Crumble the fresh yeast into the well and add a pinch of the sugar. Pour the milk over the yeast in a thin stream, mixing gently in small circles with a wooden spoon as you pour, to dissolve the yeast. Cover the bowl with a clean dishcloth and set aside for 15 minutes. (If using instant yeast, place the flour, yeast, sugar, and salt in a large bowl. Add the grated lemon peel and make a well in the middle of the flour mixture. Whisk the milk and egg yolk together and pour into the well. Start stirring, adding the butter in rough chunks, and then knead by hand in the bowl until a shaggy dough starts to develop. Proceed to the kneading portion of Step 3.)

3 When the mixture in the well is thick and bubbling, add the ¼ cup plus 2 tablespoons/75g of sugar and the egg yolk, butter, grated lemon peel, and salt; mix until combined—the dough will be a little shaggy to start. Scrape this mixture out onto a floured surface and knead for a few minutes, until smooth. You may need to add a little flour to keep the dough from sticking, but don't add too much; you want the dough to be soft and slightly floppy. Form the dough into a ball and place it in the prepared pan. Cover with a clean dishcloth and put in a warm, draft-free place for 1 hour.

4 Using your fingers, gently deflate the dough and push it out evenly to fit the pan (without making a raised edge), or remove the paper from the pan, lay it on your work surface, and roll out the dough evenly until it fits the indentations of the pan on the paper, and then transfer the paper and dough back to the pan. Using your fingers, make dimples all over the dough. Cover with the dishcloth again and set aside for 20 to 30 minutes, or until slightly puffy.

5 While the dough proofs again, preheat the oven to 350°F/180°C. Peel, core, and quarter the apples, and then cut them into ½-inch/12mm chunks. Place the chunks in a bowl and toss with the lemon juice.

6 After the proofing time is up, scatter the apple chunks evenly all over the dough. It will seem like a lot of apples, but this is just fine. Gently push them down into the dough. Then sprinkle the remaining 3 to 4 tablespoons/40 to 50g of sugar over the apples.

7 Place the pan in the oven and bake for 50 to 55 minutes, or until any visible cake is golden brown and some of the apples are toasted.

8 Remove the pan from the oven and place on a rack to cool for 30 minutes. Using the parchment paper as a sling, remove the cake from the pan and place on a cutting board. Cut the cake into squares or rectangles and serve. The cake is best eaten the day it is made, but it can be wrapped in aluminum foil and kept for 1 additional day at room temperature.

PFLAUMENSTREUSELKUCHEN
Yeasted Plum Cake with Streusel

MAKES 1 (9 BY 13-INCH/23 BY 33CM) CAKE

This late-summer classic is beloved all over the German-speaking world, where it shows up as soon as the first dark blue damson plums make their way into markets. In southern Germany it's also known as *Zwetschgendatschi*. *Zwetschgen* and *Pflaumen* are slightly different varieties of the prune plum. German folk wisdom purports that *Zwetschgen* are drier than *Pflaumen* and therefore better for cakes, since they don't release as much water when they bake, while the moister *Pflaumen* make for very good jam (see page 265). In the United States, the plum to use in this recipe is the Italian prune plum. Definitely don't substitute regular round plums for prune plums here, as they have less flavor and far more moisture and are not as delicious when cooked.

Pflaumenkuchen is almost always made with a yeasted base covered with a thicket of halved or quartered plums, stuck into the dough at a 45-degree angle so their tips stick up jauntily, even after baking. I like to add lemon peel to the yeasted dough for an added hint of flavor. A well-made *Pflaumenkuchen* will be so thickly covered in plums that you can barely see the cake below. Between the yeasted base and the copious amounts of sweet-sour fruit, *Pflaumenkuchen* is beloved precisely because it's not too sweet.

The recipe here calls for *Streusel*, but you can definitely leave it off if you want a simpler cake. You can scatter the plums with sliced almonds, which will toast and crisp in the oven but then go soft again as the cake cools and the fruit moistens the nuts. Or you can leave the fruit more or less unadorned, save for a sprinkling of sugar and cinnamon, which pairs beautifully with the dusky flavor of the plums. *Streusel* or no *Streusel*, according to every German I polled, the only thing that is nonnegotiable when it comes to *Pflaumenkuchen* is that it must be served with whipped cream, lightly sweetened (*Schlagsahne*).

A variation of this cake, known as *Kirschstreuselkuchen*, is made with canned or jarred sour cherries instead of plums. To make it, simply add 1 additional tablespoon of sugar to the dry ingredients for the dough. Once the dough has been rolled out to fit the pan, dimple the top with your fingertips. Drain a 24-ounce/680g jar of pitted sour cherries, discarding the juice, and distribute the cherries evenly over the dimpled dough. Top with the *Streusel* and bake as directed. Like *Pflaumenstreuselkuchen*, *Kirschstreuselkuchen* is best served slightly warm or at room temperature.

DOUGH

1²/₃ cups, scooped and leveled, minus 1 tablespoon/200g all-purpose flour, plus more for kneading

3 tablespoons granulated sugar

1 teaspoon instant yeast

Grated peel of ½ organic lemon

Pinch of salt

½ cup/120ml whole milk

3 tablespoons/40g unsalted high-fat, European-style butter, melted and cooled

1 egg yolk

TOPPINGS

1¼ pounds/580g Italian prune plums

1 cup, scooped and leveled/120g all-purpose flour

⅓ cup/70g granulated sugar

½ teaspoon ground cinnamon (optional)

Pinch of salt

5 tablespoons/70g unsalted high-fat, European-style butter, softened

Schlagsahne (page 267), for serving (optional)

1 Line a 9 by 13-inch/23 by 33cm metal baking pan with parchment paper, letting the sides hang over the edge to function as a sling after baking.

2 To make the dough: In a large bowl, stir together the flour, sugar, yeast, lemon peel, and salt. Then mix in the milk, butter, and egg yolk. The dough will be a bit shaggy. Dump it out onto a floured work surface and knead it for 5 minutes. It should be silky smooth. You might want to add a bit more flour to keep the dough from sticking as you knead, but don't add too much—the dough should still be soft and slightly floppy.

3 Form the dough into a ball and place in the prepared pan. Cover the pan with a clean dishcloth and place in a warm, draft-free location for about 1 hour, or until the dough has doubled in bulk.

4 In the meantime, prepare the toppings: Halve and pit the plums, then quarter them. Set aside. For the *Streusel*, mix together the flour, sugar, cinnamon, and salt in a bowl. Cut the butter into cubes and add to the flour mixture. Using your fingertips, rub the butter into the flour mixture until bean-size pieces develop. The *Streusel* should not be entirely uniform; a good mixture of smaller and larger pieces is desirable. Cover and refrigerate the *Streusel* until ready to use.

5 Preheat the oven to 350°F/180°C. Using your fingertips, gently deflate the dough and push it out evenly to fit the pan, creating a 1-inch-/2.5cm-high edge. The rest of the dough should be uniformly ⅛ inch/3mm thick.

6 Starting at the edges, push the plum quarters skin-side down into the dough at a 45-degree angle. Each row of plum quarters should slightly overlap with the preceding row, so that none of the yeasted dough is exposed when finished. Sprinkle the *Streusel* evenly over the plums.

7 Bake for 40 to 45 minutes, or until the crust is golden brown and the edges of the *Streusel* are browning.

8 Remove the pan from the oven and place on a rack to cool slightly. Using the parchment paper as a sling, remove the cake from the pan and set it on a cutting board. Cut into squares and serve slightly warm or at room temperature, with the *Schlagsahne* if desired. The cake is best the day it is made but can be wrapped in aluminum foil and kept for 1 additional day at room temperature.

BIENENSTICH
Honey-Almond Caramel Cake

MAKES 1 (9 BY 13-INCH/23 BY 33 CM) CAKE

Literally translated, *Bienenstich* means "bee sting," which is what you risk when you serve this sticky-topped cake alfresco. Its honeyed almond caramel is a powerful lure for wasps far and wide. It's even more tantalizing to caramel lovers, though. And luckily for everyone except the wasps, their season is short, but you can make this cake all year long—even though here in Germany it's considered a summer cake.

Although a few rare *Bienenstich* recipes call for a regular cake batter, most recipes call for a yeasted, not-too-sweet base, which makes for a nice contrast to that sweet topping. Several years ago, when I was working on my first book, my friend and food blogger Deb Perelman wrote to ask for my help sourcing a good recipe for *Bienenstich*. It was her mother's favorite cake, and she was determined to make it for her. I pointed her in the direction of a few recipes and went on my merry way, while Deb, true to form, went deep into *Bienenstich* research and development and made about six different versions before settling on one she was happy with. Luckily for me, Deb was generous enough to allow me to adapt her glorious topping here. It is sticky, gooey, crunchy, caramel perfection.

There is a big debate within Germany about whether *Bienenstich* must be split in half and filled with custard or vanilla pudding to be able to be called *Bienenstich* or that is simply a regional variation. I like the simplicity of unfilled *Bienenstich* and the fact that it's much easier to eat. But who am I to stand in the way of vanilla pudding lovers? For a filled *Bienenstich*, bake this recipe and then make a batch of your favorite vanilla pudding (or heck, buy some). Once the cake has fully cooled, slice it horizontally in half using a serrated knife. Spread the fully cooled pudding thickly over the bottom half. Cut the top piece into 10 rectangles, and then put them back together

on top of the pudding. This assembly will make the cutting and serving less messy. Nevertheless, serve—and eat—with a fork and knife.

YEASTED CAKE

1²/₃ cups, scooped and leveled, minus 1 tablespoon/200g all-purpose flour, plus more for kneading

1 teaspoon instant yeast

¼ cup/50g granulated sugar

3 tablespoons whole milk

⅛ teaspoon salt

1 egg

3½ tablespoons/50g unsalted high-fat, European-style butter, at room temperature

TOPPING

9 tablespoons plus 1 teaspoon/130g unsalted high-fat, European-style butter

½ cup/100g granulated sugar

4½ tablespoons/95g honey

3 tablespoons heavy cream

¼ teaspoon salt

2¼ cups/190g blanched sliced almonds

1 To make the cake: Place the flour, instant yeast, and sugar in a bowl. Stir in the milk, salt, and egg, and then knead in the butter. When the dough has come together, scrape it out onto a very lightly floured work surface and knead until smooth and no longer sticky, adding a bit of flour only if necessary. You want the dough to remain as soft and floppy as possible. Form into a ball and place in a clean bowl. Cover with a clean dishcloth and set in a warm, draft-free spot to rise for 1 hour.

continued

BIENENSTICH, CONTINUED

2 Preheat the oven to 350°F/180°C. Line a 9 by 13-inch/ 23 by 33cm metal baking pan with parchment paper, letting the sides hang over the edge to function as a sling after baking. When the dough has proofed for 1 hour, remove the paper from the pan, lay it on your work surface, and roll out the dough until it fits the indentations of the pan on the paper, and then transfer the paper and dough back to the pan. Cover with the dishcloth and set aside.

3 To make the topping: Place the butter, sugar, honey, cream, and salt in a small saucepan and bring to a boil over medium heat. Let the mixture simmer for 3 to 5 minutes, stirring frequently, until it goes from yellow to a slightly darker, duller cream color. Stir in the almonds and remove from the heat. Set aside to cool for 10 minutes.

4 Scrape the topping evenly over the dough. Place in the oven and bake for 20 to 25 minutes, or until the topping is golden brown and the almonds are crisping.

5 Remove the pan from the oven and let cool on a rack for 20 minutes. Using the parchment paper as a sling, remove the cake from the pan and set it on a cutting board. Cut into squares before serving. The cake is best eaten the day it is made but can be wrapped in aluminum foil and kept for 1 additional day at room temperature.

MOHNSTREUSELKUCHEN
Poppy-Seed Streusel Cake

MAKES 1 (9 BY 13-INCH/23 BY 33CM) CAKE

A sweet, warm, yeasty cake is a delicious base for everything from butter and sugar to fruit. But its best supporting role may be under a thick and creamy layer of ground poppy seeds and ground almonds that have swelled up in hot milk, are flavored with almond extract and honey, and lightened with beaten egg whites. Topped with a crisp, sweet-salty cap of *Streusel*, *Mohnstreuselkuchen* is the kind of cake that arouses fierce loyalties.

Although baked goods with poppy seeds are seen all over Germany these days, the heavy use of poppy seeds in sweet baking is traditional in eastern Europe, which is why these cakes and loaves are more commonly made in Germany's eastern states and in Austria. The way poppy seeds are used in cakes and sweet breads can generally be divided into two categories: Cooked into a milky pudding of sorts, thickened with ground nuts, semolina, or cornstarch, used as a thick cake filling that's almost gray in color. Or they are used more sparingly, but less adulterated with other ingredients, and layered into spiral buns or braided wreaths. Poppy seeds have always been rather expensive, so whether they are processed into a gritty black filling or a creamier gray one is not just a difference in taste; it's also a marker of wealth. The darker the filling, the less it has been adulterated with other ingredients.

It's especially nice to have this recipe in your back pocket when fresh fruit is in short supply. There's something about it that makes it particularly cozy and warming in colder months. And unlike other yeasted cakes, which are really only good on the day they are made, this cake's thick layer of poppy-seed filling keeps the base from drying out, so it still tastes very good a few days after baking.

I like using fresh yeast here, for its moisture and flavor, but instant yeast can easily be used instead.

DOUGH

1⅔ cups, scooped and leveled, minus 1 tablespoon/ 200g all-purpose flour, plus more for kneading

⅓ ounce/10g fresh yeast, or ½ teaspoon instant yeast

3 tablespoons granulated sugar

½ cup/120ml whole milk, lukewarm

¼ teaspoon salt

Grated peel of ½ organic lemon

3 tablespoons/40g unsalted high-fat, European-style butter, melted and cooled

1 egg, beaten

STREUSEL

1¼ cups, scooped and leveled, minus 1 tablespoon/ 150g all-purpose flour

¼ cup plus 2 tablespoons/75g granulated sugar

¼ teaspoon salt

¼ teaspoon baking powder

5 tablespoons plus 1 teaspoon/75g unsalted high-fat, European-style butter, softened

½ teaspoon vanilla extract

POPPY-SEED FILLING

1 cup/240ml whole milk

5 tablespoons plus 1 teaspoon/75g unsalted butter

¼ teaspoon salt

1⅔ cup/250g poppy seeds, ground (see page 7)

½ cup/100g granulated sugar

⅓ cup/50g whole almonds, finely ground

2 tablespoons honey

1 tablespoon cornstarch

1 teaspoon almond extract

3 eggs

continued

1 To make the dough: If using fresh yeast, place the flour in a large bowl and a make a well in the middle. Crumble the yeast into the well. Add a pinch of the sugar. Pour a couple of spoonsful of the milk into the well, stirring with a fork to dissolve the yeast until it's bubbly and somewhat smooth. Cover the bowl with a clean dishcloth and set aside for 10 minutes. (If using instant yeast, skip this step and simply mix all the dough ingredients together [using only half of the beaten egg, and reserving the rest for the *Streusel*], until a shaggy dough comes together. Proceed to the kneading in Step 2.)

2 Remove the dishcloth and scatter the remaining sugar and the salt around the sides of the bowl. Add the remaining milk and the grated lemon peel, the butter, and half of the beaten egg; reserve the rest of the egg to use in the *Streusel*. Stir until a shaggy dough comes together, and then scrape out onto a floured surface and knead until smooth and no longer sticky. You may have to add some flour as you work, but try not to add too much; you want the dough to be relatively soft and floppy. Form into a ball and place back in the bowl. Cover with the dishcloth and place somewhere warm and draft-free for 1 to 1½ hours.

3 In the meantime, make the *Streusel*: Place the flour, sugar, salt, and baking powder in a bowl. Cube the butter and work into the flour mixture. Then mix the vanilla extract with the beaten egg reserved from the dough and add to the flour mixture. Using your fingertips, work the ingredients together until well combined and both lima bean- and pea-size clumps form. Refrigerate the *Streusel* until ready to use.

4 To make the poppy-seed filling: Place the milk, butter, and salt in a saucepan and bring to a boil. Stir in the ground poppy seeds and sugar. Remove from the heat and set aside for 10 minutes.

5 Line a 9 by 13-inch/23 by 33cm metal baking pan with parchment paper, letting the sides hang over the edge to function as a sling after baking. Remove the paper from the pan, lay it on your work surface, and roll out the dough until it fits the indentations of the pan on the paper. Then transfer the paper and dough back to the pan. Cover again with the dishcloth and set aside for 20 to 30 minutes, until slightly puffy.

6 When the poppy-seed filling has cooled for 10 minutes, stir in the ground almonds, honey, cornstarch, and almond extract. Separate 2 of the eggs, putting the egg whites in a spotlessly clean bowl. Stir the remaining 1 whole egg and 2 egg yolks into the filling.

7 Preheat the oven to 350°F/180°C. Whip the egg whites until they hold stiff peaks. Fold them into the poppy-seed filling until no streaks remain.

8 Use your fingers to dimple the dough all over. Spread the filling over the dough and smooth the top. Remove the *Streusel* from the refrigerator and work through it with your fingers a couple of times to break up the clumps. Sprinkle the *Streusel* evenly over the filling. Bake for 45 minutes, or until the *Streusel* is faintly golden and crisp.

9 Let cool on a rack for 20 minutes. Using the parchment paper as a sling, transfer the cake to a cutting board. The cake may be served warm or at room temperature. Wrapped in aluminum foil, it will keep for up to 3 days.

GUGELHUPF
Yeasted Cake with Rum-Soaked Raisins

MAKES 1 (9-INCH/23 CM) CAKE

Gugelhupf, an old-fashioned yeasted cake studded with raisins and fragrant with lemon peel, rum, and copious amounts of butter, might be my favorite cake in this entire book. With a wonderful yeasty, buttery crumb and an enchanting old-world fragrance, this *Gugelhupf* is as good for dessert as it is for breakfast. I like to think of it as the northern cousin of Italian *panettone*.

Gugelhupf has more origin stories (and spelling variations) than you can shake a stick at. Some say it originated at the royal Austrian court in the nineteenth century and swiftly became an iconic cake in the German baking canon. It was purportedly Emperor Franz Josef I's favorite cake and, via the French members of his court, was exported to Alsace, where it came to be known as *kouglof* or *kugelhof*. Others say it was Marie Antoinette, an Austrian by birth, who brought *Gugelhupf* to France. In France, it is said that *Gugelhupf* originated all the way back with the Three Kings, who traveled through France on their way home from Bethlehem and were presented, on a pit stop in Ribeauvillé, with a cake made in the shape of their turbans. Turban-shape cake molds have been found in Roman excavations, proving that no matter the origin, *Gugelhupf* has long been a part of the human tradition—with good reason!

Nowadays, traditional yeasted *Gugelhupf* can be difficult to find in Germany—most home bakers and bakeries use *Gugelhupf* molds to bake buttery pound cakes and then call these imposters *Gugelhupf*, much to the distress of traditionalists everywhere. I urge you to try the real thing; you'll find yourself squarely in our camp henceforth.

You will need a stand mixer for this recipe unless you are endowed with Olympian muscles. The dough, which is wet and sticky, must be beaten for 10 full minutes, until it sheets off the mixer's beaters. This helps with the cake's lightness despite the plentiful quantities of eggs and butter in the batter.

Gugelhupf is traditionally a relatively small cake. This recipe, in fact, can be divided and baked in two *Gugelhupf* pans. But with only one *Gugelhupf* pan on hand at the time of testing, I decided to wing it, cramming the entire amount of dough into the pan. What resulted was a cake that shot out of the pan during baking, towering a good 3 to 4 inches/8 to 10cm over the edges of the pan. It was glorious and yielded wonderfully tall wedges. I liked it so much that I wouldn't bake it any other way again. If you don't have a *Gugelhupf* pan, you can use a Bundt pan, but reduce the baking time by 5 to 10 minutes.

You can either dust the finished *Gugelhupf* with confectioners' sugar for your afternoon tea or leave it unadorned for a less-sweet breakfast of the gods. I hope you love it as much as I do.

I think it's worth seeking out fresh yeast to make *Gugelhupf*. It gives the cake a wonderful bounce and flavor. But instant yeast can also be used.

continued

GUGELHUPF, CONTINUED

¾ cup/110g raisins

2½ tablespoons dark rum

4 cups, scooped and leveled/500g all-purpose flour

1¼ ounces/35g fresh yeast, or 1½ teaspoons instant yeast

¾ cup/150g granulated sugar

1 cup/240ml whole milk

10½ tablespoons/150g unsalted high-fat, European-style butter, plus more for the pan

5 eggs, at room temperature

Pinch of salt

Grated peel of 1 organic lemon

2 to 3 tablespoons confectioners' sugar (optional)

1 Put the raisins in a small bowl and pour the rum over the raisins. Set aside to soak.

2 If using fresh yeast, put the flour in the bowl of a stand mixer and make a well in the middle. Crumble the yeast into the well and add a pinch of the sugar. Heat ½ cup/120ml of the milk just to lukewarm and pour slowly over the yeast, stirring gently with a fork or wooden spoon to draw in just a little bit of flour and dissolve the yeast. Cover the bowl with a clean dishcloth and let sit for 15 minutes. (If using instant yeast, whisk it into the flour and proceed to Step 3.)

3 In the meantime, melt the butter and let it cool slightly, and then pour it into a second bowl. Whisk in the remaining sugar and then the eggs, salt, and grated lemon peel until smooth. Then whisk in the remaining milk (all of the milk if instant yeast is being used). Whisk in the raisins and rum.

4 Fit the stand mixer bowl onto the base of the machine and attach the flat beater. With the motor on low speed, slowly mix in the butter mixture until combined. Turn up the motor slightly and beat the batter for 10 minutes (set a timer). The dough should be falling off the beater in sheets and will be very wet and sticky. It will look more like cake batter than bread dough.

5 Very generously butter a *Gugelhupf* pan and scrape the batter into the pan, distributing it evenly. Cover the pan with the dishcloth and let sit for 20 to 30 minutes. Preheat the oven to 400°F/200°C.

6 Bake the *Gugelhupf* on a rack in the bottom third of the oven for 50 to 60 minutes, rotating halfway through. If it browns too quickly, loosely cover it with a piece of aluminum foil. The cake is ready when it is a deep golden brown.

7 Place the pan on a rack to cool for 15 to 20 minutes before turning it upside down and removing the pan. Let the cake cool completely before serving. Dust with confectioners' sugar just before serving, if desired. This cake is best the day it's baked, but it will keep for 2 to 3 days in an airtight container or wrapped tightly in plastic wrap.

SCHOKOLADEN-GUGELHUPF
Chocolate-Stuffed Yeasted Cake

MAKES 1 (9-INCH/23CM) CAKE

This recipe is for anyone who has fond memories of eating dark chocolate on white bread at snack time. Imagine a rich yeasted dough, made with a touch more sugar than usual, rolled out and filled with a textured chocolate-almond filling, rolled into a cylinder, and fitted into a *Gugelhupf* pan. In the oven, the loaf expands and pushes upward, making for gorgeously tall slices later on. A cross section of the cake shows the chocolate filling spiraling into the white strands of sweetened bread dough. It's hard to know how to classify this cake: breakfast treat or afternoon snack? Either way, it's heavenly.

I stumbled across the recipe in a cookbook I'd dug up at a thrift store in my sleepy little corner of Charlottenburg when I first started doing research for this book. The book, *Das Grosse Buch vom Backen*, called this cake a *Schokoladen-Napfkuchen*, which to contemporary German ears sounds a lot like a chocolate pound cake. But with its yeasted dough and the fact that you bake it in a *Gugelhupf* pan, there was no way around the fact that this was a sister cake to *Gugelhupf*. So after some recipe tweaking, that's how I rechristened it.

The filling has a touch of rum in it, which adds a nicely rounded flavor but no booziness. I feel comfortable feeding a slice of it to my three-year-old son. If serving this in the afternoon, you could dust the top with some sifted confectioners' sugar for more of a finished look. If you bake this in a Bundt pan, reduce the baking time by 5 to 10 minutes.

DOUGH

4¼ cups, scooped and leveled/530g all-purpose flour, plus more for kneading

1½ teaspoons instant yeast

½ cup plus 2 tablespoons/125g granulated sugar

¼ teaspoon salt

1 cup minus ½ teaspoon/235ml whole milk

7 tablespoons/100g unsalted high-fat, European-style butter, at room temperature, plus more for the pan

1 egg

FILLING

7 ounces/200g bittersweet chocolate (minimum 50% cacao)

1½ cups/150g ground almonds

½ cup/100g granulated sugar

¼ teaspoon salt

3 tablespoons dark rum

½ cup/120ml whole milk

1 To make the dough: Place the flour, yeast, sugar, and salt in a large bowl. Stir in the milk, butter, and egg. Knead together in the bowl for 1 minute, and then dump out onto a lightly floured work surface. Knead the dough until smooth and no longer sticky, about 5 minutes. You may need to add a little flour, but try to resist adding too much; you want the dough to stay as soft and floppy as possible. Form the dough into a ball and place back in the bowl. Cover with a clean dishcloth and let rise in a warm, draft-free spot for 1 hour.

2 While the dough rises, make the filling: Break the chocolate into pieces and process in a small food processor until finely chopped. Put the chocolate in a mixing bowl and add the almonds, sugar, and salt. Then stir in the rum and milk and mix well. Set aside.

continued

3 Liberally butter a *Gugelhupf* pan and set aside. Gently tug the risen dough out of the bowl and onto your work surface and roll out to a 12 by 16-inch/ 30 by 40cm rectangle. Spread the chocolate mixture evenly all over the dough, leaving a 1-inch/2.5cm border only on one of the long sides. Roll up the dough tightly, starting from the opposite long side. Carefully gather up the long roll and place in the prepared pan, pinching the ends together. Cover with the dishcloth and let the cake rise for 30 minutes.

4 Meanwhile, preheat the oven to 350°F/180°C.

5 Place the pan in the oven and bake for 1 hour, or until the top sounds slightly hollow when tapped.

6 Remove the pan from the oven and let cool on a rack for 25 minutes before gently unmolding the cake from the pan. Let the cake cool almost completely before slicing with a large serrated knife. The cake is best the day it is made, but it will keep for an additional day if wrapped tightly in plastic wrap and stored at room temperature.

SCHLESISCHE MOHNROLLE
Silesian Poppy-Seed Roll

MAKES 2 (18-INCH-/45CM-LONG) LOAVES

For five years, my husband and I lived around the corner from a little family-run neighborhood bakery called Hutzelmann. In addition to a wide array of breads and rolls, the bakery specializes in Silesian pastries and cakes: moist and heavy poppy-seed-stuffed yeasted rolls, thick and fluffy *Streuselkuchen*, *Quark*-filled sugar buns, and sugar-spangled apple fritters, among many other delicacies. When this book was still just a kernel in my mind, I spent a morning in the bakery, watching the bakers (all men) in their white shirts and pants as they painted huge trays of cakes and buns with a thick sugar icing, formed enormous pans of braided cakes, and kneaded bread, loaf after loaf after loaf.

The current owner, Elisabeth Hutzelmann-Hochreiter, is descended from a long line of *Konditoren* (pastry makers) who were originally from Silesia, which is now part of Poland. In the 1920s, her uncle and father moved to Berlin, where they both opened bakeries. Today, "our" Hutzelmann is the only one remaining. Ms. Hutzelmann-Hochreiter's husband, a tall and majestic-looking Bavarian, is the bakery's *Bäckermeister* (master baker).

Like many independent bakeries in Germany, Hutzelmann is struggling. Ingredient costs are going up, while the prices of industrially produced breads and cakes at rival chain bakeries are at rock bottom. Ms. Hutzelmann-Hochreiter is pessimistic about her bakery's long-term survival. It's deeply frustrating to witness the precarious existence of this rare kind of bakery in Germany, a country with such deep reverence for handicraft, artisanship, and culture. I can only hope that Hutzelmann's loyal customers keep coming back and that the bakery continues to find new fans. We left the neighborhood when we bought an apartment in the neighboring district, and I still haven't found anywhere else that comes close to Hutzelmann's.

It's hard to pick favorites among all of Hutzelmann's wonderful offerings, but if I were forced to, I'd choose the *Mohnrolle* (poppy-seed roll). I like to buy a plump slice off the thick, *Streusel*-topped yeast roll filled with a pitch-black poppy-seed filling so heavy and damp that each bite is almost juicy. I always swear to myself that I'll eat only half, saving the rest for the next day. But of course it takes just a few minutes after finishing the first half for me to make quick work of the second half. Every single time!

This is my approximation of Hutzelmann's sublime roll. You make a batch of lemony yeasted dough, roll it out, and spread over it a thick, gravelly poppy-seed filling flavored with almond extract and a hint of cinnamon for warmth. The dough is rolled up and topped with *Streusel* and baked until the dough is golden brown and the *Streusel* is light golden. The *Streusel* makes a crunchy textural contrast to the soft, sweet loaves; plus, it gives the final cake a more finished texture. Don't worry if the rolls split during baking: a sugar glaze gilds the lily.

For a simpler, more streamlined roll, you can leave off the *Streusel* and glaze, though keep in mind that the loaves will be slightly drier. In this case, once the loaves have fully cooled, brush each one with 1 to 2 tablespoons of melted butter and then sift 2 to 3 tablespoons of confectioners' sugar evenly over the top of each.

As for the real thing, you'll just have to come to Berlin: Hutzelmann is located at Wilmersdorfer Strasse 19 in Charlottenburg. Come hungry.

continued

STREUSEL

1 cup, scooped and leveled, minus 1 tablespoon/
120g all-purpose flour

¼ cup plus 2 tablespoons/75g granulated sugar

⅛ teaspoon salt

5 tablespoons plus 1 teaspoon/75g unsalted high-fat,
European-style butter, softened, cut into cubes

DOUGH

¾ ounce/20g fresh yeast, or 1 teaspoon instant yeast

½ cup/120ml whole milk, lukewarm

2½ tablespoons granulated sugar

2 cups, scooped and leveled/250g all-purpose flour,
plus more for kneading

2 tablespoons/30g unsalted high-fat,
European-style butter, at room temperature

Grated peel of ½ organic lemon

1 egg yolk

¼ teaspoon salt

FILLING

1⅓ cups/200g poppy seeds, ground (see page 7)

1 cup/240ml whole milk

3 tablespoons/40g unsalted butter

1 cup/200g granulated sugar

½ cup/75g raisins

¼ cup/35g finely chopped almonds

¼ cup/30g unseasoned dried bread crumbs

1 egg

1½ teaspoons almond extract

½ teaspoon ground cinnamon

1 to 2 tablespoons unsalted butter, for brushing

GLAZE

1¼ cups/150g confectioners' sugar

2 tablespoons water

1 tablespoon freshly squeezed lemon juice

1 To make the *Streusel*: Place the flour, sugar, salt, and butter in a mixing bowl. Using your fingers, work the butter into the other ingredients until the mixture clumps and looks like wet sand. Set aside.

2 To make the dough: If using fresh yeast, crumble the yeast into a mixing bowl. Pour the milk over the yeast and whisk to dissolve, adding a pinch of the sugar. Cover the bowl with a clean dishcloth and set aside for 10 minutes. Then stir in the remaining sugar and the flour, butter, grated lemon peel, egg yolk, and salt. (If using the instant yeast, simply stir all the dough ingredients together at once and then proceed immediately to the kneading phase.) Turn out onto a floured work surface and knead until smooth and no longer sticky, adding a little flour if necessary, about 7 minutes. The dough will be relatively floppy; resist adding too much flour.

3 Form the dough into a ball and place in a bowl. Cover with the dishcloth and let rise in a warm, draft-free place for 1 hour. Line a baking sheet with parchment paper.

4 While the dough rises, make the filling: Place the poppy seeds in a mixing bowl. Heat the milk until just boiling. Remove from the heat and add the butter to melt. Pour the milk mixture over the poppy seeds and stir. Add the sugar, raisins, almonds, bread crumbs, egg, almond extract, and cinnamon; mix well. Set aside to cool.

5 Heat the oven to 350°F/180°C. Gently punch down the risen dough and scrape out onto your work surface. Divide into 2 equal pieces. Roll out each piece evenly to a 14 by 17-inch/35 by 43cm rectangle. Divide the cooled poppy-seed mixture between the pieces of dough and, using an offset spatula, smooth the filling evenly all over each piece of dough, leaving a 1½-inch/4cm border on all sides. Starting from a long side, gently roll up each

piece of dough completely. Transfer both rolls to the prepared baking sheet, seam-side down, and cover with the dishcloth. Let rest for 20 minutes.

6   Before baking, melt the remaining 1 to 2 tablespoons of butter and brush the loaves with it. Press handfuls of the *Streusel* gently onto the buttered dough. Bake in the bottom third of the oven for 40 minutes, rotating halfway through. After 15 minutes, cover the roll with aluminum foil so it doesn't brown too much. When the loaves are done, they will be golden brown and sound hollow when tapped. The *Streusel* should be a pale gold.

7   Place the baking sheet on a rack. To make the glaze: Place the confectioners' sugar in a clean bowl. Whisk the water and lemon juice into the sugar until smooth and creamy. Drizzle evenly over the still-warm *Streusel*. Then let the loaves cool completely before slicing crosswise into thick slices and serving. They are best eaten the day they are made. You can wrap any leftovers in plastic wrap and keep for an additional day or two.

ROSENKUCHEN
Spiced Cocoa Pinwheel Cake

MAKES 1 (10-INCH/25CM) CAKE

Rosenkuchen (rose cake) is the lovely, lyrical name for a cake pan crammed full of filled and sliced yeasted buns, their rings unfurling like rose petals. In the United States, we mostly think of rolls iced cinnamon buns when we think of rolled, filled buns. But in Germany, buns are filled with everything from rum-plumped raisins and marzipan to *Pflaumenmus* to nut pastes. When the buns are cut thinly and then nestled together in a cake pan, they fuse, both in proofing and during baking, to produce a gorgeously whorled and craggy cake. Rather than pull the buns apart after baking, you cut wedges out of the cake to serve.

In this version of *Rosenkuchen*, the buns are filled with a simple and comforting mixture of sugar, cocoa, and cinnamon, plus lots of melted butter to keep them moist. Alternatively, you could fill the buns with the poppy-seed filling on page 100, the hazelnut filling on page 107, or the almond filling on page 104. When the cake has cooled, I like to drizzle a lemon glaze over the top, which not only finishes the cake aesthetically, but gives each bite a little extra juicy succulence.

I use a 10-inch/25cm pan to prepare this cake, which produces a 1½-inch-/4cm-high cake with lots of pretty little pinwheels and a satisfying filling-to-cake ratio. You can make it in a 9-inch/23cm pan, but the cake will be slightly thicker.

DOUGH

3 cups, scooped and leveled/375g all-purpose flour, plus more for kneading

1 teaspoon instant yeast

¼ cup/50g granulated sugar

¼ teaspoon salt

½ cup plus 1½ tablespoons/140ml whole milk

1 egg

5 tablespoons plus 1 teaspoon/75g unsalted high-fat, European-style butter, melted and slightly cooled

FILLING

5 tablespoons plus 1 teaspoon/75g unsalted butter, melted

½ cup/100g granulated sugar

2 tablespoons cocoa powder

1½ teaspoons ground cinnamon

GLAZE

13 tablespoons/100g confectioners' sugar

1½ tablespoons freshly squeezed lemon juice

1½ tablespoons water

1 Line a 10-inch/25cm cake pan with parchment paper, letting the sides hang over the edge to function as a sling after baking.

2 To make the dough: Place the flour, yeast, sugar, and salt in a large bowl. Stir in the milk, egg, and butter and knead in the bowl for 1 minute before dumping the dough out onto a lightly floured work surface. Knead until smooth and no longer sticky, about 5 minutes. You may need to add a little flour as you knead, but try to resist adding too much; you want the dough to stay as soft and floppy as possible. Form into a ball and return the dough to the bowl. Cover with a clean dishcloth and place in a warm, draft-free spot for 1 hour to rise.

3 After 1 hour, gently tug the risen dough out of the bowl and roll it out to a 15 by 20-inch/38 by 50cm rectangle.

4 To make the filling: Brush the dough very liberally with the melted butter. You will have some left over. In a small bowl, whisk together the sugar, cocoa powder, and cinnamon. Sprinkle the sugar

mixture evenly all over the buttered dough. Starting from a long side, roll up the dough tightly. Slice into ¾-inch-/2cm-thick slices. Arrange the slices, cut-side up, in the prepared pan, taking care not to lose too much of the sugar mixture as you transfer the slices from your work surface to the pan. Drizzle the remaining melted butter evenly all over the slices. Cover the pan with the dishcloth and set aside for 30 minutes.

5 Preheat the oven to 350°F/180°C. When ready to bake, remove the dishcloth (the rolls will have puffed up slightly) and place the pan in the oven. Bake for 35 to 40 minutes, or until the rolls are golden brown and dry but soft to the touch. Remove the pan from the oven and let cool completely.

6 To make the glaze: Whisk together the confectioners' sugar, lemon juice, and water until smooth; the mixture will be quite thick. Drizzle the icing evenly over the top of the cake. Serve in wedges. The cake is best eaten the day it is made, but will keep for 1 day at room temperature, wrapped well in plastic wrap.

KRANZKUCHEN

Braided Almond-Cream Wreath

MAKES 1 (13-INCH/33CM) WREATH

If *Schlesische Mohnrolle* (page 99) is my favorite thing to buy at Hutzelmann, our favorite bakery in Berlin, then *Kranzkuchen* is my husband's. Max has a soft spot for *Kranzkuchen*, an almond-paste and rum-raisin–stuffed sweet wreath. He has tried many *Kranzkuchen* in his life, but he says that absolutely none come close to Hutzelmann's version, sold in thick slabs all year long. It is glorious: sticky and rich, winey with rum and almond paste, chewy, and flaky all at once.

I tried many times to re-create their *Kranz* (which means "wreath") at home and never quite got it right, but in the process I developed this recipe, which is pretty darn good. Forming the wreath requires a bit of moxie because once you roll up the almond-cream-filled dough and slice it lengthwise, you have to wrap the 2 strands around each other without allowing the filling to leak too much. After baking, when the *Kranzkuchen* is golden brown and shiny from the apricot glaze and topped with a drizzled glaze, it's as beautiful as it is delicious. I suggest you bake this when you have a lot of people to feed at once—it's best the day it is made.

DOUGH

3¼ cups, scooped and leveled, minus 1 tablespoon/
400g all-purpose flour, plus more for kneading

1½ teaspoons instant yeast

⅓ cup/70g granulated sugar

¼ teaspoon salt

¾ cup plus 1 tablespoon/190ml whole milk

1 egg

8 tablespoons/115g unsalted high-fat,
European-style butter, at room temperature

FILLING

⅔ cup/100g raisins

3 tablespoons dark rum

Juice of ½ lemon

1 pound/455g almond paste

¼ cup/50g granulated sugar

1 egg white

1 to 2 tablespoons whole milk

3½ tablespoons/50g unsalted butter,
at room temperature

¼ teaspoon salt

GLAZE

½ cup/150g smooth apricot jam

13 tablespoons/100g confectioners' sugar

2 tablespoons water

1 To make the dough: In a large bowl, stir together the flour, yeast, sugar, and salt. Then add the milk and egg and stir briefly. Add the butter and knead the dough briefly by hand in the bowl. Scrape it out onto a lightly floured work surface and continue to knead it for several minutes. You may need to add 1 to 2 additional tablespoons of flour, but resist the urge to add more; the dough should be quite soft and rich. You won't be able to knead it as long as other yeast doughs, but try to get it to a point where it's no longer too sticky and can be formed into a ball.

2 Place the ball back in the bowl. Cover the bowl with a clean dishcloth and place in a warm, draft-free place for 1 hour to rise.

3 To make the filling: Place the raisins in a small bowl and add the rum and lemon juice. Set aside to macerate for 30 minutes.

continued

4 Heat the oven to 350°F/180°C. Line a baking sheet with parchment paper. In a medium bowl, combine the almond paste, sugar, egg white, 1 tablespoon of milk, butter, and salt; knead together by hand until well combined. Knead in the raisins and their macerating liquid. The mixture should be creamy but will still hold its shape when spread. If necessary, mix in the remaining 1 tablespoon of milk. Set aside.

5 When the proofing hour is up, gently tug the dough onto a work surface. Roll out the dough to a 13 by 16-inch/33 by 40cm rectangle. You can pull the edges out to form neat corners.

6 Scrape the filling onto the dough and, using a bench scraper, spread the mixture out evenly over the dough, leaving a 1-inch/2.5cm border on one of the long sides. Starting from the other long side, roll up the dough. Using a sharp bench scraper, cut the roll of dough in half lengthwise, leaving about 1 inch/2.5cm at one end still attached. Working quickly, twist the 2 strands around each other all the way down the length of the roll. Then form the wrapped dough strands into a circle. Next, slice through the end that you left attached and tuck the end pieces at both ends underneath each other to make a neat closure.

7 Transfer the wreath to the prepared pan (you may need someone to help you do this) and bake for 45 minutes at the second-lowest rack position, rotating halfway through. When finished, the loaf will be golden brown all over and should sound slightly hollow when tapped. It will still be quite soft.

8 To make the glaze: Just before the end of the baking time, heat the apricot jam over medium-high heat until loose and bubbling. When the wreath emerges from the oven, immediately brush it all over with the hot jam. Place the pan on a rack to cool.

9 When the wreath has almost fully cooled, sift the confectioners' sugar into a small bowl and whisk in the water. Whisk until smooth and lump-free. You want a thick but pourable glaze. Add more sugar or a drop more water as needed. Drizzle the glaze back and forth over the entire wreath. Wait 1 hour for the glaze to set and the cake to cool completely and then slice and serve. The cake is best eaten the day it is made, but it can be kept at room temperature, loosely wrapped in plastic wrap, for 2 additional days.

NUSSZOPF
Glazed Nut Braid

MAKES 1 (15-INCH/38CM) LOAF

This *Nusszopf*, a sweet and cakey yeasted braid filled with a lush hazelnut filling that is exposed when you slice the roll lengthwise and braid it, is similar in concept to the *Kranzkuchen* (page 104), only a little less rich and bombastic. The yeasted base is flavored with some lemon peel, and the filling is leaner, made with both ground and chopped hazelnuts, egg whites, and some bread crumbs to give it ballast. I like to add a tiny bit of cinnamon, which gives the filling a warm, toasty flavor without turning it into a cinnamon-roll-flavored treat. This kind of filled and braided sweet bread is also known as a *Striezel* in southern Germany and Austria.

If you're thinking this is way too complicated to attempt, let me assure you that it is actually far simpler than it looks. Once you've made the yeasted dough and filling, you roll out the dough to a large rectangle and cover it evenly with the filling. Then you roll up the dough. This roll gets cut in thirds lengthwise; I like to use a sharp bench scraper for this, but a big knife will do, too. I leave one end of the roll uncut while I braid the 3 strands of dough together. Then I cut the top through. At that point, I transfer the braid to the baking sheet. You may need help with this at first—four hands are better than two. But I promise that as you get more experienced with this, you'll eventually be able to do it on your own. All that's left, once the braid is on the baking sheet, is to tuck both ends of the braid under the loaf to create a neat beginning and end. Voilà! You will be so impressed with yourself.

Nusszopf is a really wonderful thing to serve on Easter Sunday or for a very special birthday breakfast. But it's equally good for afternoon celebrations. The thick, moist filling and the lemon glaze keep the braid from drying out quickly, so it actually is still good the day after it's baked, unlike most other yeasted sweet breads.

DOUGH

3¼ cups, scooped and leveled, minus 1 tablespoon/ 400g all-purpose flour, plus more for kneading

1½ teaspoons instant yeast

⅓ cup/70g granulated sugar

Grated peel of 1 organic lemon

½ teaspoon salt

¾ cup/175ml whole milk

2 egg yolks

7 tablespoons/100g unsalted high-fat, European-style butter, at room temperature

FILLING

2 cups/200g toasted, skinned, ground hazelnuts (see page 7)

¾ cup/100g finely chopped hazelnuts

¾ cup/150g granulated sugar

½ cup/120ml whole milk

2 egg whites

1 teaspoon vanilla extract

½ teaspoon ground cinnamon

¼ teaspoon salt

1 to 2 tablespoons unseasoned dried bread crumbs (optional)

GLAZE

1 cup/100g confectioners' sugar

2 tablespoons freshly squeezed lemon juice

continued

1 To make the dough: In a large bowl, stir together the flour, yeast, sugar, grated lemon peel, and salt. Pour in the milk and egg yolks and stir briefly. Add the butter and knead the dough briefly by hand in the bowl. Then scrape it out onto a floured work surface and knead it for several minutes. Resist adding too much flour as you knead. When the dough is ready, it should be quite smooth and no longer sticky.

2 Form the dough into a ball and place back in the bowl. Cover the bowl with a clean dishcloth and place in a warm, draft-free place for 1 hour. The dough will not double in size but will be puffier and looser than before.

3 Heat the oven to 350°F/180°C. Line a baking sheet with parchment paper.

4 To make the filling: In a medium bowl, combine the ground hazelnuts, chopped hazelnuts, sugar, milk, egg whites, vanilla extract, cinnamon, and salt; mix together until well combined. The mixture should be creamy but on the firm side. If the mixture is too loose, stir in 1 to 2 tablespoons of bread crumbs. Set aside.

5 When the proofing hour is up, scrape out the dough onto a work surface. Roll out the dough to a 13 by 16-inch/33 by 40cm rectangle. You can pull the edges out to form neat corners. Scrape the filling onto the dough and, using a bench scraper, spread the mixture out evenly over the dough, leaving a 1-inch/2.5cm border on the long sides and spreading the mixture to the edges of the short sides. Starting from one of the long sides, roll up the dough gently but briskly and then, using a sharp bench scraper, cut the dough in thirds lengthwise, leaving 1 inch/2.5cm at one end uncut. Working quickly, braid the three strands together, tucking in the ends to make a neat finish. Now slice through the end that you left attached and tuck those ends under, too.

6 Transfer the braided loaf to the prepared baking sheet and bake for 55 minutes at the second-lowest rack position, rotating halfway through. If the loaf browns too quickly, cover loosely with a piece of aluminum foil. When finished, the loaf should be golden brown all over and should sound slightly hollow when tapped. Let cool on a rack.

7 When the loaf has almost fully cooled, make the glaze: Sift the confectioners' sugar into a small bowl and whisk in the lemon juice to make a thick but pourable mixture. Whisk until smooth and lump-free. Add more sugar or a drop more water as needed. Drizzle the glaze back and forth over the entire loaf. Wait another hour for the glaze to set, and then slice and serve. The loaf is best eaten the day it is made, but it can be kept at room temperature, loosely wrapped in plastic wrap, for 2 additional days.

MOHNZOPF
Poppy-Seed Braid

MAKES 2 (14-INCH-/35CM-LONG) LOAVES

The dough for this absolutely stunning poppy-seed braid (faux-braid, to be precise, but more on that in a minute) is actually quite unusual: it is a mix of yeasted dough and short-crust dough kneaded together. It's called *Zwillingsteig* (twin dough) and was popular in bygone times in cakes made with fresh fruit, but the style has gone by the wayside in recent decades. It is making a bit of a comeback, though, as all good things do. *Zwillingsteig* is a richer, moister dough than regular yeasted doughs, as you can probably imagine, and keeps for a little while longer, too.

Here it's rolled out and spread with a creamy, vanilla-scented poppy-seed filling and, as in the *Kranzkuchen* (page 104) and *Nusszopf* (page 107), is rolled up into a big log. But unlike the other two, which are then cut lengthwise and braided together, in this recipe you use a pair of sharp shears to snip the log crosswise at regular intervals. The snipped pieces of the roll are then peeled back, alternating to the left and the right, creating a gorgeous loaf that appears braided and will impress absolutely everyone who sees it.

The recipe makes 2 relatively large loaves, great if you're baking for a larger group or if you have a particularly lovely neighbor you'd like to share one with. Otherwise, you can freeze one of the loaves in a large plastic freezer bag. Defrost by setting the loaf out at room temperature for 3 to 4 hours before serving, and then warming it slightly in a 200°F/95°C oven. Don't leave it in the oven for more than few minutes or it will dry out. This works best with an unglazed loaf.

SHORT CRUST

3 tablespoons/40g granulated sugar

2/3 cup, scooped and leveled/85g all-purpose flour

3/4 teaspoon baking powder

4 tablespoons plus 1 teaspoon/60g unsalted high-fat, European-style butter, softened, cut into cubes

1 egg yolk

YEAST DOUGH

3/4 ounce/20g fresh yeast, or 1 teaspoon instant yeast

1 teaspoon salt

2 tablespoons plus 1 teaspoon granulated sugar

1/2 cup plus 1 tablespoon/135ml water, lukewarm

1/2 teaspoon vanilla extract

2 tablespoons/30g unsalted high-fat, European-style butter, at room temperature

1 egg

2 1/3 cups, scooped and leveled, plus 1 tablespoon/300g all-purpose flour, plus more for kneading

FILLING

3/4 cup/105g poppy seeds, ground (see page 7)

1/4 cup/50g granulated sugar

2 tablespoons semolina

1/8 teaspoon salt

2 tablespoons/30g unsalted butter

1 cup minus 2 teaspoons/225ml whole milk

1 egg

1/2 teaspoon vanilla extract

1 1/2 teaspoons dark rum

GLAZE

1 1/4 cups/125g confectioners' sugar, plus more if needed

2 tablespoons water

continued

1 To make the short crust: Place the sugar, flour, baking powder, butter, and egg yolk in a bowl and quickly knead together until well combined. Shape into a disk and set aside. This dough can be made up to 1 day in advance, wrapped in plastic wrap, and refrigerated, but it should be brought to room temperature before combining it with the yeast dough.

2 To make the yeast dough: If using fresh yeast crumble the fresh yeast into a large mixing bowl and sprinkle with the salt and sugar. Set aside for 10 minutes. Stir in the water and vanilla extract; add the butter, egg, and flour and stir. (If using instant yeast, simply stir all the dough ingredients together and proceed immediately to the kneading phase.) Dump the shaggy dough out onto a lightly floured work surface and knead until smooth and elastic, about 3 minutes. Resist adding too much more flour as you knead; the dough should remain as soft as possible.

3 Roll out the yeast dough to about 1-inch/2.5cm thickness and place the disk of short crust on top of the dough. Fold the yeast dough over the short crust and knead together by hand until fully combined, about 2 minutes. Shape into a ball, place in a bowl, and cover with a clean dishcloth. Set in a warm, draft-free spot to rise for 1 hour.

4 In the meantime, make the filling: Mix the ground poppy seeds, sugar, semolina, and salt in a saucepan. Add the butter and milk. Place the pot over medium-high heat and, stirring constantly, bring to a boil. Immediately remove from the heat and set aside to cool. When it is lukewarm, stir in the egg, vanilla extract, and rum. Set aside.

5 Line a baking sheet with parchment paper. After the dough has proofed, divide it in half and set one piece aside. Roll out the other half to a 12 by 14-inch/30 by 35cm rectangle. Spread the dough evenly with half of the poppy-seed filling, leaving no border. Starting from one of the long sides, roll up the dough tightly. Transfer the dough to the prepared baking sheet. Repeat with the second piece of dough and the remaining filling.

6 Hold a pair of kitchen shears perpendicular to one loaf, 1 inch/2.5cm from the top of the roll, and snip the dough almost all the way through, leaving about 1-inch/2.5cm of the dough uncut, which will function as a hinge. Repeat, moving down the loaf, at 1-inch/2.5cm intervals. When finished, set aside the shears and, using your fingers, gently separate and twist out each snipped segment, alternating to the left and right of the roll, so that the cut sides of each segment face upward. Tug gently at the segments so that each segment on the left side of the loaf slightly overlaps with the one in front of it, and the same on the right. Repeat with the second loaf. Cover the baking sheet with the dishcloth and set the loaves aside to proof for 30 minutes.

7 Preheat the oven to 400°F/200°C.

8 Remove the dishcloth and place the baking sheet in the oven. Bake for 40 minutes, or until the loaves are a deep golden brown. You may need to cover them with a piece of aluminum foil in the last 10 to 15 minutes of baking. Remove the baking sheet from the oven and place on a rack to cool.

9 To make the glaze: When the loaves have fully cooled, whisk together the confectioners' sugar and water until completely smooth. Brush the glaze thinly over the loaves. Let the glaze set before serving. The *Mohnzopf* is best served the day it is made, but it can be kept for an additional day by wrapping it tightly in plastic wrap.

TORTES AND STRUDELS

If yeasted cakes are the day dresses of German baking, then the tortes in this chapter are its fancy evening gowns. From the towering wonder that is a *Schwarzwälder Kirschtorte* (page 123) to the restrained and elegant *Mohntorte* (page 126), these are celebration recipes. But lest you think that elegant and cream-filled tortes are more of an after-dinner kind of thing, I must assure you that even these are still considered *Kaffeezeit* treats, to be eaten in the afternoon with good coffee or hot tea.

The *Kaffeeklatsch* started in the seventeenth century as a way for high-class German women, who couldn't assemble in public places but longed for community, to get together and talk. A group of women would take turns hosting the *Kaffeeklatsch* each month, laying the table with fine linens and china. While times have changed, the tradition of a beautifully set table and fancy home-baked tortes hasn't.

Reflecting the influence that Austrian food culture has had on Germany over the centuries, many of the recipes in this chapter hail from Austria, not Germany. Generally speaking, Austrian cuisine is considered more elegant and refined than German. And in fact, on a trip to Vienna and the Burgenland with my husband last year, I was struck by the delicacy and sophistication of the food.

The flourless *Mohntorte* and legendary *Sachertorte* (page 128) require a bit more skill than the simple batter cakes earlier in the book, while the *Linzertorte* (page 134)—which according to most Germans and Austrians actually belongs to Christmas, but I could not restrict that kind of deliciousness to one month a year—requires more patience than skill, since it must rest for at least 3 days before being eaten. Yes, really.

Strudel also comes from Austria and is one of its finest exports. I have given recipes for three different versions here, but the sky is the limit when it comes to *Strudel* fillings. Almost any fruit will do. Oh, and in case you're feeling intimidated, I always thought *Strudel* was far too complicated for the home cook to achieve, but if writing this book taught me anything, it was that making *Strudel* is actually quite simple. It's all about confidence.

Other recipes in this chapter reflect regional diversity to a much larger degree than the simpler cakes in previous chapters. For example, the *Heidjertorte* (page 119) is a specialty from the Lüneburg Heath, where buckwheat and cranberries grow and are paired together in the torte. The *Friesentorte* (page 122) is a standard-bearer of the East Frisian islands in the north of Germany, while the *Träubelestorte* (page 136), filled with a sweet-sour redcurrant meringue, is one of Swabia's most beloved desserts.

RÜBLITORTE
Carrot-Nut Torte

MAKES 1 (10-INCH/25CM) TORTE

About the only thing that Swiss *Rüblitorte* has in common with American carrot cake is the carrot. The torte is made with ground almonds and just a whisper of flour, as well as stiffly beaten egg whites, so it is light and nubby where the American one is rich and heavy. *Rüblitorte* is scented with only a faint whiff of cinnamon and freshly grated citrus peels, which lets the flavor of the nuts and carrots shine. And instead of ivory swaths of cream cheese frosting, it is sheathed in a thin lemon glaze, decorated with toasty sliced almonds, and—perhaps most important—topped with a ring of tiny handmade almond-paste carrots.

I call for the batter to be baked in a 10-inch/25cm pan because I like the more austere look of the slightly shorter wedge and because the ratio of lemon glaze to pebbly crumb is higher when it's spread out in a larger pan. But if you'd prefer to bake it in a 9-inch/23cm pan, that's fine; just remember to increase the baking time accordingly. *Rüblitorte* needs a rest period after baking to develop both flavor and moisture, so you must plan for at least a day or two between baking and serving the torte. And whatever you do, don't skip those handmade carrots.

Unsalted butter, for the pan

¾ cup, scooped and leveled, plus 1 tablespoon/100g all-purpose flour, plus more for the pan

10½ ounces/300g (6 small) carrots

1⅔ cups/250g blanched whole almonds (see page 7)

1 teaspoon baking powder

5 eggs, separated

¾ cup plus 2 tablespoons/175g granulated sugar

¼ teaspoon ground cinnamon

Grated peel of 1 organic lemon

Grated peel of 1 organic orange

¼ teaspoon salt

3½ ounces/100g almond paste

Orange food coloring or red and yellow food coloring

Green food coloring (optional)

8 to 10 pistachios (optional)

½ cup/40g blanched sliced almonds (optional)

2 cups/200g confectioners' sugar

3 to 4 tablespoons/45 to 60ml freshly squeezed lemon juice

1 Preheat the oven to 350°F/180°C. Butter a 10-inch/25cm cake pan and dust with flour.

2 Finely grate the carrots. You should have about 2 lightly packed cups. Set aside.

3 Place the whole almonds in the bowl of a food processor and process until finely ground but not yet turned to paste. Transfer to a bowl and whisk in the flour and baking powder.

4 Place the egg yolks and granulated sugar in the bowl of a stand mixer fitted with the whisk attachment and start whipping together. With the motor running, add the cinnamon and grated citrus peels. Continue to whip for 5 minutes. Add the grated carrots to the egg mixture and whip until combined.

5 Place the egg whites in a separate bowl and whip with a handheld mixer until large bubbles form; add the salt and beat until stiff peaks form.

6 Remove the bowl from the stand mixer and fold in half of the flour mixture. Then fold in half of the beaten egg whites. Fold in the remaining flour mixture. Finally, fold in the remaining egg whites until well combined.

continued

7 Scrape the batter into the prepared pan and smooth the top. Place in the oven and bake for 60 minutes, or until the torte is a rich golden brown and a tester inserted into the middle comes out clean.

8 Remove the pan from the oven and place on a rack to cool completely. Only when the torte has fully cooled can you unmold it from the pan by turning the pan upside down.

9 While the cake cools, prepare the almond-paste carrots: If using pistachios for the carrot tops, place all of the almond paste in one bowl and add food coloring drop by drop, kneading well until the almond paste is orange. If using almond paste for the carrot tops, before coloring the almond paste transfer one-eighth of it to a separate bowl and color with green food coloring.

10 When the almond paste is an even orange, divide it into 12 pieces and roll each piece into a carrot shape. You can, if desired, mark the carrots with the tines of a fork for added flair. Poke a hole in the top of each carrot with a toothpick.

11 If using pistachios for the carrot tops, split each nut in half and then into quarters. Stick 2 quarters of each pistachio into the top of each carrot. If using almond paste, divide it into 12 roughly equal pieces. Roll each out into 3 small pieces and, using the toothpick, insert them into the top of each carrot. Set the carrots aside on a piece of plastic wrap.

12 Place the sliced almonds in a small skillet and toast over medium heat, tossing and stirring constantly, until golden brown and fragrant. Remove from the heat and set aside to cool completely.

13 Prepare the glaze by placing the confectioners' sugar in a bowl and stirring in the lemon juice. You want the glaze to be thick and more spreadable than pourable. With the help of an offset spatula, spread the glaze all over the top and sides of the fully cooled torte. Working quickly before the glaze sets, press the toasted, sliced almonds onto the sides of the torte. Arrange the almond-paste carrots evenly on the top of the cake around the perimeter, tapered ends pointing toward the middle of the cake. When you cut the cake, each slice should have a carrot on top. When the glaze has set, cover the torte with plastic wrap and let it rest at room temperature for 1 to 2 days before serving.

HANNCHEN-JENSEN-TORTE
Meringue Cream Cake

MAKES 1 (10-INCH/25CM) TORTE

Oh, *Hannchen-Jensen-Torte*, my own personal tormenter. I first discovered this oddly named layer cake at a birthday party in the countryside outside Berlin years ago. I wrote in my first book, *My Berlin Kitchen*, about how much I loved it and how hard a recipe it was to crack (my first try resulted in a cake with a raw center at the fiftieth anniversary party of some of my favorite people on Earth). When that book was published, the *Wall Street Journal* ran an excerpt from that chapter. I mentioned my struggles with the recipe, but also the fact that the name remained impenetrable to me. I had no idea where it came from or what it meant. (I called it *Hannchen Jansen*, because that's what my friend who first gave me the recipe called it.) No one I asked, no book I read, no website I searched could help me.

I got the answer, almost a year after that article was posted, from a man named Ragnar Heil. He commented on the piece, saying that his grandparents had often gone to the North Sea for vacation and, while there, had stayed at a bed-and-breakfast run by a woman named (wait for it) Hannchen Jensen. The fruit-and-cream-filled, meringue-topped torte had been her creation, albeit with mandarin oranges instead of the gooseberries I called for (which is how it was first served to me). Later still, I found out that this kind of multilayered torte filled with cream and fruit—usually handfuls of gorgeously sour and jewellike redcurrants or softer, milder raspberries—is also known as *Himmelstorte* (heaven torte) or *Schwimmbadtorte* (swimming pool torte). Hoo! Are you still with me?

At first, I thought I wouldn't include a recipe for this type of torte in the book; after all, I'd covered it before. But after my assistant Maja's lobbying, I started wondering if I shouldn't change my mind. *Himmelstorte* with red currants is one of her favorites and she made

a compelling case. Then, shortly before I finished writing this book, a family friend asked if she could send me her favorite cake recipe to try; I guess I wasn't even surprised when it turned out to be this one.

So, ladies and gentlemen, without further ado, I present to you *Hannchen-Jensen-Torte* or *Himmelstorte*, however you'd like to call it: 2 cake layers topped with crunchy, almond-capped meringue and filled with a vanilla-scented whipped cream and fruit—anything from canned mandarin oranges to gooseberries. It is bombastic, beautiful, and most deserving of all the attention it has gotten from me over the years. A celebration cake, for sure.

If you have a good source of redcurrants when they are in season, then substitute 2 to 3 cups of stemmed redcurrants for the mandarin oranges. You may, in this case, want to increase the sugar in the whipped cream by a teaspoon, but it's not mandatory. The cake can also be made with fresh raspberries or canned gooseberries.

CAKE

8½ tablespoons/120g unsalted butter, at room temperature

½ cup/100g granulated sugar

4 eggs, separated

1⅓ cups, scooped and leveled, plus 1 tablespoon/ 175g all-purpose flour

1½ teaspoons baking powder

¼ teaspoon salt plus a pinch of salt

¼ cup/60ml whole milk

1 cup/125g confectioners' sugar

⅔ cup/60g blanched sliced almonds

continued

FILLING

2 (11-ounce/310g) cans mandarin oranges

1¾ cups/420ml whipping cream

2 teaspoons granulated sugar

¾ teaspoon vanilla extract

1 Preheat the oven to 350°F/180°C. Line two 10-inch/25cm pans with a sheet of parchment paper, letting the paper hang over the sides to function as a sling after baking.

2 To make the cake: Place the butter and granulated sugar in the bowl of a stand mixer fitted with the flat beater attachment and beat together for 5 minutes, scraping down the sides once. Beat in the egg yolks one at a time, beating for 30 seconds after each addition.

3 In a separate bowl, mix together the flour, the baking powder, and the ¼ teaspoon of salt. Beat this mixture into the batter, and then follow with the milk. Beat until the batter is well combined.

4 In a separate, very clean bowl, whip the egg whites with an electric mixer until large bubbles form. While whipping, add the remaining pinch of salt and continue to whip until the mixture is thick and white and soft peaks form. Then, whipping constantly, add the confectioners' sugar in spoonsful. Whip until stiff peaks form.

5 Divide the batter, which will be relatively stiff, equally between the two prepared pans. Using an offset spatula, spread the batter out evenly. This will seem difficult; persist. Then spoon half of the egg whites into one of the two pans and spread evenly. Use the spatula or the back of a spoon to create gentle peaks and valleys in the meringue. Sprinkle with half of the sliced almonds. Place the pan in the oven and bake for 30 minutes, or until the almonds and meringue are golden brown. Remove from the oven and place on a rack to cool.

6 Toward the end of the baking time of the first layer, spoon the remaining meringue into the second cake pan, again making gentle peaks and valleys, and sprinkle with the remaining sliced almonds. As soon as the first layer comes out, place the second one in the oven and bake for 30 minutes. Remove from the oven and let cool on a rack.

7 When both layers have completely cooled (they will have sunk down a bit), remove from the pans using the parchment paper as a sling. Peel off the parchment paper and place one layer on a cake platter or stand.

8 To make the filling: Drain the mandarin oranges and cut them in half crosswise. Place the whipping cream, granulated sugar, and vanilla extract in a bowl and whip until stiff. Gently fold the drained mandarin oranges into the whipped cream.

9 Scrape the whipped cream mixture onto the cake layer on the platter or stand. Spread out evenly to cover the whole round.

10 Using a heavy knife, cut the remaining cake round into 12 even wedges. This will make cutting and serving the cake later easier and less messy. Transfer the wedges to the top of the filling and arrange back together. The cake can now be set aside for up to 4 hours or served immediately. Remember to cut through the cream and bottom cake layer before serving.

HEIDJERTORTE
Lingonberry Buckwheat Cream Torte

MAKES 1 (9-INCH/23CM) TORTE

My assistant, Maja, introduced me to this delicate and unusual three-layer torte, which comes from the Lüneburg Heath in the western German state of Lower Saxony. Both buckwheat and lingonberries are native to the heath, and both have a faint and pleasing bitterness that is absolutely inspired when combined. The torte is also completely gluten-free.

To make the torte, you must first make a towering buckwheat sponge cake and slice it into thirds horizontally. Then you combine lingonberry preserves, which have a taste reminiscent of American cranberry sauce, only less biting and acidic, with whipped cream. The layers of cake are sandwiched back together with the gorgeously hued sweet-sour cream, and the cake is thickly enrobed in more whipped cream and smoothed out as flat as can be. (You can also decorate the top of the torte with rosettes of reserved whipped cream and lingonberries for a more bakery-style torte as in the photo.) When a piece is cut out, the gorgeous pink-and-buff-striped interior is revealed.

Maja prefers to eat the torte when it has had time to settle and ripen. She bakes the torte on one day, fills it with cream and preserves the next day, and serves it on the third day (refrigerating it in between). And indeed, the torte is much easier to slice when it has rested for at least a day. But I tried the torte several hours after it was freshly filled and frosted and again a couple of days later, and I confess I preferred it freshly made. The light and airy quality of the torte is precisely what I like about it. And although the amount of cream called for seems eye-popping, the astringent preserves keep the torte from becoming too rich or overwhelming.

Unsalted butter, for the pan

6 eggs, separated

¾ cup/150g granulated sugar, plus 2 teaspoons for the whipped cream

3 tablespoons hot water

⅛ teaspoon salt

1 cup, scooped and leveled, plus 2 tablespoons/150g buckwheat flour

2 teaspoons baking powder

3¾ cups/900ml whipping cream

1½ cups/400g lingonberry preserves

1 Preheat the oven to 350°F/180°C. Line the bottom of a 9-inch/23cm springform pan with parchment paper and butter the sides.

2 Place the egg yolks and the ¾ cup sugar in the bowl of a stand mixer fitted with the whisk attachment; turn the motor on to medium-high. Slowly add the hot water and beat for 5 minutes.

3 In a separate, very clean bowl, whip the egg whites and salt with an electric mixer until the egg whites hold stiff peaks.

4 Mix the buckwheat flour and baking powder together and sift over the egg yolk mixture. Fold in until well combined. Then fold the whipped egg whites into the batter until no white streaks remain. Scrape the batter into the prepared pan, smooth the top, and place the pan in the oven.

continued

5 Bake for 40 to 45 minutes, or until the top is pale golden brown and a skewer inserted into the middle comes out clean. Remove the pan from oven and let cool completely on a rack before removing the springform ring. Gently turn the cake upside down to remove the pan bottom and parchment paper. Turn the cake right-side up again.

6 Place 1½ cups/360ml whipping cream in a clean bowl and beat until soft peaks form. Fold in the lingonberry preserves, reserving 2 to 3 tablespoons for a garnish.

7 Slice the cake into thirds horizontally. Spread the bottom layer evenly with half of the lingonberry cream. Place the middle layer on top. Spread that layer with the remaining lingonberry cream. Top with the top layer.

8 In a separate, clean bowl, whip the remaining 2¼ cups/540ml of cream with the 2 teaspoons of sugar until stiff peaks form. Frost the top and sides of the torte with the whipped cream, reserving about 1 cup for the garnish.

9 Place the reserved whipped cream in a pastry bag fitted with the tip of your choice to decorate the top of the torte (one suggestion is to pipe rosettes around the rim of the cake). Then use the reserved lingonberry preserves to garnish (by, for example, spooning a little bit on top of each piped rosette). Refrigerate the torte for at least 6 hours and up to 24 hours before serving. Remove the cake from the refrigerator and let sit at room temperature for 30 minutes before serving it.

FRIESENTORTE
Plum Cream Torte

MAKES 1 (9-INCH/23CM) TORTE

I first caught wind of the glorious cream- and jam-filled *Friesentorte* on television. A reporter for a local show had gone to a bakery on the North Sea island of Amrum to see a master *Konditor* put together the local specialty: rounds of crisp puff pastry sandwiched together with epic amounts of jet-black roasted plum butter and great drifts of whipped cream.

A few months later, I spotted *Friesentorte* in the wild: behind the bakery case at my local organic grocery store. I bought a slice, of course, and went straight home to eat it. Research! It was even better than I imagined. The toasty, gently spiced flavor of the plum butter is just the right match for vanilla-flavored whipped cream, while the buttery-crisp shards of puff pastry anchor it. The textural contrasts—crisp, creamy, smooth, and sticky—are inspired. And believe it or not, it isn't as sweet as you might think, especially if you stick to the amount of sugar called for to sweeten the whipped cream.

The torte is a cinch to make, because it calls for pre-made puff pastry (high-quality all-butter puff pastry, if possible) and jam from your pantry (see page 265 for how to make your own *Pflaumenmus* and page 2 70 for where to buy it). All you have to do, really, is whip the cream.

You can make the torte look prettier and fancier by preparing a third 9-inch/23cm round of puff pastry. Before baking, cut the pastry into 12 equal wedges. After the wedges have baked and cooled, arrange them in a circle on top of the top layer of whipped cream, at a 45-degree angle, like the arms of a windmill.

1 sheet frozen store-bought puff pastry (2 sheets, if making the windmill top described above)

2½ cups/600ml whipping cream

3 tablespoons granulated sugar

1½ cups/450g homemade *Pflaumenmus* (see page 265) or store-bought

Confectioners' sugar, for dusting (optional)

1 Preheat the oven to 425°F/220°C. Line a baking sheet with parchment paper.

2 Unroll the puff pastry and then, using a rolling pin, roll it out until the rectangle measures approximately 9 by 18 inches/23 by 46cm. Prick the pastry all over with a fork. Using a 9-inch/23cm round cake pan as a guide, cut out 2 rounds of pastry. Bake one round of pastry on the baking sheet for 12 to 14 minutes, or until well browned and crisp. Then bake the second round, along with the trimmings. Let cool completely on a rack. If making the windmill top described above, bake a third round, reserving the remaining puff pastry for a different use.

3 Place the whipping cream and granulated sugar in a bowl and beat until quite stiff. Set aside.

4 To assemble the torte, dab a bit of whipped cream on a cake plate. Place one round of puff pastry on top. The cream on the bottom will anchor the pastry. Spread ¾ cup/225g of the *Pflaumenmus* evenly all over the pastry, leaving a ¼-inch/6mm border. Scrape half of the whipped cream over the *Pflaumenmus* and spread evenly. Top with the second piece of pastry and repeat with the remaining jam and whipped cream. Crumble the trimmings over the top of the torte. Or cut the third round of puff pastry into 12 wedges and arrange on the whipped cream, as described above. Chill in the freezer for up to 30 minutes. Dust with confectioners' sugar, if desired, before slicing with a very sharp knife and serving. The torte is best eaten when the pastry is still crisp.

SCHWARZWÄLDER KIRSCHTORTE
Black Forest Torte

MAKES 1 (9-INCH/23CM) TORTE

If there is a better example of a standard-bearing German cake, I have yet to find it. Next to pretzels and sausages, Black Forest cake has become synonymous with Germany abroad. Here in Germany, the kirsch-soaked chocolate layer cake is actually most beloved by the older generations and is considered too fussy and dated for most young bakers. In fact, when you do come across one at a bakery, which is not that often (at least in Berlin), it's decorated with curlicues of whipped cream, glacé cherries, and chocolate sprinkles and appears more retro than appetizing.

When I was fourteen, I accompanied my friends Joanie and Dietrich on a two-week visit to Dietrich's cousins who live near Kassel, in Hessen. Karl and Ischen (a German nickname for Luise, pronounced "EES-yen") are dairy farmers. And the days we spent at their home—seeing piglets being born at the farm across the road, waking up at dawn to watch Karl milk his herd, falling asleep on an honest-to-goodness goose-down-filled mattress in a small room under the eaves—were more than enough to make a lifelong impression on this teenage city kid who'd merely grown up with stories of Laura Ingalls Wilder's farm life in her head. Completing the picture of rural bliss, Ischen is a master home baker. That's no overstatement; she regularly wins regional baking competitions. It was at her home that I tried *Schwarzwälder Kirschtorte* for the first time. I can still remember the very moment I took my first bite. That's how good it was.

To make *Schwarzwälder Kirschtorte*, you start by baking a plump, cocoa-flavored sponge cake. This is split into thirds and dribbled with kirsch, that potent cherry brandy, before being layered with whipped cream and sour cherries and cloaked in even more whipped cream.

A few thoughts on decorating the torte: For an elegant finish, use a bench scraper to smooth out the whipped cream that covers the top and sides until it's as neat as possible. Then pipe little rosettes of reserved whipped cream on the top of the cake (one for each of the slices) and dot each rosette with a reserved sour cherry. If you prefer a more retro finish, you can cover the top of the cake in piped cream rosettes (you may need more whipped cream for this; adjust the quantities accordingly). In both instances, however, you must coat the sides of the cream-covered cake with grated bittersweet chocolate. Without the chocolate, it just won't read as a real *Schwarzwälder Kirschtorte*. The easiest way to frost the torte is to swathe it in whipped cream and then coat the top and sides of the cake generously with handfuls of grated bittersweet chocolate. Then decorate the top with sour cherries, one for each slice. To grate the chocolate, I use the large holes on a box grater and then try to work as quickly as possible as I fling them onto the cake, so that they don't melt in my hands.

What's essential is that you must let the torte rest a bit before serving so the flavors meld and the cake layers get good and moist. A minimum of 4 hours is good—refrigerated, of course.

A note on the kirsch: Traditionalists say there should be enough kirsch in the cake to make you tipsy after one slice. Depending on your taste, though, you can reduce the amount you use. I like a less alcoholic cake, so I've given a range for you to choose from, depending on your taste and whom you're baking for.

continued

CAKE

6 eggs, separated

¼ teaspoon salt

¾ cup plus 1 tablespoon/180g granulated sugar

¾ cup, scooped and leveled, minus 1 tablespoon/100g cake flour

⅓ cup plus 1 tablespoon/50g cocoa powder

⅓ cup plus 1 teaspoon/50g cornstarch

FILLING AND TOPPING

1 (24-ounce/680g) jar or can pitted sour cherries in sugar water

1 tablespoon cornstarch

3 cups/720ml whipping cream

3 tablespoons granulated sugar

3 to 6 tablespoons/45 to 90ml kirsch

Large chunk of bittersweet chocolate, chilled, for grating

1 Preheat the oven to 400°F/200°C. Line the bottom of a 9-inch/23cm springform pan with parchment paper.

2 To make the cake: Place the egg whites in the bowl of a stand mixer fitted with the whisk attachment. Add the salt; begin whisking on medium speed, and then increase the speed. As the egg whites whip and froth, slowly add the sugar in small increments. Beat until the egg whites are thick and glossy and at least tripled in volume. The sugar should be fully dissolved (you can pinch a bit of the mixture between thumb and forefinger to see whether it's still grainy).

3 Lower the speed and beat in the egg yolks, one at a time. Turn off the machine.

4 In a separate bowl, sift together the flour, cocoa powder, and cornstarch. Gently shake this mixture over the whipped eggs. Using a spatula, gently but

thoroughly fold together until the batter is smooth and creamy and no streaks remain. Scrape the batter gently into the prepared pan and smooth the top. Bake for 25 minutes.

5 Remove the pan from the oven and let cool on a rack for 30 minutes. Run a thin knife around the edged of the cake, then remove the springform ring. Turn the cake upside down, remove the bottom of the pan and the parchment paper, and let the cake cool completely.

6 To prepare the filling and topping: Drain the sour cherries over a bowl, reserving the juice. Set aside 13 to 15 cherries for the top of the cake. Pour the cherry juice into a measuring cup and add enough water to come up to ¾ cup plus 2 tablespoons/200ml (you may have enough juice without needing to add water—it depends on the jar of cherries you buy). Pour 2 tablespoons of the juice into a separate bowl and stir in the cornstarch until no lumps remain. Set aside. Pour the remaining juice into a saucepan.

7 Bring the pan of juice to a boil. Add the drained cherries, bring to a boil again, and then immediately stir in the cornstarch mixture. Let cook over medium heat until the mixture thickens slightly. Remove from the heat and let cool—the mixture will continue to thicken as it cools.

8 Whip the cream and sugar together until very thick. Set aside.

9 Cut the fully cooled chocolate cake horizontally into 3 equal layers. Place the bottom third on a cake platter. Sprinkle evenly with 1 to 2 tablespoons of kirsch. Scrape some of the whipped cream into a pastry bag fitted with a round tip and pipe 3 concentric rings onto the cake round. Fill the rings with half of the sour cherry mixture. Gently place the second round of cake on top and repeat

the process with the kirsch, whipped cream, and cherry mixture. Place the third round of the cake on top and sprinkle with the remaining kirsch. Frost the top and sides of the cake with the remaining whipped cream, and then arrange the reserved cherries on top of the cake.

10 Grate the bittersweet chocolate and scatter it over the top and sides of the cake. How much you use is up to you. Refrigerate the cake for at least 4 hours and up to 24 hours before serving. If refrigerating for 4 hours, remove from the refrigerator 30 minutes before serving. If chilling for longer, remove from the refrigerator 1 hour before serving. The cake will keep, lightly wrapped in plastic wrap, for several days.

MOHNTORTE
Flourless Poppy-Seed Torte

MAKES 1 (9-INCH/23CM) TORTE

This classic inky-black, flourless torte from the Austrian sweet kitchen is a stunner to behold. Flat-topped and stark in its black-and-white simplicity, it never fails to enchant. The unusual texture of the torte, airy with egg whites and creamy-gravelly from the ground poppy seeds and nuts, is part of its appeal. But its flavor, dusky and haunting, with a faint hint of acidity from the almost imperceptible line of redcurrant jelly running through the torte, is what makes people fall in love with it.

The torte batter, which is gluten-free, is baked in a 9-inch/23cm pan and cut in half once fully cooled. The halves are glued back together with tart redcurrant jelly, which gives the torte some backbone. I like to sift confectioners' sugar on top—if you have a cake stencil to sift over, this is an exceptionally good torte for it. You can, alternatively, glaze it with a thick lemon glaze like the one for the *Rüblitorte* (page 114). It should be served with a nice dollop of *Schlagsahne* (lightly sweetened whipped cream).

The recipe here uses an equal mix of ground walnuts and almonds (they should be as finely ground as possible without turning to paste). You can, however, use only one or the other, if you prefer.

12 tablespoons plus 1 teaspoon/175g unsalted high-fat, European-style butter, at room temperature, plus more for the pan

6 tablespoons/50g confectioners' sugar, plus more for dusting

5 eggs, separated

2 tablespoons dark rum

Grated peel of 1 organic lemon

1 cup minus 1 tablespoon/90g ground almonds

1 cup minus 1 tablespoon/90g ground walnuts

1⅓ cups plus 1 tablespoon/210g poppy seeds, ground (see page 7)

⅛ teaspoon salt

½ cup plus 2 tablespoons/125g granulated sugar

⅓ cup/100g redcurrant jelly

Schlagsahne (page 267), for serving

1 Preheat the oven to 350°F/180°C. Line the bottom of a 9-inch/23cm springform pan with parchment paper. Butter the sides.

2 Place the butter and confectioners' sugar in the bowl of a stand mixer fitted with the whisk attachment and beat together for 30 seconds; add the egg yolks, one at a time, and continue beating until the mixture is very light and fluffy. Scrape down the sides, and then beat in the rum and grated lemon peel. Continue beating until the mixture is thick and glossy. Beat in the almonds, walnuts, and poppy seeds, beating just until combined.

3 Place the egg whites in a separate, very clean bowl and add the salt. Using a handheld mixer, whip at high speed until the egg whites start to form large bubbles. Add the granulated sugar very slowly, a spoonful at a time, whipping all the while. When all the sugar has been whipped into the egg whites, continue to whip until the mixture is quite stiff and glossy.

4 Scrape one-third of the egg white mixture into the batter and fold in to lighten. Scrape another one-third of the egg white mixture into the batter and fold it in gently but thoroughly. Scrape the final one-third of the egg white mixture into the batter and fold it in gently but thoroughly until no white streaks remain. Scrape the batter into the prepared pan and smooth the top.

5 Place the pan in the oven and bake for 50 to 55 minutes, rotating the pan halfway through. The cake will be pulling away from the edges of the pan and a thin skewer inserted into the middle of the torte should come out clean. Remove the pan from the oven and let cool on a rack for 5 minutes before removing the springform ring and turning the cake upside down on the rack. Remove the pan bottom and peel off the parchment paper. Let the cake cool completely upside down.

6 Place the jelly in a small saucepan over medium heat and heat until runny. Remove from the heat and let cool briefly. In the meantime, slice the torte in half horizontally. Spread the jelly evenly all over the top of the bottom layer. Place the top layer of the torte over the jelly. (If you have a cake stencil, place it on the torte now.) Sift confectioners' sugar over the top of the torte. Set the torte aside at room temperature for 1 day before serving with the *Schlagsahne*. The torte will keep, lightly wrapped in plastic wrap, for several days.

SACHERTORTE
Glazed Chocolate Torte

MAKES 1 (9-INCH/23CM) TORTE

If you asked me what was the dark-horse recipe in this book, the one that most caught me by surprise in the recipe-testing phase of this book, it would have to be this *Sachertorte*. I confess that I had never really given *Sachertorte* much thought before. I knew that it had been developed by an apprentice *pâtissier* at the court of an Austrian royal in the early nineteenth century. I knew it had a chocolate crumb and a chocolate glaze. I knew that the Hotel Sacher and its rival, the Demel bakery, did a brisk worldwide mail-order business in *Sacher Torten* and *Sachertorten* (only Hotel Sacher has the copyright on the name, which is why Demel's version, and everyone else's, must be called *Sachertorte*). But I still wrote it off as the kind of cultural obsession that was probably more disappointing than delicious in real life. How special could a chocolate cake be?

Well, I was wrong. Sometimes the hype is real. And in this case, the hype is very, very real. This may be the most special chocolate cake I've ever had—and I've had lots.

The texture of *Sachertorte* is what I find most amazing: its crumb is velvety and light, almost frothy, and yet it's also deeply chocolaty—improbably so for such a light sponge. A layer of apricot jam gives the cake a faintly fruity note, and a thin, cooked chocolate glaze bestows on the cake its famously glossy, minimalist coating. Not to overstate things, but this *Sachertorte* is nothing short of quietly majestic. It's the kind of cake I'd like to request for my birthday for the rest of my years on Earth.

There is much discussion about whether a true *Sachertorte* (or *Sacher Torte*) should be split in half and filled with apricot jam as well as having it on the top of the cake, or if it should be left whole and only topped with jam before you glaze it. I like the split and filled cake, if only because it gives an already special thing a little extra pizzazz. But leave it whole, by all means, if you are so inclined. What's important is that your apricot jam be completely smooth, otherwise the finishing chocolate glaze will not be smooth. Use an immersion blender to puree your apricot jam before heating it and, for good measure, press it through a fine-mesh sieve to catch any remaining lumps.

If you'd like to decorate the glazed cake with thin curlicues of monochromatic script, fill a pastry bag fitted with a very small round tip for letter writing with some of the remaining chocolate glaze. Working quickly, while the glaze is still warm, decorate the top of the cake with the words you'd like and a few choice curlicues. Less is more with this one. Any excess chocolate glaze that collects on the parchment paper or baking mat while you are glazing the cake can be scraped up and used for hot chocolate. (Heat milk on the stove, and then whisk in a few spoonsful of solidified glaze.)

You will note that the instructions tell you to wedge a wooden spoon handle in the oven door. This is, most likely, a holdover from olden times when ovens were not the highly calibrated appliances they are today and needed circulating air from outside to keep the oven from running too hot. But since *Sachertorte* must be baked at a relatively low temperature anyway, so that it develops that wondrously light yet creamy texture, I kept the wooden handle trick. Who wants to mess with tradition?

CAKE

4¼ ounces/120g bittersweet chocolate (minimum 50% cacao)

8½ tablespoons/120g unsalted high-fat, European-style butter, plus more for the pan

6 eggs, separated

13 tablespoons/100g confectioners' sugar

¼ teaspoon salt

⅓ cup plus 1 tablespoon/80g granulated sugar

9½ tablespoons, scooped and leveled/80g cake flour, plus more for the pan

¼ cup plus 1 teaspoon/40g cornstarch

FILLING

1 cup/300g smooth apricot jam

2 tablespoons dark rum

GLAZE

1 cup/200g granulated sugar

½ cup/120ml water

5¼ ounces/150g bittersweet chocolate (minimum 50% cacao), chopped

Schlagsahne (page 267), for serving

1 Preheat the oven to 350°F/180°C. Line the bottom of a 9-inch/23cm cake pan with parchment paper. Butter and lightly flour the sides of the pan.

2 To make the cake: Place the chocolate and butter in a metal bowl set over a saucepan of simmering water and melt, stirring, until smooth. Set aside.

3 Place the egg yolks in the bowl of a stand mixer fitted with the whisk attachment. Place the whites in a separate, very clean bowl.

4 Add the confectioners' sugar to the yolks and start to whip together until fluffy, creamy, and pale, about 5 minutes. With the motor on, slowly drizzle in the melted chocolate mixture and beat until fully incorporated.

5 Add the salt to the bowl of egg whites and start beating them with a whisk or electric mixer. When the whites show soft peaks, slowly add the granulated sugar as you continue to beat. Continue to beat until the sugar has dissolved and the egg whites are stiff and glossy.

6 In a separate bowl, sift together the flour and cornstarch.

7 Fold one-third of the flour mixture into the egg yolk mixture. Fold one-third of the egg whites into the egg yolk mixture. Repeat with the next one-third of the flour and then the egg whites, and then fold in the remaining flour and then the egg whites, until no white streaks remain.

8 Gently scrape the batter into the prepared pan and smooth the top. Place in the oven and then wedge the handle of a wooden spoon in the oven door. Bake for 10 minutes and then remove the spoon; turn the heat down to 275°F/135°C and bake for 40 to 45 minutes longer, or until a tester inserted into the center of the cake comes out clean.

9 Place the cake pan on a rack for 10 minutes to cool, and then invert the cake, remove the pan, and peel off the parchment paper. Let the cake cool completely upside down. Once it has fully cooled, slice it in half horizontally. Place the rack on top of a piece of parchment paper or a nonstick baking mat.

continued

10 To make the filling: Place the jam and rum in a small pan, bring to a boil, and continue to boil for a minute or two. Let cool slightly, and then spread half of the mixture evenly on top of the bottom cake layer. Place the second layer on top of the jam and press down slightly. Spread the remaining jam over the top and sides of the cake. Let cool completely.

11 To make the glaze: Place the sugar and water in a small pan and bring to a boil. Let boil over high heat for 5 minutes. Remove from the heat, add the chopped chocolate, and stir until the chocolate has melted. Place the pan over medium-high heat and bring to a boil; immediately remove from the heat and let stand, stirring occasionally, for 7 to 8 minutes. The mixture will be smooth, glossy, and pourable and will coat the back of a spoon.

12 Slowly pour the warm chocolate glaze evenly all over the cake, letting the excess drip down the sides. If possible, avoid using a spatula to spread the glaze—it will stay glossiest if not touched. Reserve a little glaze in the pan to pour over any uncoated patches on the sides so that the entire cake is coated evenly and thoroughly. Gently wedge two spatulas under the cake to transfer it to a serving plate. Let the glaze set completely before cutting and serving the cake with *Schlagsahne* alongside. The cake will keep for 3 to 5 days at room temperature, loosely wrapped in plastic wrap or in a large airtight container.

NUSSTORTE VON HAMMERSTEIN
Glazed Hazelnut Torte

MAKES 1 (9-INCH/23CM) TORTE

I never thought I had much of an opinion about hazelnuts. I resented finding them in my bowl of morning *Müsli* as a kid; for some reason, they were always unpleasantly chewy and rancid—and a rancid hazelnut is a foul thing indeed. But of course I loved them when paired with chocolate, as in the occasional treat of Nutella; and later, as a young woman in New York, I was happy to discover the rich, toasty flavor of roasted, skinned hazelnuts in salads made with roasted beets or earthy-sweet squash. Either way, though, I just wasn't that passionate about them. For the most part, I suppose, I ignored hazelnuts.

Then I married my husband. And my husband has intense feelings about them (pistachios, too). He doesn't have much of a sweet tooth, but you can almost guarantee that if there are hazelnuts in whatever you're peddling, he'll have some. Hazelnut ice cream, hazelnut chocolate, hazelnut cake—he likes it all.

So I was delighted when my friend and baking guru Joanie told me about a hazelnut torte that she has been making for decades, ever since her art school friends, the von Hammersteins, wrote down their family recipe for her. The torte features 3 whole cups of ground hazelnuts, lightened only by beaten egg whites. The torte is split and filled with a thin layer of raspberry jam (redcurrant would also be very nice here) and iced with a lemon glaze. Both provide welcome hits of bright acidity against the rich crumb of the torte.

The ground hazelnuts make the torte exceptionally moist, and it keeps well for several days. As with other nut-based tortes, it is essential to let it rest for a day or two before being served so that the flavors have a chance to ripen and the texture improves. For a slightly more grown-up torte, you can leave the lemon juice out of the sugar glaze and substitute the same amount of dark rum.

12 tablespoons/170g unsalted butter, at room temperature, plus more for the pan

1⅓ cups/270g granulated sugar

7 eggs, separated

4 tablespoons/60ml freshly squeezed lemon juice

½ teaspoon vanilla extract

2¾ cups/275g toasted skinned, ground hazelnuts (see page 7)

½ cup, scooped and leveled, plus 1 tablespoon/ 70g all-purpose flour

¼ teaspoon salt

½ cup/150g raspberry jam

1½ cups plus 2 tablespoons/200g confectioners' sugar

6 to 12 toasted skinned hazelnuts (see page 7), whole or halved, for decoration

1 Preheat the oven to 350°F/180°C. Line the bottom of a 9-inch/23cm springform pan with parchment paper and butter the sides.

2 Place the butter and granulated sugar in the bowl of a stand mixer fitted with the whisk attachment and whip until light and fluffy. With the motor running, add the egg yolks, one at a time, beating until fully incorporated. When all the yolks have been incorporated, whip the mixture for an additional 7 minutes (set a timer). Beat in 2 tablespoons/30ml of the lemon juice and the vanilla extract.

3 In a separate bowl, mix together the ground hazelnuts and flour. Briefly beat into the butter mixture until just combined.

4 In a separate, very clean bowl, whip the egg whites until large bubbles form and then add the salt. Continue to whip until the egg whites hold stiff peaks. Stir one-third of the beaten egg whites into the cake batter to lighten it. Fold another one-third of the egg whites into the batter gently but thoroughly to lighten it further. Then fold the remaining one-third of the egg whites into the batter until no white streaks remain. Scrape the batter into the prepared pan and smooth the top.

5 Place in the oven and bake for 50 to 55 minutes, or until the cake is golden brown and a skewer inserted into the middle comes out clean. Remove the pan from the oven and let cool for 30 minutes on a rack before removing the springform ring. Let the cake cool completely.

6 Slice the cake in half horizontally. Place the jam in a small pan and warm briefly over medium heat to loosen it. Spread it evenly all over the top of the bottom half of the cake. Place the top half of the cake on top.

7 Place the confectioners' sugar in a small bowl and stir in the remaining 2 tablespoons/30ml of lemon juice until the mixture is smooth. Spread the glaze evenly over the top and sides of the cake. Arrange the whole or halved hazelnuts around the rim of the cake. Let the cake rest for at least 1 day and up to 3 days before serving. The cake does not need to be wrapped as it ripens. Once sliced, the cake can be wrapped in aluminum foil and will keep for up to 1 week.

LINZERTORTE
Spiced Almond Jam Tart

MAKES 1 (10-INCH/25CM) TORTE

The legendary *Linzertorte*, a rich, gently spiced jam tart with a lattice top, hails from the Austrian town of Linz and has, over the decades, become an integral part of German baking as well. In both countries, it's considered a wintertime classic thanks to the inclusion of ground almonds and warm spices in the dough. There are a hundred and one ways to make *Linzertorte*, and I baked many different *Linzertorten* in the quest for the perfect recipe. In some, the dough was too thick and crumbly; in others it was too heavy and greasy. Some had cocoa powder in the crust, others ground hazelnuts. None of them were quite right, but I was able to cobble together tips, tricks, and ingredients from each round of baking until I finally developed the best *Linzertorte* I've ever had.

In this recipe, the dough is made with ground almonds and equal amounts of butter, sugar, and flour. The grated peel of a lemon adds brightness to the crust, and the cooked egg yolks kneaded into the dough make it meltingly tender. I learned from the Austrian food writer Katharina Seiser that it is imperative to let a freshly baked *Linzertorte* rest for at least 3 days at room temperature before it is served. This tip was an absolute game changer. The rest period not only allows the flavor of the crust to mellow, but the consistency of the torte changes too, becoming more like a confection than a cake. A good Austrian baker will always make a *Linzertorte* several days in advance of guests coming. Don't refrigerate the *Linzertorte* during this rest period—the refrigerator is far too damp a place. Instead, wrap it well in aluminum foil and place it in a cool room in your house.

Some experts say that *Linzertorte* must be made with redcurrant jam to be truly traditional, but I found old Austrian cookbooks that also suggested using apricot or raspberry jam. In fact, I found I liked raspberry jam the best. What all three jams have in common is a tartness that's necessary to counterbalance the sweetness and spicy crust. A sweeter jam like strawberry or blueberry would push this over the edge into cloying territory.

When you first spread the jam on the crust, you will probably think it's not enough. Don't worry; it is. The trick with *Linzertorte* is that the jam should really be only a thin layer, which allows the delicious crust to shine.

10½ tablespoons/150g unsalted high-fat, European-style butter, at room temperature

¾ cup/150g granulated sugar

1¼ cups, scooped and leveled, minus 1 tablespoon/150g all-purpose flour

1 cup/100g ground almonds

¾ teaspoon ground cinnamon

½ teaspoon ground cloves

¼ teaspoon salt

⅛ teaspoon ground allspice

Grated peel of 1 organic lemon

1 tablespoon freshly squeezed lemon juice

2 hard-boiled egg yolks

1 raw egg yolk

¾ cup/220g raspberry jam

Milk or beaten egg, for brushing

1 Place the butter, sugar, flour, almonds, cinnamon, cloves, salt, allspice, grated lemon peel, and lemon juice in a large mixing bowl. Press the cooked egg yolks through a fine-mesh sieve into the bowl. Add the raw egg yolk. Using your fingers, quickly work all the ingredients together until you have a cohesive dough. Form into a disk, wrap tightly in plastic wrap, and refrigerate for at least 1 hour and up to 48 hours.

2 When you are ready to bake, heat the oven to 350°F/180°C. Line a 10-inch/25cm cake pan with parchment paper, letting the sides hang over the edge to function as a sling after baking. Alternatively, you can use a 10-inch/25cm fluted tart pan with a removable bottom, which does not have to be lined. Take the dough out of the refrigerator. Cut off one-quarter of the dough and set aside. Press the remaining dough into the prepared pan, making a ½-inch/12mm-thick crust.

3 Scrape the jam onto the crust and spread it evenly.

4 Roll out the remaining dough to ⅛-inch/3mm thickness, and then cut it into ½-inch/12mm strips. Lay the strips over the jam to form a lattice. Brush all the strips and crust with a little milk or beaten egg.

5 Place the pan in the oven and bake for 45 minutes, or until the jam is bubbling and the edges of the crust and the strips are a deep golden brown. Remove from the oven and let cool completely (a minimum of 4 hours) before wrapping in aluminum foil. Place the foil-wrapped torte in a cool place that is not the refrigerator, which would be too damp, for a minimum of 3 days before serving. The foil-wrapped torte or leftovers will keep for 2 weeks.

TRÄUBELESTORTE
Redcurrant Meringue Torte

MAKES 1 (9-INCH/23CM) TORTE

In Swabia, in southwestern Germany, redcurrants are called *Träubele* (Swabian dialect for "little grapes"). That's why this torte, a cakey crust pressed into a springform pan and filled with an almond meringue studded with fresh redcurrants, is called *Träubelestorte*. Elsewhere in Germany, it's also known as *Johannisbeer-Baiser-Kuchen*, which is what I asked for and received as the cake on my fifth birthday. I can still remember it well! But no matter what it's called, the most salient detail of this torte is that it requires redcurrants. No other fruit will do, I'm afraid.

Here in Germany, currant canes are practically weeds. When currants are in season, the markets burst with little baskets of them. Far more sour than most of the berries people are used to eating in the United States, redcurrants are used by Germans (and other northern Europeans) to make gorgeous ruby-hued jelly or a fruit pudding made with sour cherries and raspberries called *Rote Grütze* (red grits), as well being paired with meringues and sweet cake batters to offset their natural astringency.

If you can find redcurrants where you live, or if you have them growing in your garden, you lucky dog, this torte is practically the best thing you can make with them. In the heat of the oven, the nutty meringue browns and puffs up, while the currants swell and then slacken. Later, when the meringue has subsided and the cake has cooled, and you've cut slices of it and placed them on plates, the pink-and-white meringue interior is so pretty against the golden brown of the crust. The top of the meringue crackles a bit, but the inside is cloudlike and light, each bite a fine balance between the sugary whipped meringue and the puckery currants. The balance of sweetness and sourness is delightful and quite typical of German baking. And though it looks substantial, *Träubelestorte* is actually relatively light.

CRUST

2 cups, scooped and leveled/250g all-purpose flour

1 teaspoon baking powder

½ cup/100g granulated sugar

Pinch of salt

1 egg

9 tablespoons plus 1 teaspoon/130g unsalted high-fat, European-style butter, softened, cut into small chunks

FILLING

4 egg whites

1¼ cups/250g granulated sugar, or 1 cup/200g for a more pronounced currant flavor

1 cup/100g ground almonds

1 pound 2 ounces/500g fresh redcurrants, washed and stemmed

1 To make the crust: Mix together the flour and baking powder in a bowl and make a well in the middle. Pour in the sugar and the salt. Crack the egg into the well and, using a fork, mix the egg gently into the flour and sugar in the center of the bowl. Then add the chunks of butter and mix briefly by hand before turning out the mixture onto a lightly floured work surface and kneading together until well combined and uniform. Wrap the dough tightly in plastic wrap and refrigerate for at least 1 hour and up to 24 hours.

2 When ready to bake, heat the oven to 400°F/200°C. Remove the dough from the refrigerator and roll or pat it out to fit a 9-inch/23cm springform pan. Transfer the dough to the pan and push the dough up the sides of the pan to form a 1-inch-/2.5cm-high edge.

3 To make the filling: Place the egg whites in the clean bowl of a stand mixer fitted with the whisk attachment and begin beating at low speed. When small bubbles form, speed up the mixer and whip the egg whites until tripled in volume. Then add the sugar in a thin stream and beat to combine. Fold in the ground almonds until well combined and then gently fold in the redcurrants. Pour the egg white mixture into the crust and smooth the top. Put the pan in the bottom third of the oven and bake for 45 to 55 minutes, or until the egg whites are browned and dry to the touch.

4 Remove the pan from the oven and cool on a rack for 15 minutes before removing the springform ring. Cool completely before serving. Keeps for 1 to 2 days in an airtight container at room temperature.

PFLAUMENSTRUDEL
Plum Strudel

MAKES 1 (23-INCH-/58CM-LONG) STRUDEL

Strudel, like many other delicious recipes in the German baking canon, actually comes from Austria and is one of those recipes that most people think of with awe, reverence, and trepidation—at least I always did. I grew up thinking *Strudel* was like Mount Everest, to be attempted only by the professionals or the Viennese. My parents, who are good cooks but not bakers, instilled this in me by speaking of their friend Christine's *Strudel* (she's Viennese) or our friend Joanie's *Strudel* in hushed, reverent tones. These *Strudel* were legendary. Complicated. Difficult. And these *Strudel* were certainly not to be attempted by the clumsy likes of us.

But when I actually tried my hand at *Strudel* making, I discovered that *Strudel*, like so many mythological baking mountains, isn't that difficult after all! In fact, it's so much simpler than you (or my parents) might think. The only thing it requires is a little bit of self-confidence when working with the dough—well, that and a lot of guests, because a true Austrian fruit *Strudel*, 2½ pounds/1.1kg of fruit wrapped in a dough made with just a scant 1¼ cups/150g of flour, is quite colossal.

Strudel dough is deceptively simple. There's not much in it: only flour, water, salt, and some oil. But the long kneading makes it very supple and elastic. It's wondrous stuff. Self-confidence comes in handy when you have to stretch the dough out to a large, gossamer rectangle. You may think that this tiny little ball of dough will never stretch that far, but it will. Just go slowly and with patience and confidence, and you'll find that the dough will do just what you ask of it. You'll also need a bit moxie when rolling the *Strudel* up and around its generous filling. You will think the dough will tear or rip, but it won't. Just trust yourself and the dough (and, if needed, have a friend help you) as you follow the instructions in this recipe.

Here Italian prune plums are paired with a mix of ground almonds and toasted, buttered bread crumbs, both of which soak up the fruit juices generated by the baking process so that the *Strudel* doesn't drown or get soggy. This recipe uses *Vanillezucker* (vanilla sugar) instead of vanilla extract in the filling. You may flinch at the amount of butter called for to baste the *Strudel*, but please try to resist. The butter is essential for getting the very simple *Strudel* dough to turn crisp and flaky in the heat of the oven. A dollop of *Schlagsahne* (lightly sweetened whipped cream) served alongside is practically mandatory.

DOUGH

1¼ cups, scooped and leveled, minus 1 tablespoon/150g all-purpose flour, plus more for dusting

Pinch of salt

3 tablespoons sunflower oil or other neutral vegetable oil

⅓ cup/80 ml water

PLUM FILLING

10½ tablespoons/150g unsalted butter

¾ cup plus 1 tablespoon/100g unseasoned dried bread crumbs

2 tablespoons *Vanillezucker* (page 267)

Pinch of salt

2¼ pounds/1kg Italian prune plums

¼ cup/50g granulated sugar

½ teaspoon ground cinnamon

1½ cups/150g ground almonds

Confectioners' sugar, for dusting

Schlagsahne (page 267), for serving

1 To make the dough: Combine the flour and salt in a small bowl. Pour the oil into the flour mixture, and then slowly add the water, using your index finger to stir. The mixture will be very wet. Continue to stir with your fingers, and as soon as the dough has come together, dump it out onto a work surface (you may lightly flour it if needed, but once you get started with kneading, you won't need to add more) and start kneading the dough. Knead for 10 minutes (set a timer; the time will pass faster than you think). At the end of the kneading, the dough should be soft, supple, and silky to the touch. Form it into a ball and place it on the work surface. Invert the bowl over the dough and let it rest for 30 minutes.

2 While the dough is resting, prepare the plum filling: Melt 5 tablespoons plus 1½ teaspoons/75g of the butter in a large skillet over medium heat. Add the bread crumbs, *Vanillezucker*, and salt. Combine gently and continue to heat, stirring constantly, until the bread crumbs are toasted, golden brown, and very fragrant, about 8 minutes. Don't let the bread crumbs burn. Set aside.

3 In another pan, melt the remaining 5 tablespoons plus 1½ teaspoons/75g butter and set aside. Pit and quarter the plums. Toss them with the granulated sugar and cinnamon. Set aside.

4 Heat the oven to 400°F/200°C. Line a baking sheet with a piece of parchment paper.

5 On your work surface, spread out a clean cotton or linen kitchen towel that measures at least 24 by 32 inches/60 by 80cm. The long side of the towel should be horizontal and the short side vertical; this is how you want the *Strudel* dough to be later when you fill it. Sprinkle flour lightly over the towel.

Place the dough in the middle of the towel and roll it out several times in both directions with a tapered rolling pin until it's about 10 by 13 inches/25 by 33cm. Then ball your hands into loose fists, put them under the rolled-out dough, and gently start stretching out the dough using the backs of your hands. Alternate with pulling on the dough gently with your fingers to continue stretching the dough. This takes patience and some confidence; you don't want to the dough to rip, but you do need to stretch out the dough with some assertiveness. If it does rip, press the dough together again around the rip. Continue stretching out the dough evenly until it measures 16 by 24 inches/40 by 60cm and is thin enough that you can see the pattern of the towel through it. Make sure you pull the edges of the dough as thin as you can, too. The dough should be uniformly thin all over.

6 Brush the dough all over with some of the melted butter. Starting at the bottom of the dough and leaving a 1¼-inch/3cm border at the bottom and sides, distribute the toasted bread crumbs lengthwise over one-quarter of the dough. Mix the almonds with the plums and pile the mixture evenly over the bread crumbs.

7 Gently pull the left and right edges of the dough over the sides of the filling, stretching slightly if necessary, and then pull the bottom edge of the dough up and over the filling as far as it will go without tearing. Working carefully, use the towel to roll up the *Strudel* tightly all the way. When the *Strudel* is completely rolled up, gently pull the top end of the dough over the *Strudel*, thinning out the dough as you go, and press it gently against the

continued

Strudel. Using the towel as a sling, gently roll the *Strudel* onto the baking sheet. You may need a second set of hands for this. You will have to gently shape the *Strudel* into a crescent so that it fits on the baking sheet. If the *Strudel* is very lumpy or larger at one end than the other, use your hands gently but firmly to form the *Strudel* into a uniform shape—it should be more or less the same thickness all the way along its length. Brush the *Strudel* liberally and thoroughly with more of the melted butter.

8 Bake the *Strudel* for 20 minutes; remove from the oven and brush liberally with more of the melted butter. Bake for another 15 minutes; remove and brush with the remaining butter. Bake for an additional 5 minutes. The *Strudel* should be flaky and browned. Remove from the oven and let cool for at least 30 minutes before serving.

9 Dust with confectioners' sugar and slice into 2-inch/5cm pieces to serve, with *Schlagsahne* alongside. *Strudel* is best the day it is made, but it will keep for 1 to 2 days at room temperature. Before serving, crisp up any leftover *Strudel* in a 350°F/180°C oven for a few minutes.

APFELSTRUDEL
Apple Strudel

MAKES 1 (14-INCH-/35CM-LONG) STRUDEL

A real Viennese apple *Strudel* is a thing of wonder: 2 pounds of fruit wrapped up in dough so thin that you're supposed to be able to read a newspaper through it after rolling and pulling it out. The *Strudel* is painted with butter repeatedly as it bakes, causing the thin layers of dough to crisp and flake right before your eyes. It's one of those kitchen miracles that never, ever fails to enchant me.

Classic apple *Strudel* always includes a small handful of rum-soaked raisins; buttery, toasted bread crumbs to soak up the baking apple juices and give the *Strudel* body; and thinly sliced apples that are only faintly spiced with cinnamon, more for a warm, rounded flavor than anything else. You could add chopped walnuts or slivered almonds if you really wanted to, but I like the purity of a nut-free filling. *Apfelstrudel* is best served slightly warm from the oven, and a dollop of *Schlagsahne* (lightly sweetened whipped cream) or scoop of good vanilla ice cream alongside is almost de rigueur. When preparing the bread crumbs, it's essential to use *Vanillezucker* (vanilla sugar) instead of vanilla extract.

If you think you see a certain similarity between traditional *Strudel* dough and phyllo or *yufka* pastry, you are on to something: those thin, flaky layers made their way from the Arab world to central Europe sometime during the Ottoman Empire. And although the stretching of the dough requires some practice, it is much easier than you might think. Once you master making *Strudel* dough and stretching it, you can fill it with countless different things—like plums (page 138) or apricots or cherries, sautéed chanterelles mixed with crushed potatoes, a savory mix of cabbage and bacon (page 163), or sweetened *Quark* (page 145).

RAISINS

½ cup/75g raisins

2 tablespoons dark rum

DOUGH

1¼ cups, scooped and leveled, minus 1 tablespoon/150g all-purpose flour, plus more for dusting

Pinch of salt

3 tablespoons sunflower oil or other neutral vegetable oil

⅓ cup/80ml water

APPLE FILLING

2¼ pounds/1kg apples (about 6 or 7 medium)

Juice of 1 lemon

¼ cup plus 2 tablespoons/75g granulated sugar

½ teaspoon ground cinnamon

8 tablespoons/115g unsalted butter

½ cup/60g unseasoned dried bread crumbs

1 tablespoon *Vanillezucker* (page 267)

⅛ teaspoon salt

Confectioners' sugar, for dusting

Schlagsahne (page 267) or vanilla ice cream, for serving

continued

1 To prepare the raisins: The day before you plan to bake, place the raisins and rum in a small nonreactive bowl and cover. Set aside for 24 hours.

2 To make the dough: The day of baking, make the dough. Combine the flour and salt in a small bowl. Pour the oil into the flour mixture, and then slowly add the water, using your index finger to stir. The mixture will be very wet. Continue to stir with your fingers, and as soon as the dough has come together, dump it out onto a work surface (you may lightly flour it if needed, but once you get started with kneading, you won't need to add more) and start kneading the dough. Knead for 10 minutes (set a timer; the time will pass faster than you think). At the end of the kneading, the dough should be soft, supple, and silky to the touch. Form it into a ball and place it on the work surface. Invert the bowl over the dough and let it rest for 30 minutes.

3 While the dough is resting, prepare the apple filling: Peel, quarter, and core the apples. Slice the quarters thinly, and then cut the slices in half crosswise. Place in a large bowl and toss with the lemon juice, sugar, and cinnamon. Add the plumped raisins and any rum left in the bowl.

4 Melt 3 tablespoons/40g of the butter in a small pan over medium-high heat; add the bread crumbs, *Vanillezucker*, and salt. Stir to coat and then cook the bread crumbs, stirring constantly, until they are golden brown and very fragrant, 5 to 8 minutes. Don't let the bread crumbs burn. Set aside.

5 Heat the oven to 400°F/200°C. Line a baking sheet with a piece of parchment paper.

6 Melt the remaining 5 tablespoons/115g of butter in a small pan and set aside.

7 On your work surface, spread out a clean cotton or linen kitchen towel that measures at least 24 by 32/60 by 80cm. The long side of the towel should be horizontal and the short side vertical; this is how you want the dough to be positioned later when you fill it. Sprinkle flour lightly over the towel. Place the dough in the middle of the towel and roll it out several times in both directions with a tapered rolling pin until it's about 10 by 13 inches/25 by 33cm. Then ball your hands to loose fists, put them under the rolled-out dough, and gently start stretching out the dough using the back of your hands. Alternate with pulling on the dough gently with your fingers to continue stretching the dough. This takes patience and some confidence; you don't want the dough to rip, but you do need to stretch out the dough with some assertiveness. If it does rip, press the dough together again around the rip. Continue stretching out the dough evenly until it measures 16 by 24 inches/40 by 60cm and is thin enough that you can see the pattern of the towel through it. Make sure you pull the edges of the dough as thin as you can, too. The dough should be uniformly thin all over.

8 Brush the dough evenly all over with some of the melted butter. On the right side of the rectangle, distribute the toasted, seasoned bread crumbs from top to bottom over one-quarter of the dough, leaving a 1¼-inch/3cm border at the edges on the top, bottom, and right.

continued

ALLE ÄPFEL VOM
ALTEN LAND! ▬
KG 3,50

9 Drain off any juices that have accumulated at the bottom of the bowl of apples and raisins, and then pile the apple mixture evenly over the bread crumbs. Gently pull the top and bottom edges of the dough over the sides of the filling, stretching slightly if necessary, and then pull the right edge of the dough up and over the filling as far as it will go without tearing. Working carefully, use the towel to roll up the *Strudel* all the way. Using the towel as a sling, gently roll the *Strudel* onto the baking sheet with the bread crumbs on the bottom. If the *Strudel* roll feels sturdy enough, you can instead transfer the roll with your hands. If the *Strudel* is lumpy or larger at one end than the other, use your hands gently but firmly to form the *Strudel* into a uniform shape—it should be the same thickness all the way along its length. Brush the *Strudel* liberally and thoroughly with more of the melted butter.

10 Place the baking sheet in the oven and bake the *Strudel* for 15 minutes; remove from the oven and brush the *Strudel* thoroughly all over with more of the melted butter. Rotate and bake for another 15 minutes; remove again and brush liberally with the remaining butter. Rotate again and bake for an additional 10 to 15 minutes. When ready, the *Strudel* should be crisp to the touch and a deep golden brown.

11 Remove the baking sheet from the oven and put it on a rack to cool for at least 20 minutes before serving. Dust with confectioners' sugar and slice into 2-inch/5cm pieces to serve, with *Schlagsahne* or vanilla ice cream alongside. *Strudel* is best the day it is made, but it keeps for 1 or 2 days at room temperature. Before serving, crisp up leftover *Strudel* in a 350°F/180°C oven for a few minutes.

TOPFENSTRUDEL
Quark Strudel

MAKES 1 (16-INCH-/40CM-LONG) STRUDEL

On a family trip to Salzburg to see dear friends a few years ago, I ordered a slice of *Topfenstrudel* (*Topfen* is the Austrian word for *Quark*) at a *Kindercafé*. Not a romantic *Kaffeehaus* with newspapers hanging on polished wooden hangers and quiet, elegant waiters ferrying cups of coffee with whipped cream across gleaming parquet floors. No, a loud, slightly grubby, child-friendly café replete with toys, dirty tables, and harried-looking parents. Halfway through the trip, I'd already seen more varieties of *Strudel* than I had ever known existed. (Apricot! Poppy seed! Sour cherry!) But a *Strudel* made with *Quark* really blew my mind. The crisp, flaky layers of *Strudel* dough paired with the creamy, grainy filling was the culinary highlight of my week. The fact that it had been served to me at a place I associated more with toddler-size *Schnitzel* and high chairs made it even more surprising.

The filling for *Topfenstrudel* is flavored with lemon peel and vanilla, relies on semolina for ballast, and includes raisins. (You can leave them out if you're a raisin loather, but they help give the filling structure and moisture.) The challenge with this *Strudel* is rolling it up, as the filling is quite liquid compared with the fruit fillings. The handy towel that the rolled *Strudel* rests on is enlisted to help coax it onto the baking sheet. (It sounds nerve-wracking, but it's easier than it sounds, especially with a partner in the kitchen to help.) Because the filling is so moist, once I've transferred the *Topfenstrudel* to the baking sheet, I prop an upside-down loaf pan against one of the long sides to keep it from spreading too much as it bakes. Still, *Topfenstrudel* will end up flatter than other *Strudels* and may split a little during baking. Never mind; the obligatory dusting of confectioners' sugar will mask any flaws.

DOUGH

1¼ cups, scooped and leveled, minus 1 tablespoon/ 150g all-purpose flour, plus more for dusting

Pinch of salt

3 tablespoons sunflower oil or other neutral vegetable oil

⅓ cup/80ml water

FILLING

2 cups/500g *Quark* (page 264), drained if necessary (see page 8)

2 eggs

⅓ cup plus 1 tablespoon/80g granulated sugar

3 tablespoons semolina

¼ teaspoon salt

Grated peel of 1 organic lemon

½ teaspoon vanilla extract

½ cup/75g raisins

5 tablespoons plus 1 teaspoon/75g unsalted butter, melted

Confectioners' sugar, for dusting

1 First, make the dough: Combine the flour and salt in a small bowl. Pour the oil into the flour mixture, and then slowly add the water, using your index finger to stir. The mixture will be very wet. Continue to stir with your fingers, and as soon as the dough has come together, dump it out onto a work surface (you may lightly flour it if needed, but once you get started with kneading, you won't need

continued

to add more) and start kneading the dough. Knead for 10 minutes (set a timer; the time will pass faster than you think). At the end of the kneading, the dough should be soft, supple, and silky to the touch. Form it into a ball and place it on the work surface. Invert the bowl over the dough and let it rest for 30 minutes.

2 To make the filling: Place the *Quark*, eggs, granulated sugar, semolina, salt, and grated lemon peel in a bowl. Whisk until smooth and well combined. Then whisk in the vanilla extract and raisins.

3 Preheat the oven to 400°F/200°C. Line a rimmed baking sheet with parchment paper.

4 On your work surface, spread out a clean cotton or linen kitchen towel that measures at least 24 by 32 inches/60 by 80cm. Lay down the towel horizontally—with a long side of the towel parallel to the edge of your countertop. Sprinkle flour lightly over the towel and spread the flour out with your hands to coat the towel all over. Place the dough in the middle of the towel and roll it out several times in both directions with a tapered rolling pin until it measures about 10 by 13 inches/25 by 33cm. Then ball your hands into loose fists, put them under the rolled-out dough, and gently start stretching out the dough using the backs of your hands. Alternate with pulling on the dough gently with your fingers to continue stretching the dough. This takes patience and some confidence; you don't want to the dough to rip, but you do need to stretch out the dough with some assertiveness. If it does rip, press the dough together again around the rip. Continue stretching out the dough evenly until it measures 16 by 24 inches/40 by 60cm and is thin enough that you can see the pattern of the towel through it. Make sure you pull the edges of the dough as thin as you can, too. The dough should be uniformly thin all over.

5 Brush the dough thinly all over with some of the melted butter. Scrape the *Quark* mixture onto one-quarter of the dough, leaving a 2-inch/5cm border on the left side. Gently pull the let side of the dough up and over the filling, cutting off any thick edges with a pair of kitchen scissors. Then pull the top and bottom sides of the dough up and over the filling, also cutting off any thick edges with the scissors. (Discard the dough scraps.) Using the towel as a sling, roll up the *Strudel* completely. Using the towel, transfer the *Strudel* to the baking sheet, making sure the seam is on the bottom of the *Strudel*. Using the parchment paper as a sling, pull the *Strudel* to the edge of the baking sheet so that the long side of the *Strudel* is up against the long side of the baking sheet. Place an upside-down loaf pan on the other side of the *Strudel* (with a bit of the parchment paper in between to keep the *Strudel* from sticking to the pan), so that the *Strudel* is penned in on both sides. Brush the *Strudel* gently and evenly all over with more of the melted butter.

6 Bake the *Strudel* for 15 minutes; remove and brush evenly with more melted butter. Return to the oven, rotating the baking sheet. Baked for another 15 minutes; remove and brush evenly with the rest of the melted butter. Return to the oven for another 10 to 15 minutes. The *Strudel* should be starting to flake and turning a deep golden brown.

7 Remove the *Strudel* from the oven and let the pan cool on a rack for 30 minutes before serving. Dust with confectioners' sugar and serve just slightly warm or at room temperature. The *Strudel* is best the day it is made, but it can be kept for an additional day at room temperature, lightly wrapped in plastic wrap. Crisp up any leftover *Strudel* in a 350°F/180°C oven before serving.

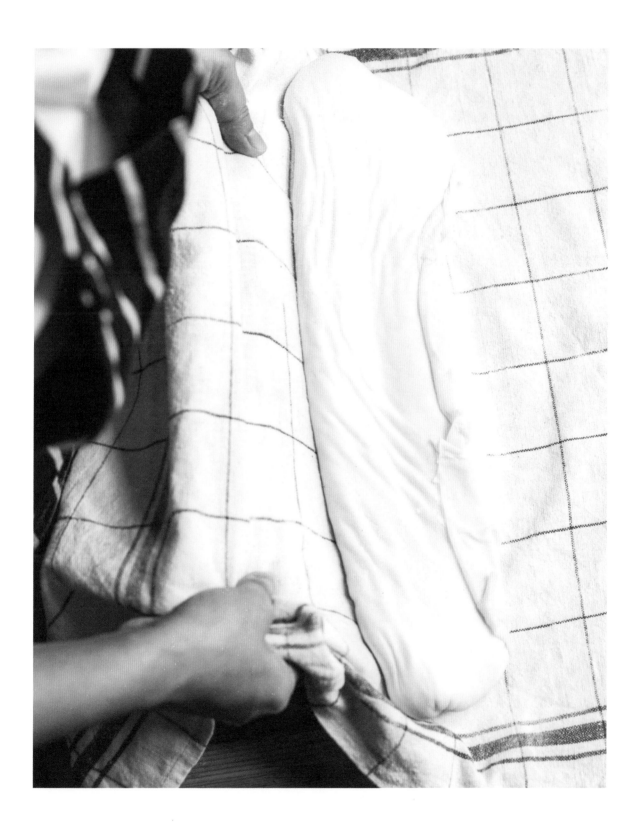

SAVORIES

Germany's savory cakes, breads, and tarts often come from wine-producing regions and are particularly well suited to pairing with wine. Savory *Gugelhupf* from the Baden region (page 168) is made to be eaten as an appetizer with wine, while *Zwiebelkuchen* (page 152), a savory tangle of onions baked atop a soft and chewy base, is traditionally served with *Federweisser*, a young and effervescent white wine that hits the market every fall. In fact, an invitation to someone's home in the fall almost certainly guarantees being served a wedge of homemade *Zwiebelkuchen* and a glass of fizzy *Federweisser*.

Some of our favorite testing days for this book were the days when we tested the recipes in this chapter. On those days, we could break for lunch with our meal fresh from the oven. If there were leftovers, my family ate them for dinner. In fact, all of the recipes in this chapter became instant favorites with my family. Hearty and satisfying, most are best suited for the colder months, like the brawny Hessian

Salzekuchen (page 156) or the flaky-skinned Austrian potato *Strudel* (page 161). But the *Grüner Kuchen* (page 154) is made to usher in the springtime and the cabbage *Strudel* (page 163) is surprisingly delicate.

A warning: This chapter is tough on vegetarians, as bacon, or *Speck*, features in almost every single recipe. It can, of course, be left out, but I find that its smoky, savory, salty flavor and chewy texture are important in many of the recipes. For some of the recipes in

this chapter, you will need a 10-inch/25cm cake pan. It's important to bake the *Zwiebelkuchen* (page 152) and *Peterlingskuchen* (page 151) in this slightly larger than normal pan, so that the ratio of topping to base makes sense. A final thing to note if you need to feed a crowd: Many of the recipes in this chapter can be easily doubled and baked in a 9 by 13-inch/23 by 33cm baking pan.

SÜDDEUTSCHE LAUCHTORTE
Creamy Leek Tart

MAKES 1 (9-INCH/23CM) TART

This southern German tart will remind some of its kissing cousin, quiche Lorraine. And in fact, the Lorraine region, also known as Lothringen in Germany, is just over the border from where this tart originates. Quiche Lorraine is a richer, creamier affair, while sweet and silky sautéed leeks star in this tart. Bacon, diced finely, studs the tangle of leeks, and cornstarch-thickened sour cream brings it all together. I love making this tart in the fall and winter, when the Berlin green markets are cleaned out of much of everything besides tubers, roots, and leeks. We eat it with a green salad to balance out its richness.

CRUST

2 cups, scooped and leveled/250g all-purpose flour

½ teaspoon salt

9 tablespoons plus 1 teaspoon/130g unsalted high-fat, European-style butter, softened, cubed

1 egg

FILLING

3½ tablespoons/50g unsalted butter

3 to 4 leeks, white and pale green parts only, halved and sliced into ¼-inch-/6mm-thick pieces

¼ cup/60ml white wine

1½ teaspoons salt

Freshly ground black pepper

⅛ teaspoon freshly grated nutmeg

2 eggs

1 cup/250g sour cream

1 tablespoon cornstarch

1 cup/125g diced *Speck* or bacon

4½ ounces/130g grated Emmentaler (Swiss) cheese (about 1½ cups)

1 First, make the crust: Place the flour, salt, butter, and egg in a bowl and knead together until well combined. Form into a disk, wrap in plastic wrap, and refrigerate for 1 hour.

2 Make the filling: Melt the butter in a large skillet over medium-high heat. Add the leeks and sauté for 5 to 7 minutes, until softened. Stir in the wine and cook for about 2 minutes. Season with the salt, plenty of black pepper, and the nutmeg. Remove from the heat. Let cool slightly.

3 Preheat the oven to 350°F/180°C.

4 Unwrap the dough leaving the plastic wrap on the top side of the disk and placing the unwrapped side on a lightly floured surface. Roll out to ¼-inch/6mm thickness. Line the bottom and sides of a 9-inch/23cm fluted tart pan with a removable bottom with the dough. Prick the dough all over with a fork. Place a piece of aluminum foil over the dough, pushing it gently out to the edges, and fill the pan with pie weights or dried beans. Bake for 15 minutes. Remove from the oven and, using the foil as a sling, remove the pie weights or beans. Maintain the oven temperature.

5 In a large bowl, whisk together the eggs, sour cream, and cornstarch. Fold in the cooked leeks, and then stir in the *Speck* and cheese. Pour the filling into the crust and smooth the top. Bake for 40 minutes, or until golden brown.

6 Remove from the oven and let cool on a rack for 30 minutes before removing the tart ring. Serve warm or at room temperature, cut into wedges. Refrigerated, the tart will keep for 1 day. It can be reheated in a 325°F/165°C oven.

PETERLINGSKUCHEN
Swabian Parsley Cake

MAKES 1 (10-INCH/25CM) CAKE

In Swabian dialect, *Peterling* is the word for parsley (*Petersilie* in High German). In this unusual cake from Swabia, in southwestern Germany, a yeasted dough is topped with chopped parsley and diced bacon, flavored lightly with nutmeg and bound with a bit of cream, sour cream, and egg. It's rare to see parsley used in such a large quantity, but it's quite wonderful; the tangy, sharp flavor of the leaves is only slightly tamed by the cream and the salty bacon.

This savory cake, which has its roots near Heilbronn in Baden-Württemberg, is served at wine festivals in early autumn to celebrate the new wine of the season.

DOUGH

1²/₃ cups, scooped and leveled, minus 1 tablespoon/200g all-purpose flour, plus more for kneading

1 teaspoon instant yeast

Pinch of granulated sugar

½ cup/120ml water

½ teaspoon salt

2 tablespoons vegetable oil, plus more for the bowl

TOPPING

2 tightly packed cups/80g flat-leaf parsley, stemmed (about 2 bunches)

2½ ounces/70g *Speck* or slab bacon, finely diced

⅓ cup/80ml heavy cream

⅓ cup/80g sour cream

1 egg

Freshly grated nutmeg

Salt

Freshly ground black pepper

1 To make the dough: Place the flour in a large bowl and make a well in the middle. Put the yeast in the well and add the sugar. Slowly pour in the water, stirring gently with a fork. Keep stirring, adding the salt and oil. As soon as the dough is starting to come together, dump it out on a lightly floured work surface and knead vigorously until the dough is smooth and silky, 4 to 5 minutes. Resist adding too much more flour as you knead; you want to the dough to remain as soft as possible. Put the dough in an oiled bowl and cover with a clean dishcloth. Place in a warm, draft-free spot and let rise for 1 hour.

2 Preheat the oven to 400°F/200°C. Line a 10-inch/25cm cake pan with a piece of parchment paper, letting the sides hang over the edge to function as a sling after baking.

3 Place the dough in the prepared pan. Gently push the dough down and out to cover the bottom of the pan and make a very slight rim, taking care not to stretch the dough so much as simply spread it out with your fingertips. The dough should be even and slightly dimpled. Cover with the dishcloth and set aside for an additional 30 minutes.

4 To make the topping: Coarsely chop the parsley and place in a mixing bowl. Add the *Speck*, heavy cream, sour cream, egg, and a few gratings of nutmeg; season with salt and pepper. Whisk to combine well. Scrape the parsley mixture evenly onto the risen dough.

5 Bake for 40 minutes, or until the crust is golden brown and the top is starting to brown. Remove from the oven and let cool on a rack for a few minutes. Using the parchment paper as a sling, remove the cake from the pan and place on a cutting board. Cut into wedges and serve hot or warm. The cake is best eaten the day it is made, but you can keep it for 1 day at room temperature, wrapped in plastic wrap. Warm leftovers in a 350°F/180°C oven before serving.

ZWIEBELKUCHEN
Savory Onion Cake

Every fall, just as the summer's last plums are fading from the markets and a definite chill has set in, the season for *Zwiebelkuchen* and the fresh, young wine known as *Federweisser* begins. From Rhineland vineyards to wine stores in Berlin, handwritten signs go up heralding the arrival of the season's first white wines and their natural partner, the simple, savory *Zwiebelkuchen*.

Zwiebelkuchen, which translates literally to "onion cake," is a yeasted bread topped with sautéed onions, *Speck*, caraway, and beaten eggs that is baked until golden brown and blistery. Wedges of it are traditionally served with those young white wines so fresh that they are still fermenting in the bottle, sending little white bubbles up to the surface constantly. Those wines—slightly sweet, very yeasty, and fizzy—pair beautifully with the soft white crumb of the *Zwiebelkuchen*.

Some variations on the *Zwiebelkuchen* yield a more quiche-like tart, with a short crust and a creamy filling. But I like this bready, rustic, dairy-free version better, and not only because it can be eaten out of hand. The sweet-savory flavor and silky-chewy texture of the onions take center stage.

I would serve this with a green salad as a light meal for a small group of people, or you can cut it into much smaller wedges and serve as a hearty appetizer.

DOUGH

1²⁄₃ cups, scooped and leveled, minus 1 tablespoon/ 200g all-purpose flour, plus more for kneading

1 teaspoon instant yeast

Pinch of granulated sugar

½ cup/120ml water

1 teaspoon salt

2 tablespoons/30ml vegetable oil, plus more for the bowl

TOPPING

1 pound 2 ounces/500g yellow onions (about 5 medium)

4 tablespoons/70ml vegetable oil

2¼ ounces/65g *Speck* or slab bacon, diced

½ to 1 teaspoon caraway seeds

Freshly ground black pepper

2 eggs

1 To make the dough: Place the flour in a large bowl and make a well in the middle. Put the yeast in the well and add the sugar. Slowly pour in the water, stirring gently with a fork. Keep stirring, adding the salt and 2 tablespoons/30ml of the oil. As soon as you have a shaggy dough, dump it out on a lightly floured work surface and knead vigorously until the dough is smooth and silky, 4 to 5 minutes. Resist adding too much flour as you knead; you want the dough to remain as soft as possible. Put the dough in an oiled bowl and cover with a clean dishcloth. Place in a warm, draft-free spot and let rise for 1 hour.

2 Line a 10-inch/25cm cake pan with a piece of parchment paper, letting the sides hang over the edge of the pan to function as a sling after baking.

3 After the dough has risen, place it in the pan. Gently push the dough down and out to cover the bottom of the pan and make only a very small rim, about ¼ inch/6mm, taking care not to stretch the dough so much as simply spread it out with your fingertips. The dough should be even and slightly dimpled. Cover with the dishcloth and set aside for an additional 30 minutes.

4   While the dough is resting, heat the oven to 400°F/200°C and prepare the topping: Thinly slice the onions into rings. Heat the oil in a medium skillet and then add the diced *Speck*. Let the *Speck* render for a few minutes, and then add the onion rings, and caraway seeds and season with pepper. Sauté over medium heat until the onions are softened, translucent, and taking on some color, 10 to 15 minutes. Take the pan off the heat and let cool slightly.

5   In a small bowl, beat the eggs and then add them to the onions, mixing well. When the 30-minute resting time is up for the dough, scrape the onion mixture evenly on top of the dough. Place the pan in the oven and bake for 40 minutes, rotating halfway through. You may find that you need to cover the onions with a piece of aluminum foil if they brown too quickly.

6   Remove the pan from the oven and let cool on a rack for a few minutes. Using the edges of the parchment paper as a sling, remove the cake from the pan. Cut into wedges and serve hot or warm. The cake is best eaten the day it is made but can be kept for 1 additional day at room temperature, wrapped in plastic wrap. To reheat, place in a 350°F/180°C oven for 5 minutes to crisp up again.

GRÜNER KUCHEN

Savory Green Onion and Bacon Cake

MAKES 1 (9 BY 13-INCH/23 BY 33CM) CAKE

When I was fourteen, I spent two weeks on a dairy farm where cousins of my friends Joan and Dietrich live near Kassel, in Hessen. A lot of memorable experiences happened on that trip, but the food memories are particularly vivid, in no small part because Dietrich's cousin Ischen is an amazing baker. That week saw my introduction to the boozy, creamy wonder that is *Schwarzwälder Kirschtorte* (page 123), but also to the rustic and simple local favorite *Grüner Kuchen,* a savory, green onion–topped bread she made for lunch one day.

Grüner Kuchen, which translates as "green cake," is a regional specialty from the area around Kassel and is traditionally eaten in the week before Easter, to celebrate Maundy Thursday, which is called *Gründonnerstag* in German (green Thursday). It's not entirely clear where the term *Gründonnerstag* comes from, but one explanation is that it is related to the pre-Christian tradition of eating new green herbs and leaves at the beginning of spring as a way of fortifying the body and soul after the long, cold winter months. Here, those greens are chopped green onions and parsley, stirred into a creamy filling and poured on top of a yeasted bread base. Traditionally, bread crumb–coated cubes of fatback, known as *grüner Speck,* are scattered across the *Kuchen.* The bread crumbs give the bacon a lovely crispness.

Making this in spring, when the wind can still have quite a nip to it, actually makes a lot of sense. *Grüner Kuchen* is rib sticking and richly flavored. But I like *Grüner Kuchen* far too much to make it only once a year, and in fact, when tender baby leeks are in season, I recommend substituting them for the green onions, making sure you use not just the white and pale green parts, but also the lower end of the dark green parts. Also, I prefer making this recipe with cubes of slab bacon rather than fatback.

DOUGH

1⅔ cups, scooped and leveled, minus 1 tablespoon/ 200g all-purpose flour, plus more for kneading

1 teaspoon instant yeast

Pinch of granulated sugar

½ cup/120ml water

½ teaspoon salt

2 tablespoons vegetable oil, plus more for the bowl

FILLING

3½ cups/60g cubed crustless white bread or 2 crustless *Brötchen* (page 172), cubed

1 cup/240ml whole milk

15 to 20 green onions

1 tightly packed cup/40g flat-leaf parsley, stemmed

2 eggs

½ cup/120g sour cream

1 tablespoon vegetable oil

½ teaspoon salt

Freshly ground black pepper

TOPPING

3½ ounces/100g slab bacon, cubed

¼ cup/30g unseasoned dried bread crumbs

1 To make the dough: Place the flour in a large bowl and make a well in the middle. Put the yeast in the well and add the sugar. Slowly pour in the water, stirring gently with a fork. Keep stirring, adding the salt and the oil. As soon as the dough is starting to come together, dump it out on a lightly floured work surface and knead vigorously until the dough is smooth and silky, 4 to 5 minutes. Try to resist adding too much more flour as you knead; you want the dough to remain as soft as possible. Put the dough in an oiled bowl and cover with a clean dishcloth. Place in a warm, draft-free spot and let rise for 1 hour.

2 In the meantime, make the filling: Place the cubed bread in a bowl and add the milk. Stir well and set aside.

3 Wash and trim the green onions. Slice them into ⅛-inch/3mm rounds all the way up to the dark green parts. Place them in a large bowl. Chop the parsley and add to the bowl with the green onions. Whisk in the eggs, sour cream, and vegetable oil. Stir in the salt and season with pepper.

4 When the bread has soaked up all of the milk, scrape it into the bowl with the green onion mixture and stir well to combine.

5 Line a 9 by 13-inch/23 by 33cm metal baking pan with parchment paper, letting the sides hang over the edge to function as a sling after baking.

6 Roll out the risen dough to fit the pan, making only a very small rim. Cover with the dishcloth and set aside for another 20 minutes. Preheat the oven to 400°F/200°C.

7 To make the topping: In a medium bowl, toss the diced bacon with the bread crumbs until well coated.

8 Scrape the filling over the prepared dough. Scatter the bacon and bread crumbs evenly over the filling.

9 Place the pan in the oven and bake for 45 minutes, or until the topping is browned and crisp. Remove the pan from the oven and let cool on a rack for 5 minutes. Using the parchment paper as a sling, remove the cake from the pan and place it on a cutting board. Cut into squares and serve hot or warm. This is best the day it is made but can be kept for 1 additional day at room temperature or refrigerated, wrapped in plastic wrap. Reheat leftovers in a 350°F/180°C oven before serving.

SALZEKUCHEN
Hessian Potato Cake

MAKES 1 (9 BY 13-INCH/23 BY 33CM) CAKE

This brawny potato cake, a specialty from northern Hessen, is a hefty stunner. A thick, imposing filling of mashed potatoes seasoned with bacon, onions, and caraway is baked on top of a very thin rye-and-wheat crust. The filling, bolstered with *Quark*, measures several inches high and holds its shape beautifully when sliced. I make this whenever I have to feed a crowd; it's hearty, delicious, and simple. Traditionally, *Salzekuchen* is served with steaming cups of coffee. Afterward, a caraway *Schnapps* is passed around for digestion.

Traditional recipes call for buying a lump of sourdough rye bread dough at the bakery to use as the base, so I spent quite a bit of time developing the recipe for the base. It's not a sourdough, but the rye flour gives the crust a bit of chew and extra flavor. *Salzekuchen* is best eaten the day it's made, but if kept for an extra day and reheated in the oven, the crust takes on a pleasing crispness.

CRUST

1 cup, scooped and leveled/100g rye flour

1⅔ cups, scooped and leveled, minus 1 tablespoon/200g all-purpose flour, plus more for kneading

1½ teaspoons instant yeast

¾ cup plus 1½ teaspoons/185ml water

1 teaspoon salt

Oil, for the bowl

FILLING

3 pounds/1.4kg russet potatoes

2 small yellow onions

1 cup/250g *Quark* (page 264), drained if necessary (see page 8)

2¾ ounces/80g diced *Speck* or slab bacon

6 tablespoons/90ml vegetable oil

2 eggs

1½ teaspoons caraway seeds

1 tablespoon salt

Freshly ground black pepper

1 To make the crust: Whisk together the rye and all-purpose flours in a large bowl. Make a well in the middle and add the instant yeast. Slowly pour in the water, stirring in the middle of the bowl to start with; add the salt and continue to stir until a shaggy dough results. Dump the dough out onto a lightly floured work surface and knead for 3 to 5 minutes, until the dough is very smooth and no longer sticky. Resist adding too much flour as you knead. The rye flour will make the dough more claylike and less springy than an all-wheat dough. Rinse out the mixing bowl, pour in a few drops of vegetable oil, and place the dough in the bowl, turning it once to coat it thinly with the oil. Cover with a clean kitchen towel and place in a draft-free spot for 1 hour.

2 Heat the oven to 400°F/200°C. Line a 9 by 13-inch/23 by 33cm metal baking pan with parchment paper, letting the sides hang over the edge to function as a sling after baking.

3 Meanwhile, make the filling: Place the potatoes in a large pot and cover with cold water by 1 inch/2.5cm. Bring to a boil over high heat and let simmer for 25 minutes, or until the potatoes are tender when pierced with a knife. While they are boiling, mince the onions.

4 When the potatoes are done, drain them and let them cool slightly, until you can comfortably work with them. Peel the potatoes and then push them through a potato ricer into a very large bowl. Alternatively, mash them with a potato masher until

smooth. Add the onions, *Quark*, *Speck*, oil, eggs, caraway seeds, and salt and pepper; mix until well combined.

5 Place the proofed rye dough in the prepared pan and gently press it out evenly to the edges of the pan. Set it aside for 5 minutes to relax, and then make a small rim by pushing the dough up the edges of the pan ¼ to ½ inch/6 to 12mm.

6 Scrape the potato mixture evenly onto the dough and smooth the top. Bake for 40 minutes, or until the top is golden brown.

7 Take the pan out of the oven and let cool on a rack for 20 minutes. Using the parchment paper as a sling, lift the cake out of the pan (you may need two people for this task) and place on a cutting board. Using a serrated knife, cut into squares or rectangles. Serve hot. This cake is best the day it is made, but it can be kept for an additional day at room temperature and warmed up in a 350°F/180°C oven before serving.

HERZHAFTER KÄSEKUCHEN
Savory Cheesecake

MAKES 1 (9 BY 13-INCH/23 BY 33CM) CAKE

This chapter is tough for vegetarians, I know, but this savory cheesecake is a notable exception: it's made entirely without bacon and, in fact, is all the better for it. The rich, nutty cheese and grated nutmeg are all the flavoring it needs. In Germany, this kind of savory cake would almost always be paired with wine and eaten as a savory snack more than a main meal.

I like to make it for brunch crowds (it's very easily doubled and made in a rimmed baking sheet) instead of the ubiquitous egg dishes, but also for simple dinners, served with a green salad. The cake here calls for Emmentaler and Gruyère cheeses, but you can play around with the kinds of cheese you'd like to use—or even use the cake as an excuse to finish up forgotten ends of cheese floating around in your refrigerator.

The crust is worth mentioning: it's a bready dough made with *Quark* and vegetable oil and approximates a yeasted base without all the fuss and time that yeasted dough requires. It's leavened with baking powder and can be mixed together, rolled out, and immediately baked. In fact, in these modern times *Quark-Öl-Teig*, as the dough is known, is often used as a base for other cakes that would typically have a yeasted base. If you are pressed for time and want to use it as a base for fruit-topped cakes like *Apfelkuchen* (page 86) or *Pflaumenstreuselkuchen* (page 88), or the *Mohnstreuselkuchen* (page 93), simply add 3 tablespoons of sugar to the dough as you knead it together. Once the dough is finished, you just have to roll it out, top it, and bake it.

CRUST

⅓ cup/80g *Quark* (page 264), drained if necessary (see page 8)

3 tablespoons plus 1 teaspoon/50ml whole milk

3 tablespoons plus 1 teaspoon/50ml vegetable oil

½ teaspoon salt

1¼ cup, scooped and leveled, minus 3 tablespoon/150g all-purpose flour, plus more for kneading

1½ teaspoons baking powder

FILLING

1 packed cup/125g grated Emmentaler (Swiss) cheese

1 packed cup/125g grated Gruyère cheese

2 eggs

¾ cup/180ml heavy cream

⅓ cup plus 1 tablespoon/100g sour cream

¼ teaspoon salt

⅛ teaspoon grated nutmeg

Freshly ground black pepper

1 Preheat the oven to 350°F/180°C. Line a 9 by 13-inch/23 by 33cm metal baking pan with parchment paper, letting the sides hang over the edge to function as a sling after baking.

2 To make the crust: First drain the *Quark* by placing it in a fine-mesh sieve and letting any excess liquid drip off for 20 to 30 minutes. Then place the *Quark* in a mixing bowl. Whisk in the milk, oil, and salt until you have a smooth, creamy mixture.

3 In a separate bowl, combine the flour and baking powder. Stir the flour mixture into the *Quark* mixture and scrape out onto a floured work surface. Knead swiftly just until a smooth dough forms.

4 Roll out the dough to fit the prepared pan, forming a ¾-inch-/2cm-high rim. Place in the oven and bake for 10 minutes.

5 While the crust is baking, make the filling: Place both grated cheeses in a large bowl. In a separate bowl, whisk the eggs, cream, and sour cream together. Then add the salt, nutmeg, and pepper. Whisk the egg mixture into the cheeses.

6 As soon as the crust has baked for 10 minutes, take it out of the oven and spread the cheese filling evenly in the hot crust. Return the pan to the oven and bake for 45 minutes, covering the tart with a piece of aluminum foil toward the end of the baking time if the top starts to brown too heavily.

7 Take the cheesecake out of the oven and let cool on a rack in the pan until warm or at room temperature. Using the parchment paper as a sling, take the tart out of the pan and place it on a cutting board. Cut into squares or rectangles and serve. The cheesecake is best the day it is made, but it will keep for a day at room temperature and can be reheated in a 325°F/165°C oven.

KARTOFFELSTRUDEL
Potato Strudel

MAKES 1 (15-INCH-/38CM-LONG) STRUDEL

My husband, Max, is a good sport. He'll eat almost anything I make with gusto. But the look in his eyes when I make something with potatoes—or, more specifically, something with onions, bacon, caraway, and potatoes—trumps everything. Yes, my husband lives up to the German national stereotype to a T.

When I first started making this *Strudel*, filled with a savory, creamy mix of mashed potatoes seasoned with Quark, onions, leeks for color and sweetness, bacon, and mint, Max could not get enough. I think I made three potato *Strudel* in as many weeks. And although the frequency with which I make it has now dropped off somewhat, it's always worth it just to see Max's glee when he comes into the kitchen and hears what's for dinner.

The filling, rich and savory, is good enough to eat on its own; in fact, you could just pile the filling into a buttered dish and bake it in the oven. Presto! You'll have made *Kartoffelauflauf,* which you can serve in big scoops with a nice green salad on the side.

Don't be intimidated by the thought of making your own *Strudel* dough. It's the simplest dough imaginable. Taking it 10 minutes to knead may be the hardest part about the whole thing. That long kneading leads to a wonderfully elastic dough, which makes the subsequent stretching and pulling until it's thin and translucent almost child's play. The lashings of butter on the dough both before and during baking are what help the dough turn flaky and crisp.

A word of warning: Depending on how tightly you roll your *Strudel,* it may burst as it bakes because of the exceptionally sturdy filling. Unlike cabbage or fruit fillings, which shrink in the oven, the potatoes,

egg, and *Quark* expand. Don't worry; the split *Strudel* will still look quite magnificent. I like to call it "appealingly rustic."

DOUGH

1¼ cups, scooped and leveled, minus 1 tablespoon/150g all-purpose flour, plus more for dusting

Pinch of salt

3 tablespoons sunflower oil or other neutral vegetable oil

⅓ cup/80ml cold water, plus more as needed

FILLING

1 pound/455g russet potatoes

½ teaspoon caraway seeds

1 cup/250g *Quark* (page 264), drained if necessary (see page 8)

½ teaspoon salt, or to taste

Freshly ground black pepper

1 to 2 teaspoons minced fresh mint leaves (optional)

2 tablespoons vegetable oil

3½ ounces/100g *Schinkenspeck* or lean bacon, finely diced (⅔ cup)

1 leek, white and pale green parts only, halved and thinly sliced

1 medium yellow onion, diced

1 egg

5 tablespoons/70g unsalted butter, melted

continued

KARTOFFELSTRUDEL, CONTINUED

1 To make the dough: Combine the flour and salt in a small bowl. Pour the oil into the flour mixture, and then slowly stir in the water. The mixture will be very wet. Continue to stir with your fingers, and as soon as the dough has come together, dump it out onto a work surface (you may lightly flour it, but once you start, you won't need to add more) and start kneading. Knead for 10 minutes (set a timer; the time will pass faster than you think). At the end of the kneading, the dough should be soft, supple, and silky. Form it into a ball and place it on the work surface. Invert the bowl over the dough and let it rest for 30 minutes.

2 While the dough rests, prepare the filling: Place the unpeeled potatoes in a pot and add cold water to cover. Cover and place over high heat until boiling. When the water boils, turn down the heat and simmer until the potatoes are tender when pierced, about 20 minutes. Drain the potatoes and, as soon as they are cool enough to handle, peel them. Mash the potatoes or put them through a ricer. Mix in the caraway, *Quark*, and salt until well combined, and season with pepper. Mix in the mint. Set aside.

3 Place the oil in a skillet over medium heat and add the bacon. Sauté for a minute or two, and then add the leek and onion and sauté until glossy and wilted, about 10 minutes. Turn off the heat.

4 Mix the egg into the potatoes and then stir in the bacon mixture until well combined.

5 Preheat the oven to 400°F/200°C. Line a baking sheet with parchment paper.

6 On your work surface, spread out a clean cotton or linen kitchen towel that measures at least 24 by 32 inches/60 by 80cm with one of the ends facing you. Sprinkle flour lightly over the towel. Place the *Strudel* dough in the middle of the towel and roll it out several times in both directions with a tapered rolling pin until it measures about 10 by 13 inches/25 by 33cm. Then ball your hands into loose fists, put them under the rolled-out dough, and gently start stretching the dough using the backs of your hands. Alternate with pulling on the dough gently with your fingers to continue stretching the dough. This takes patience; you don't want to the dough to rip, but you do need to stretch the dough with some assertiveness. If it does rip, press the dough together again. Continue stretching the dough evenly until it measures 16 by 24 inches/40 by 60cm and is thin enough that you can see the towel through it. Make sure you pull the edges of the dough as thin as you can, too. The dough should be uniformly thin.

7 Brush the dough thinly and evenly all over with some of the melted butter. Scrape the potato mixture over one-quarter of the dough along a short side, leaving a 1¼-inch/3cm border at the edges. Gently pull the top and bottom edges of the dough over the filling, stretching slightly if necessary, and then pull the right edge of the dough over the filling. Use the towel to roll up the *Strudel* completely. Pull the end of the dough over, thinning out the dough as you go, and press it gently against the *Strudel*. Using the towel as a sling, gently roll the *Strudel* onto the baking sheet, seam-side down.

8 Brush the *Strudel* all over with the melted butter. Bake for 15 minutes; remove and brush all over with more of the melted butter, and then bake for another 15 minutes. Remove and brush with the remaining melted butter. Bake for a final 15 minutes.

9 Place the pan on a rack for 10 minutes. Then slice the *Strudel* into thick pieces and serve immediately. *Strudel* is best the day it is made, but it will keep at room temperature for an additional day or two and can be crisped up in a 325°F/165°C oven.

KRAUTSTRUDEL
Cabbage Strudel

MAKES 1 (16-INCH-/40CM-LONG) STRUDEL

I have a lot of favorite recipes in this book, but this one has to be up at the top. Imagine a crackling, flaky, buttery crust encasing silky strands of sautéed cabbage, chewy bits of bacon, and the occasional savory crunch of a caraway seed, which in German cuisine is considered cabbage's soul mate. Now that you have that image in front of you, you can understand why a 16-inch-/40cm-long *Strudel* will feed only four to six people—one measly slice per person is most certainly not enough.

You might not think it by looking at the list of ingredients, but *Krautstrudel* is a surprisingly delicate dish. After all, it's mostly made up of tender shreds of cabbage and gorgeous, crackling thin pastry layers. In Austria, a slice of this would be considered a light meal and one that would absolutely be eaten in summer, when the first fresh cabbages appear in the fields.

Strudel dough is a cinch to make, requiring only a very thorough kneading. And stretching it out until it's thin enough is much easier than it seems. In other words, don't be afraid to make *Strudel* at home. It's easy. I promise!

DOUGH

1¼ cups, scooped and leveled, minus 1 tablespoon/150g all-purpose flour, plus more for dusting

Pinch of salt

3 tablespoons sunflower oil or other neutral vegetable oil

⅓ cup/80ml cold water, plus more if needed

FILLING

2 tablespoons olive oil or vegetable oil

5¼ ounces/150g *Speck* or slab bacon, diced

1 large yellow onion, diced

1 small head green cabbage, cored and shredded

¼ teaspoon salt

1 teaspoon caraway seeds

Freshly ground black pepper

3½ tablespoons/50g unsalted butter, melted

1 First, make the *Strudel* dough: Combine the flour and salt in a small bowl. Pour the oil into the flour mixture, and then slowly add the water, using your index finger to stir. The mixture will be very wet. Continue to stir with your fingers, and as soon as the dough has come together, dump it out onto a work surface (you may lightly flour it, if needed, but once you get started with kneading, you won't need to add more) and start kneading the dough. Knead for 10 minutes (set a timer; the time will pass faster than you think). At the end of the kneading, the dough should be soft, supple, and silky to the touch. Form it into a ball and place it on the work surface. Invert the bowl over the dough and let it rest for 30 minutes.

2 While the dough rests, prepare the cabbage filling: Put the oil in a large skillet over medium heat. Add the *Speck* and then the onion. Sauté for several minutes, until the onion is translucent. Add the shredded cabbage and stir well. Cook for 10 minutes, stirring often. Toward the end of the cooking time, stir in the salt and caraway seeds, and season with pepper. Turn off the heat and set aside.

3 Preheat the oven to 400°F/200°C. Line a baking sheet with parchment paper.

4 On your work surface, spread out a clean cotton or linen kitchen towel that measures at least 24 by 32 inches/60 by 80cm. The long dimension of the

continued

towel should be horizontal. Sprinkle flour lightly over the towel. Place the *Strudel* dough in the middle of the towel and roll it out several times in both directions with a tapered rolling pin until it measures about 10 by 13 inches/25 by 33cm. Then ball your hands into loose fists, put them under the rolled-out dough, and gently start stretching out the dough using the backs of your hands. Alternate with pulling on the dough gently with your fingers to continue stretching the dough. This takes patience and some confidence; you don't want to the dough to rip, but you do need to stretch out the dough with some assertiveness. If it does rip, press the dough together again around the rip. Continue stretching out the dough evenly until it measures 16 by 24 inches/40 by 60cm and is thin enough that you can see the pattern of the towel through it. Make sure you pull the edges of the dough as thin as you can, too. The dough should be uniformly thin all over.

5 Brush the dough all over with some of the melted butter. Scrape the cabbage mixture over one-quarter of the dough along the bottom side, leaving a 1¼-inch/3cm border at the edges. Gently fold the sides of the dough over the filling, stretching slightly if necessary, and then pull the bottom edge of the dough over the filling. Working carefully, use the towel to roll the *Strudel* tightly over the remaining dough. When the *Strudel* is all rolled up, pull the end of the dough over, thinning out the dough as you go, and press it gently against the *Strudel*. Using the towel as a sling, gently roll the *Strudel* onto the baking sheet, seam-side down. You may need a second set of hands for this. You may have to shape the *Strudel* into a crescent so that it fits on the baking sheet. Brush the *Strudel* liberally with more of the melted butter.

6 Bake the *Strudel* for 15 minutes; remove from the oven and brush liberally with more of the melted butter. Bake for another 15 minutes; remove and brush with the remaining butter. Bake for an additional 10 minutes. The *Strudel* should be flaky and browned.

7 Remove from the oven and let cool for 5 to 10 minutes before serving. Slice into 2-inch/5cm pieces and serve. *Strudel* is best the day it is made, but it will keep at room temperature for an additional day or two and can be crisped up in a 325°F/165°C oven.

KARTOFFEL-KÄSE DINNEDE
Swabian Potato-Cheese Flat Bread

MAKES 4 FLAT BREADS

It's no wonder that Alsace in France and Swabia in Germany share many of the same culinary traditions—they are just over the border from each other. The Swabian version of Alsatian *Flammekueche* or *tarte flambée* is called *Dinnede* in dialect; it has a slightly thicker crust and is slipper shaped. It is spread thinly with sour cream and then topped with everything from sliced onions and cubed bacon, like *Flammkuchen*, or various other combinations, including paper-thin slices of raw potatoes and cheese.

My favorite version layers thinly sliced onions and potatoes on top of sour cream that's flavored with a whisper of ground nutmeg and judicious grindings of black pepper. Then I sprinkle a few handfuls of savory grated cheese on top for good measure. The high oven heat blisters the shreds of cheese. The base gets crackly-crisp. And the onions, insulated by the potato slices, steam more than brown, retaining their sharp flavor, while the potatoes get soft and fudgy. When these flat breads come fresh from the oven on a crisp winter evening, your family will find it hard not to devour them like a pack of starving hyenas.

The amount given here makes four *Dinnede*, which will serve four to six people quite amply, with a nice green salad to follow. Keeping the thin base layer of sour cream, try these toppings in various combinations with one another: slivered onions, diced bacon, thinly sliced potatoes, grated cheese, and thinly sliced apples, which add a welcome fresh and sweet-tart note to the richer toppings. For a bit of extra color, I like to add a shower of minced chives to the tops of my *Dinnede* right when they come out of the oven.

DOUGH

4 cups, scooped and leveled/500g all-purpose flour, plus more for kneading

2 teaspoons salt

1 teaspoon instant yeast

1½ cups/360ml water

TOPPING

2 large yellow onions

3 to 4 large Yukon gold potatoes

1 cup/250g sour cream

Salt

Freshly ground black pepper

Freshly grated nutmeg

1 packed cup/125g grated Comté or Gruyère cheese

Chives, minced (optional)

1 First, make the dough: Place the flour in a large bowl. Whisk in the salt and yeast. Slowly pour in the water as you stir with your fingers or a wooden spoon. As soon as the dough starts to come together, scrape it out onto a floured work surface and knead until smooth, about 3 minutes, adding a little flour if needed. When the dough is smooth, form into a ball and place back in the bowl. Cover with a clean dishcloth and set in a warm, draft-free spot for 1½ hours, or until doubled.

2 Preheat the oven to 475°F/245°C. Line two baking sheets with parchment paper.

3 Once the dough has proofed, prepare the topping: Slice the onions in half, and then slice very thinly in half-moons. Peel the potatoes and then slice very thinly just before using.

4 Divide the dough into quarters. Leave 3 of the portions in the bowl. On a lightly floured surface, roll out one dough piece to an 8 by 13-inch/20 by 33cm oval. Transfer the dough to one of the prepared baking sheets. Using your fingertips, dimple the dough about ½ inch/12mm around, creating a small

raised edge. Spread one-quarter of the sour cream evenly over the dough, except for the edge. Sprinkle a pinch or two of salt and freshly ground pepper over the sour cream, and then sprinkle with a few gratings of nutmeg. Distribute one-quarter of the sliced onions evenly over the sour cream. Follow by distributing one-quarter of the sliced potatoes over the onions. Sprinkle one-quarter of the cheese evenly over the potatoes. Set the topped dough aside for 10 minutes. Repeat with the second baking sheet and another one-quarter of the ingredients.

5 Slide the first baking sheet into the oven and bake for 15 minutes, or until the crust is golden brown and the cheese is bubbling. Remove the pan from the oven and immediately slide the parchment paper and flat bread onto a cutting board. Sprinkle one-quarter of the chives over. Cut and serve immediately. Place the second baking sheet in the oven and bake as before.

6 Repeat with the remaining dough and toppings. (Alternatively, roll out all the pieces of dough and top them at the same time. Bake as many as can fit in your oven on a single rack.) The flat breads do not keep.

SPECK-WALNUSS GUGELHUPF
Bacon-Walnut Gugelhupf

MAKES 1 (9-INCH/23CM) CAKE

Unlike the traditional sweet, yeasted *Gugelhupf* (page 95), which both the Austrians and the Alsatians lay claim to, the origins of this savory *Gugelhupf*—which is made with a mix of rye and wheat flour—are much clearer. Baden, a strip of land in southwestern Germany that borders France and is considered the source of some of Germany's best food, is the home of this savory cake.

The dough is flavored liberally with ground caraway. Tiny cubes of sautéed bacon and onions and creamy chunks of chopped walnuts are distributed throughout. Instead of butter and milk moistening the dough, it's made with a hefty portion of sour cream, which gives the freshly baked *Gugelhupf* a finely sandy crust. I urge you to make one for your next dinner party—cut wedges of it warm from the oven and pass them around with flutes of Champagne or glasses of white wine for an absolutely killer hors d'oeuvre. If you don't have a *Gugelhupf* pan, you can make this in a Bundt pan. Just remember to start checking the cake about 15 minutes before the baking time is up.

Savory *Gugelhupf* is best when freshly made and still warm, but it can be kept for a day and reheated in a hot oven. Or you can follow my assistant Maja's brilliant suggestion: make savory French toast for dinner (or breakfast!). Just soak slices of the leftover *Gugelhupf* in beaten egg and milk and fry them in a pan until golden. A fresh green salad alongside hits the spot.

I like using fresh yeast here, for the extra flavor and moisture it brings to the loaf, but instant yeast can be substituted.

2¾ cups, scooped and leveled, plus 1 tablespoon/ 350g all-purpose flour, plus more for the pan

1½ cups, scooped and leveled/150g rye flour

¾ ounce/20g fresh yeast, or 1 teaspoons instant yeast

Pinch of sugar

½ cup/120ml water, lukewarm

5¼ ounces/150g *Speck* or slab bacon, finely diced (about 1 cup)

1 medium yellow onion, finely diced

1 egg

¾ cup plus 1 tablespoon/200g sour cream

1 teaspoon ground caraway seeds

¾ teaspoon salt

Freshly ground black pepper

1 cup/100g walnuts, coarsely chopped

Unsalted butter, for the pan

1 If using fresh yeast, whisk both flours together in a large bowl and make a well in the middle. Crumble the yeast into the middle of the well. Add the pinch of sugar. Pour ¼ cup/60ml of the water very slowly into the well, stirring gently with a fork to dissolve the yeast and incorporate some of the flour. Cover the bowl with a clean dishcloth and set aside for 15 minutes. (If using instant yeast, stir together with the flour, set aside, and proceed with Step 2.)

2 While the yeast is proofing, place a sauté pan over medium-high heat and cook the diced *Speck* in the pan for 5 to 8 minutes. Scrape the *Speck* out of the pan and onto a plate. Place the diced onion in the pan and sauté until glassy and golden from the residual bacon fat, 5 to 8 minutes. Set aside.

3 In a medium bowl, whisk together the egg, sour cream, caraway seeds, salt, and the remaining ¼ cup/60ml water, and then season with pepper. (If using instant yeast, add all of the water and the sugar.) Then whisk in the *Speck*, onion, and walnuts.

4 Remove the dishcloth from the bowl of flour and slowly pour the sour cream mixture into the bowl, stirring as you go. Knead the dough in the bowl by hand. It will be quite messy and sticky at first but will come together as the rye flour hydrates and you continue to mix. Make sure you get all the flour at the bottom of the bowl incorporated into the dough. When the dough is well combined and no longer sticky, form it into a rough ball and leave it in the bowl. Cover with the dishcloth and place in a warm, draft-free spot for 1 hour.

5 Liberally butter a 9-inch/23cm *Gugelhupf* pan, and then flour it lightly.

6 When the dough has finished proofing, gently pull it out of the bowl and knead it once or twice. Form it into a 16-inch/40cm cylinder and place this in the prepared pan so that it lies evenly. Press the ends together. Cover the pan with the dishcloth and set aside in a warm, draft-free spot for 30 minutes. Preheat the oven to 350°F/180°C.

7 After 30 minutes, remove the dishcloth and place the pan in the oven. Bake for 55 to 60 minutes, or until the loaf is golden brown and sounds hollow when tapped. Remove from the oven and let cool on a rack for 10 to 15 minutes before turning upside down and removing the pan. Let the *Gugelhupf* cool for 30 minutes before cutting into it. The *Gugelhupf* is best the day it is made, but it will keep for 1 to 2 days, wrapped in aluminum foil, and can be crisped up in a 350°F/180°C oven.

BREADS AND ROLLS

People associate a lot of things with Germany: beer, for one, and *Oktoberfest*, sausages and soft pretzels, cars and no-speed-limit highways, villainy and unequaled repentance, Christmas markets and soccer, and, of course, bread. Like Italy's pasta or France's wine, German bread is a touchstone and a vast subject. By some estimates, Germany boasts more than three hundred different kinds of bread. Three hundred! It is hard to fathom.

From dark, sour, grainy rye loaves studded with sunflower seeds or flaxseeds to intricately braided celebration breads, it seems that every single tiny corner of Germany has its own bread tradition. For all of Germany, bread is an essential part of everyday life. From the millions of *Brötchen* (white rolls), split and spread with butter and lined with a slice of ham for breakfast each morning, and the *Pausenbrot* (two slices of grainy dark bread spread with butter and a slice of cheese or ham) that every child takes to school for snack time, to the national weeknight dinner of *Abendbrot*—literally, "evening bread"—where slices of bread are set out on the table along with soft butter, cold cuts, slices of cucumber, and halved tomatoes to round out the meal, bread makes up an enormous part of the quotidian diet.

While Germans' annual consumption of bread (117 pounds/53kg per person) is dwarfed by that of, say, Turkey (more than 220 pounds/100kg per person), the variety of breads available here is unparalleled. And bread is *the* food that Germans identify most strongly with. My father likes to tell the story of family friends from Lübeck who spent a year in California on a sabbatical. At the end of the year, before flying back to Germany, they came to Boston for a few days to stay with my father and my stepmother. At dinner one evening, the boys bit into pieces of the good sourdough bread my father had sliced for dinner. Immediately, they looked at each other and in hushed wonder exclaimed, "*Echtes Brot!*" (Real bread!).

For home bakers, making these heavy, fragrant, sour breads at home is not that feasible. In fact, Sam Fromartz of the *Washington Post* and author of *In Search of the Perfect Loaf* told me that German bakers consider their breads too complicated and difficult for a layperson to make at home, unless you are a singularly devoted bread baker with access to bakery-grade sourdough starters and all the different grinds of grains, such as rye and spelt, that are required.

But I was pleased to discover, in the course of writing this book, that there are some German rolls and breads that can easily be made at home. I've collected a selection of different kinds here: all-purpose rolls that are great for breakfast or dinner, rich and savory rolls that are best eaten with a soup or salad as part of a hearty meal, sweet rolls for breakfast, and a few braided celebration breads. I've also included two recipes for sweet rolls that are considered afternoon snack material. In other words, they are too rich and sweet for breakfast, but are excellent with a cup of coffee or tea as a pick-me-up or after-school treat in the afternoon.

A note on yeast: As already mentioned in the pantry information (see page 6), you will notice that the recipes in this chapter call for either fresh (cake) yeast or instant yeast, also known as bread-machine yeast. Fresh yeast can be hard to find in the United States, but if you are lucky enough to have a retailer in your area who sells it, then by all means use it—it produces breads, rolls, and cakes that are particularly lofty, with great flavor. Fresh yeast must be dissolved, usually in lukewarm milk or water, before being used. However, instant yeast, which is added directly to the dry ingredients, is a great substitute. The rule of thumb is that 1 teaspoon of instant yeast is roughly equivalent to 20g or ¾ ounce of fresh yeast. I don't recommend using active dry yeast, which can be unreliable.

BRÖTCHEN
Classic Breakfast Rolls

MAKES 8 ROLLS

Plain white *Brötchen*—also known as *Semmeln*, *Weck*, or *Schrippen*, depending on which region of Germany you are in—are a German bakery classic. With thin, crisp crusts and a cottony white interior, *Brötchen* are a must on every weekend breakfast table, where they often share the spotlight with grainier whole wheat rolls. On Sunday mornings, you'll often see people hurrying home for breakfast carrying a big bag of bakery rolls bought fresh that morning.

Sadly, fewer and fewer bakeries actually make their own *Brötchen* these days, preferring to buy frozen, industrially produced rolls from Poland as a cost-saving measure. This is, in my opinion, a culinary tragedy for Germany with repercussions for the culture at large. I am fortunate to have a traditional, family-run bakery just around the corner that still makes all its own breads, rolls, and cakes. My family likes to eat the darker, seeded rolls first with savory toppings like cheese and ham, saving the white *Brötchen* for "dessert" at the end of breakfast, to be spread with jam or honey.

Inspired by Lutz Geissler, a geologist turned food blogger whose passion project is mastering homemade bread (his blog *Plötzblog*—in German—can be found at ploetzblog.de and is a treasure trove for bread-baking enthusiasts), I discovered that making bakery-quality *Brötchen* at home, both crackle-crusted and deliciously fluffy, is actually quite simple, as long as you have a little time to invest. You make a simple yeast dough—I adapted Geissler's recipe for *Brötchen* (he found the recipe in an old German cookbook published in the 1930s) but reduced the yeast by one-third—and then form rolls, which you refrigerate overnight. Geissler's recipe has you bake the rolls after proofing them twice at room temperature, but I prefer the refrigeration method, which not only allows the rolls to develop flavor without overproofing, but also means I can have freshly baked rolls for breakfast.

The next day, when it's time to bake the rolls, I slide a pan of ice cubes onto the oven floor just as I put the rolls in to bake. The humidity created by the melting ice helps the rolls develop their signature crackly surface.

I use fresh yeast in this recipe because I find it gives the rolls a particularly good flavor and a wonderful rise. But if you cannot find fresh yeast where you live, you can substitute instant yeast.

½ cup plus 2 tablespoons/150ml whole milk

½ cup plus 2 tablespoons/150ml warm tap water

⅓ ounce/10g fresh yeast, or ½ teaspoon instant yeast

4 cups, scooped and leveled/500 g all-purpose flour, plus more for kneading

1¼ teaspoons salt

2 handfuls of ice cubes, for baking

1 Line a baking sheet with parchment paper.

2 Set aside 1 tablespoon of the milk, storing it in the refrigerator, and mix the remaining ½ cup plus 1 tablespoon/135ml of milk with the water. If using fresh yeast, crumble the yeast into a large mixing bowl and stir in the milk mixture. Continue to stir until the yeast has fully dissolved. Add the flour and salt to the bowl and stir until a shaggy ball comes together. (If using instant yeast, just mix the milk, water, yeast, flour, and salt together at once, and stir until a shaggy ball comes together.) Dump out onto a floured work surface and knead until the dough is very smooth and no longer sticky. The dough will be quite firm.

3 Place the ball back in the bowl, cover with a clean kitchen towel, and let rise for 1 hour in a warm, draft-free spot. Gently punch down the dough, and then divide into 8 equal pieces (if you

have a scale, you can weigh them out). Roll into ovals that are approximately 3½ inches/9 cm long and 2 inches/5cm wide. Place on the prepared baking sheet, leaving 3 inches/8cm between the rolls. Cover the baking sheet with plastic wrap and refrigerate overnight.

4 The next morning, remove the baking sheet from the refrigerator. Place a metal cake or roasting pan on the bottom of the oven and preheat the oven to 450°F/230°C.

5 When the rolls have sat at room temperature for 20 minutes, brush them evenly with the reserved 1 tablespoon of milk and slash them lengthwise with a sharp knife (the cut should be about ¾ inch/2 cm deep). Then, working quickly, dump the ice cubes into the pan at the bottom of the oven and immediately slide the baking sheet of rolls into the oven.

6 Bake for 20 to 25 minutes, or until the rolls are crusty and golden and sound hollow when tapped. Remove from the oven and let cool on a rack before serving. The rolls are best eaten the day they are made but can be crisped up in a 350°F/180°C oven a day after baking. The rolls also freeze well. To freeze them, the freshly baked rolls must be completely cooled. Place them in a plastic freezer bag and freeze for up to 1 month. To defrost and serve warm, place the frozen rolls on a baking sheet in a 350°F/180°C oven for 5 to 8 minutes.

MOHNHÖRNCHEN
Poppy-Seed Crescent Rolls

MAKES 10 ROLLS

When my husband goes to the bakery on weekend mornings for a bag of assorted *Brötchen* for our breakfast, he always has the baker slip in a couple of these fluffy and tender poppy-seed crescent rolls to eat for "dessert," spread with jam, honey, or Nutella, after the heavier seeded rolls have been eaten with slices of ham or cheese. Since they are made with white flour, *Mohnhörnchen* are considered by some to be less wholesome than their darker brethren, but I suspect that they are no less beloved.

Meike Peters, the blogger at *Eat in My Kitchen* (eatinmykitchen.meikepeters.com) is originally from the Cologne area and has fond memories of finding *Mohnhörnchen* and other enriched white breads at traditional bakeries in the area. The rolls were barely sweet and fluffy but not too airy. Sadly, these traditional bakeries are becoming more and more difficult to find, so Meike set about developing this recipe herself so that she could have fantastic *Mohnhörnchen* whenever the mood struck her.

Meike's recipe is simple, but it really delivers: These *Mohnhörnchen* are by far the best I've ever had. They are puffy and tender, but still substantial enough to require happy chewing. When you break one open, the crumb is gorgeously twisted from the rolling. I love that the rolls subtly straddle the line between sweet and salty. We usually eat these for breakfast, but I've had them at lunchtime too, with a small salad or soup, and they are just as good then. Meike's original recipe uses instant yeast, but I like the extra ballast that fresh yeast gives the rolls.

The rolls are at their best when freshly made. But I discovered a trick to reviving them the next day: Split day-old rolls in half horizontally. Melt a little butter in a pan and toast the split rolls in the pan cut-side down until golden brown. Serve immediately with a dab of jam or just plain—and preferably with a cup of hot, milky coffee for dunking.

ROLLS

¾ ounce/20g fresh yeast, or 1 teaspoon instant yeast

3 tablespoons granulated sugar

1 teaspoon salt

3 tablespoons/40g unsalted butter

1 cup minus 1 tablespoon/220ml whole milk

1 egg, at room temperature

4 cups, scooped and leveled/500g all-purpose flour, plus up to 2 tablespoons as needed, and more for dusting

TOPPING

1 egg yolk

1 teaspoon whole milk

1 to 2 tablespoons poppy seeds

1 Line a baking sheet with parchment paper.

2 To make the rolls: If using fresh yeast, crumble the yeast into a small bowl. Sprinkle in the sugar and salt. (If using instant yeast, stir the yeast, sugar, salt, and flour together in a bowl and proceed to Step 3.)

3 Melt the butter and combine with the milk. The mixture should be lukewarm. Whisk in the egg.

continued

4 If using fresh yeast, pour the egg mixture into the bowl with the yeast mixture and add the flour. (If using instant yeast, pour the egg mixture into the bowl with the flour mixture.) Stir together until shaggy; dump out onto a lightly floured work surface and knead by hand for 5 to 7 minutes, or until the dough is smooth and silky. If the dough seems too sticky, you can add up to 2 tablespoons more flour, but no more; you want the dough to stay as soft as possible.

5 Form the dough into a ball and place back in the bowl. Cover with a clean dishcloth and place in a warm, draft-free spot to rise for 1 hour.

6 Punch down the dough and knead briefly. Divide the dough into 10 equal portions (about 3 ounces/85g each). Roll out each portion of dough into a triangle that is about 8 inches/20cm long on each side. Starting with a long side (not a tip), roll up each piece and form into a crescent roll with the tip secured underneath. Place the rolls on the prepared baking sheet. Alternatively, you can roll the original ball of dough out to a 15-inch/38cm round and cut the round into 10 equal wedges. Roll up the wedges and form them into crescents. Cover the baking sheet with the dishcloth and place in a warm, draft-free spot for 20 minutes.

7 Meanwhile, preheat the oven to 425°F/220°C.

8 When the rolls have proofed again, make the topping: Beat the egg yolk with the milk for an egg wash. Remove the dishcloth and brush the rolls thinly with the egg wash. Sprinkle the poppy seeds over them.

9 Place the baking sheet in the oven and bake for 15 minutes, or until the rolls are a rich golden brown. They will be very soft to the touch. Remove the baking sheet from the oven and let cool on a rack for 15 minutes before serving. The rolls are best eaten the day they are made.

SEELEN
Swabian Spelt Caraway Rolls

MAKES 8 (10-INCH-/25CM-LONG) ROLLS OR 12 SMALLER ONES

I find bread baking endlessly entertaining—it never ceases to amaze me that a few humble ingredients, combined with time and a bit of moisture and heat, can produce crusty, flavorful, chewy loaves of bread. *Seelen*, classic Swabian spelt rolls flavored with caraway, are a great project for home bakers and even novice bread bakers who have a bit of confidence (required for shaping the rolls).

Seelen, which means "souls" in German, were traditionally made around All Saints' Day and given to the poor as alms. Nowadays, they're eaten all year long. Swabians in Berlin speak longingly of their favorite bakers' *Seelen* back home; the few bakeries in Berlin that make *Seelen* apparently don't do a particularly good job of it. (Most Germans who grew up elsewhere and then moved to Berlin find the bread situation here to be dismal.)

Traditionally, they are made with white spelt flour and topped with topped with flaky salt and caraway seeds. You can substitute whole grain spelt flour in this recipe, but keep in mind that the rolls will be slightly heavier and darker. When freshly made, their crust is thick and crackling and their crumb is moist and sour. One- and two-day-old *Seelen* are less crusty and chewier, sort of like bagels, and still quite delicious.

The recipe requires you to make a pre-ferment, but that's nothing more than a mixture of flour, water, and yeast that ferments for several hours at room temperature to get nice and sour before being mixed into the main batter. The pre-ferment gives the dough better flavor and a nice ropy texture.

Instead of kneading the dough into rolls, you pull off pieces of dough and twist them into shape. I found it helped if I kept a bowl of water nearby while I worked, both to keep the bread dough from sticking to my fingers and to twist it. The unbaked rolls will look a little gnarly. This is as it should be. First of all, these are rustic rolls. And second, in the heat of the oven, a lot of the smaller lumps and warts smooth out. I guarantee you'll be impressed with your finished rolls, no matter how funny they looked when you first formed them.

Please note: The dough is quite moist and floppy and can't really be kneaded, so it's essential to use a stand mixer for this recipe.

PRE-FERMENT

1⅔ cups, scooped and leveled/200g white spelt flour

1 cup/240ml water

¼ teaspoon instant yeast

DOUGH

6⅔ cups, scooped and leveled/800g white spelt flour

2 cups/480ml water

1 teaspoon instant yeast

1 tablespoon salt

1 teaspoon granulated sugar

1 tablespoon whole milk

1 tablespoon caraway seeds

1 tablespoon flaky sea salt, such as Maldon

2 large handfuls of ice cubes, for baking

1 To make the pre-ferment: Mix together the flour, water, and instant yeast in a medium bowl until smooth. Cover with a clean dishcloth and let rest at room temperature for 12 to 14 hours.

continued

2 To make the dough: Place the flour in the bowl of a stand mixer fitted with the dough hook and add the water, yeast, salt, sugar, and milk; scrape in the entire batch of pre-ferment. Turn on the machine and stir the mixture at low speed for 12 minutes.

3 Remove the dough hook, cover the bowl with the dishcloth, and let sit for 45 minutes. (Wash the dough hook.)

4 Put the dough hook back on the machine and mix at low speed for 1 minute. Again remove the dough hook, cover the bowl, and let sit for 45 minutes. (Wash the dough hook.)

5 Put the dough hook back on the machine and mix at low speed for 1 minute. Remove the dough hook, cover the bowl, and let sit for 20 minutes.

6 Line two baking sheets with parchment paper. Fill a medium bowl with cold water and place it on your work surface next to the first baking sheet. Wet your hands in the bowl of water and pull off a piece of dough to form into a roll. The size of the piece of dough you pull off is approximate: for larger rolls, to serve two, the dough will need to be divided into 8 portions; for smaller rolls, to serve one, the dough will be divided into 12 portions. The dough will be quite elastic, so you'll have to use some force to shape it. Dip the piece of dough in the water. Lift it up out of the water, twist it a few times,

and lay the twisted piece of dough on the prepared baking sheet. The rolls will be on the messy side; this is part of their appeal. Also, some of the ragged edges smooth out in the oven. Repeat the process, leaving 1 to 2 inches/2.5 to 5cm between the rolls, until the baking sheet is full (4 large rolls or 6 small ones will fill a sheet). Set aside for 20 minutes. Leave the remaining dough in the bowl until it's time to form the second batch.

7 Preheat the oven to 475°F/245°C. Position a rack in the middle of the oven. Place a metal cake or roasting pan at the bottom of the oven.

8 After the rolls have rested for 20 minutes, sprinkle them evenly with half of the caraway seeds and half of the flaky salt. Working quickly, dump half of the ice cubes in the pan in the oven and slide the baking sheet onto the middle rack. Bake for 25 minutes (for smaller rolls) or 35 minutes (for for larger rolls), or until the rolls are golden brown, risen, and cracked.

9 Remove the baking sheet from the oven and let cool on a rack for 15 to 20 minutes. Repeat with the remaining dough and ice cubes.

10 The rolls can be served hot, warm, or at room temperature. They are best the day they are made but will keep at room temperature in a bread box for 2 days.

HEISSWECKEN
Raisin-Spice Buns

MAKES 20 BUNS

Heisswecken, beautifully burnished little raisin buns, are a regional specialty from northern Germany, which explains the inclusion of cardamom—a spice that would have been available only to the Hanseatic cities in earlier centuries and is nonexistent in baking recipes from the rest of Germany. *Heisswecken*, or "hot buns," were traditionally made before the Lenten fast and can be traced back all the way to medieval times. Historically, the buns were doused with hot milk and served with spoons, a practice that I can personally attest to being quite a delightful way of using up stale *Heisswecken*.

Another thing that sets *Heisswecken* apart from other small buns in the German baking tradition is the way they are formed. Instead of pieces of dough being plucked off from a batch of dough and then rolled and baked, the whole batch of dough is rolled out and rounds are stamped out with a round cutter, as you would with scone or biscuit dough. As a result, the buns bake up with beautiful loft and can be nicely split in half crosswise and buttered.

The crumb is light and cottony, while the tops, glazed with an egg wash, go deeply bronze in the oven. I love the contrast between the buns' crisp top and fluffy interior. A fresh batch of *Heisswecken* at breakfast would be a fine treat indeed, but any leftovers can be served the next day. For each serving, place a bun in a bowl and pour ½ cup/120ml of hot milk over it. Let the bun soften for a minute or two and then serve with a spoon.

DOUGH

4 cups, scooped and leveled/500g all-purpose flour, plus more for kneading

1½ teaspoons instant yeast

⅓ cup plus 1 tablespoon/80g granulated sugar

¼ teaspoon salt

½ teaspoon ground cardamom

½ cup/120ml whole milk

2 eggs, at room temperature

7 tablespoons/100g unsalted high-fat, European-style butter, at room temperature

½ cup/75g raisins or dried currants

⅓ cup/50g chopped candied citron peel

EGG WASH

1 egg yolk

1 teaspoon whole milk

1 Line a baking sheet with parchment paper.

2 To make the dough: Place the flour, yeast, sugar, salt, and cardamom in a large bowl. Add the milk, eggs, and butter, cut into rough chunks. Knead together by hand for a minute or two in the bowl, and then dump out on a lightly floured work surface and knead until smooth and no longer sticky, about 5 minutes. Pat out the dough slightly. Place the raisins and citron peel on top, fold the dough around them and knead until everything has been well distributed. Form the dough into a ball and place in the large bowl. Cover with a clean dishcloth and set in a warm, draft-free spot to rise for 1 hour.

continued

3 After 1 hour, gently tug the risen dough out of the bowl and onto your work surface. Roll out the dough with a rolling pin until it is ½ inch/12mm thick. Using a 2.5-inch/6cm round biscuit cutter, cut out rounds of dough and place them on the prepared baking sheet, leaving ½ inch/12mm between the buns. Knead together the scraps, roll out again, and stamp out the remaining buns.

4 Preheat the oven to 400°F/200°C. Cover the buns with the dishcloth and let rise for 20 minutes.

5 To make the egg wash: Whisk together the egg yolk and milk and then brush it thinly over the tops of the risen buns.

6 Place the baking sheet in the oven and bake for 15 minutes. The buns will be deeply bronzed on top.

7 Remove the pan from the oven and let cool on a rack for 10 minutes before removing the buns from the baking sheet. Serve warm or at room temperature. The buns are best the day they are made, but will keep at room temperature for 1 day.

ROGGENBRÖTCHEN
Rye Rolls

MAKES 10 ROLLS

Rye rolls are ubiquitous all throughout Germany. There are probably as many different versions of them as there are municipalities in the country. They can be found plain; flavored with ground fennel, coriander, and caraway; studded with tiny pieces of shredded carrots; or topped with pumpkin seeds or sunflower seeds, among many variations. Most often they are made with sourdough, emphasizing rye's naturally sour and grassy flavor. *Roggenbrötchen* are satisfyingly hearty, best paired with a rib-sticking pea soup or else split, buttered, and topped with a slice of ham or cheese.

A time-honored trick for achieving that trademark sourdough flavor without the hassle of making a real sourdough starter at home is to use buttermilk in the dough and a small amount of yeast, and then letting the dough proof overnight at room temperature. Rye flour has far less gluten than wheat flour, so to make it manageable for the home baker, equal amounts of both flours are called for in this recipe. You will need a stand mixer to beat the dough, which is very sticky and thick.

I like to shape the dough into relatively small rolls. While they are delicious when still crisp and warm from the oven, I like them equally the next day, when their crumb is cool and delectably chewy.

To flavor the rolls with what Germans call *Brotgewürz*, or bread spices, add ⅛ teaspoon each of ground fennel, ground coriander, and ground caraway to the bowl in the first step. If instead you would like to add shredded carrots to the rolls, finely shred a medium carrot and add to the bowl in the first step. To cover the rolls with pumpkin seeds or sunflower seeds, after the final 40-minute proofing stage brush the rolls thinly with water and sprinkle the tops of the rolls with seeds of your choice, pressing them into the dough very lightly before baking.

2½ cups, scooped and leveled/250g rye flour

2 cups, scooped and leveled/250g all-purpose flour, plus more for shaping

½ teaspoon instant yeast

1½ teaspoons salt

½ teaspoon granulated sugar

1 cup/240ml buttermilk

⅔ cup/160ml water

2 handfuls of ice cubes, for baking

1 Place the two flours, yeast, salt, and sugar in the bowl of a stand mixer fitted with the dough hook. In a separate bowl, whisk together the buttermilk and water. Turn the motor to low speed to start mixing and pour in the buttermilk mixture. When the flour mixture has been moistened, increase the speed to medium-high and mix for 2 minutes. Then increase the speed to high for 5 minutes. The dough will be creamy and very sticky. Scrape off the dough hook, scrape down the sides of the bowl if necessary, and cover the bowl with a clean dishcloth. Let the dough sit at room temperature for 12 hours.

2 After the dough has finished proofing, liberally dust your work surface with a generous handful or two of all-purpose flour. Line a baking sheet with parchment paper. Gently scrape the risen dough out of the bowl and onto the floured work surface. Using a bench scraper and with heavily floured hands, divide the dough into 10 equal pieces. Keeping your hands floured, gently roll each piece into a ball and place on the prepared baking sheet. The dough is very soft, so the balls will be flattish. Cover the baking sheet with the dishcloth and set aside for 40 minutes.

3 Preheat the oven to 475°F/245°C. Place a metal cake or roasting pan at the bottom of the oven.

4 When the rolls have proofed for 40 minutes, working quickly, dump the ice cubes into the pan at the bottom of the oven and immediately slide the baking sheet into the oven. Bake for 23 to 25 minutes, or until the rolls are golden brown, have a crisp crust, and sound hollow when tapped. Remove the pan from the oven and place on a rack to cool for 20 to 30 minutes before serving. The rolls are best eaten the day they are made but can be kept for up to 5 additional days in a plastic bag or airtight container. Leftover rolls should be placed in a 400°F/200°C oven for 5 minutes to soften and freshen up.

ROSINENBRÖTCHEN

Whole Wheat Raisin Buns

MAKES 12 ROLLS OR 24 MINI ROLLS

One of Berlin's oldest organic bakeries, Weichardt Brot, is located on a sleepy residential street in Wilmersdorf, a western neighborhood of Berlin. Heinz Weichardt and his wife, Mucke, have run the bakery since the early 1970s and are at the bakery every day, Heinz—outgoing and gregarious—often at the front, and Mucke at the back working in the office. Weichardt Brot specializes in the hearty, grain-stuffed, dark, sour loaves that are so emblematic of German baking. The bakery even stone grinds its own organic flours in a huge mill that you can see from the sidewalk.

But what I love best about Weichardt—more than the bread or the bronze door handle shaped like a croissant or their legendary chocolate cream torte, which sells out every morning by noon at the latest and for which I sadly have no recipe—is that every time a child enters the bakery, a little whole grain raisin bun is plucked from a basket behind the counter and given to the child, free of charge.

Rosinenbrötchen are one of most enduring traditions of a childhood in Germany. Traditional ones are made with white flour, but when whole grain flours started showing up in the 1970s, whole wheat or spelt flour *Rosinenbrötchen* became popular. Wholesome and simple, slightly sweet but not remotely cakelike, they please both a small child's palate and a parent's conscience. I make them by adding raisins to a beloved old recipe of Bernard Clayton's that uses a mix of regular and whole wheat flour, a bit of lemon peel, and some butter and honey for suppleness and sweetness. You mix and shape the buns in the evening, and then let the buns proof slowly overnight

in the refrigerator so that you can bake them first thing in the morning for breakfast. (Once they have fully cooled, you can freeze the remaining buns and defrost them individually as needed.)

My son, who has loved *Rosinenbrötchen* since before he could stand, and who always knows what to ask for when we get within spitting distance of the bakery, was suitably impressed when I first pulled a homemade one from the oven for him. I hope your children (and you!) like them, too.

3 cups, scooped and leveled/375g all-purpose flour, plus more for kneading

1 tablespoon instant yeast

2½ teaspoons salt

2 cups/480ml water

¼ cup/80g honey

3 tablespoons plus 1 teaspoon/45g unsalted butter, at room temperature

Grated peel of 1 organic lemon

2⅔ cups, scooped and leveled, minus 1 tablespoon to 3 cups, scooped and leveled, plus 2 tablespoons/ 325 to 390g whole wheat flour

1½ cups/225g raisins

Vegetable oil, for brushing

2 large handfuls of ice cubes, for baking

1 Place the all-purpose flour, yeast, salt, water, honey, butter, and grated lemon peel in the bowl of a food processor fitted with the short plastic dough blade. Pulse to make a batterlike dough. With the machine running, pour in 1½ cups/195g of the

whole wheat flour. Blend well. Turn off the machine and let the batter rest for 3 minutes, until the whole wheat flour has been absorbed. Turn on the machine and gradually add 1 to 1½ cups/130 to 195g whole wheat flour. Turn off the machine, remove the lid, and feel the dough. It should be soft and a bit sticky, but a solid (not hard) mass.

2 Turn on the machine and knead for 45 seconds, or until the dough pulls away from the sides of the bowl. Turn the dough out onto a lightly floured work surface, and start kneading by hand. The dough may be sticky at first. Add a sprinkle or two of all-purpose flour, if necessary, as you knead. Depending on how long your dough was kneaded in the machine, you may be kneading for up to 10 minutes, adding flour as needed until the dough is smooth and elastic. Test to see if you've kneaded enough by slapping your hand on the dough, holding it there for a count of 10, and then lifting your hand. If bits of dough stick or cling to your hand, continue to knead, adding flour. If your hand comes off clean, the dough's ready for the next step.

3 Add the raisins and knead until well distributed. Form the kneaded dough into a ball and cover it with a clean dishcloth or plastic wrap. Let it rest for 20 minutes. Line a baking sheet with parchment paper.

4 Knead the dough for 30 seconds to press out any air bubbles. Cut the dough into 12 equal pieces.

For mini rolls, cut into 24 pieces. Roll each piece of dough between your hands to form a ball. Place each ball on the prepared baking sheet, flattening slightly with the palm of your hand.

5 Brush the rolls thinly with vegetable oil. Cover with plastic wrap loosely enough to allow the rolls to rise but sealed around the edges to hold in the moisture. Place the baking sheet in the refrigerator overnight.

6 The next morning, remove the baking sheet from the refrigerator and let the rolls sit, covered, at room temperature for 25 minutes while heating the oven to 400°F/200°C. Place a metal cake or roasting pan on the floor of the oven to heat as the oven heats.

7 Uncover the rolls. Place them in the oven, and then quickly and carefully place the ice cubes in the hot pan on the bottom of the oven and close the oven door. Bake for 25 to 30 minutes (or 15 to 20 minutes for mini rolls), or until the rolls are browned and sound hollow when tapped on the bottom.

8 Remove the baking sheet from the oven and transfer the rolls to a rack to cool. Serve slightly warm or let cool completely before freezing. Freshly baked, completely cooled rolls can be frozen (packaged in plastic freezer bags) for up to 3 months. To defrost and serve warm, place the frozen rolls on a baking sheet in a 350°F/180°C oven for 5 to 8 minutes.

KÄSE-KÜMMEL-BRÖTCHEN
Caraway-Cheese Rye Rolls

MAKES 16 ROLLS

In the United States, go to any Jewish deli and the rye breads for sale will almost always be studded with caraway. In fact, most Jewish Americans think rye bread must have caraway in it to be authentic. In Germany, however, caraway is a regional addition to rye breads—in fact, most rye breads and rolls here are made without it. You can go to any bakery in Germany and find a selection of rye breads with varying amounts of rye—100 percent (these are very dark, sour loaves with an almost sticky texture), 70 percent (often a flattish loaf with a very firm crust and crumb), 50 percent (studded with sunflower seeds or flaxseeds, for example), or 30 percent, which is called a *Mischbrot* (mixed bread) and is no longer considered as nutritious as a higher-percentage rye.

Rye is an interesting grain with low gluten, which is why kneading it can be such a sticky, frustrating affair. Rye has a sour, grassy flavor that is delicious in sourdough breads, and it is often paired with all-purpose flour, making for an easier dough to tame. In Germany, rye is almost exclusively used in bread recipes, though there are a few rare examples of using rye flour in cookies (see, for example, the *Lebkuchen-Powidltatschkerln* on page 224).

These plump and glossy rye rolls are made with a mix of all-purpose and rye flour, the rye contributing a delicately sour note. Buttermilk tenderizes the rolls and enhances the faint hint of sour flavor. Cheese and caraway are kneaded into the dough for a rich, spicy flavor. The baked rolls freeze terrifically well and are all-around crowd-pleasers. I like to serve them with a bowl of tomato soup, or split and fill them with a thin slice or two of ham for lunch (or breakfast).

1¼ cups plus 2 tablespoons/330ml buttermilk, at room temperature

½ ounce/15g fresh yeast, or ¾ teaspoon instant yeast

Pinch of sugar

1 teaspoon salt

1 teaspoon ground caraway seed

2¾ cups, scooped and leveled, plus 1 tablespoon/350g all-purpose flour, plus more for kneading

1½ cups, scooped and leveled/150g rye flour

3½ tablespoons/50g unsalted butter, melted and cooled

2 lightly packed cups/200g grated Emmentaler (Swiss) cheese

1 egg yolk

1 teaspoon water

Poppy seeds, caraway seeds, or toasted sesame seeds, for sprinkling

2 large handfuls of ice cubes, for baking

1 If using fresh yeast, pour the buttermilk into a large bowl. Crumble in the fresh yeast. Add the sugar and stir together with a wooden spoon, using the back of the spoon to dissolve the yeast. Add the salt and ground caraway to the bowl; pour in the flours and the cooled butter, stirring as you go. The dough will be ragged and thick. (If using instant yeast, stir the yeast, sugar, salt, ground caraway, and flours together in a large bowl. In a separate bowl, mix together the buttermilk and the cooled, melted butter. Pour the buttermilk mixture into the flour, stirring as you go. The dough will be ragged and thick.)

2 Add the grated cheese to the bowl and, using your hands, incorporate as best you can. Then dump the shaggy mixture out onto a lightly floured work surface, scrape out the bowl, and begin kneading.

3 The dough will seem impossible to work with at first, but continue to knead, and as the minutes tick by, you will see the dough slowly start to take shape. Try to resist adding more flour as you knead. Keep in mind that the rye flour will keep the dough from having the springiness of an all-wheat loaf. Keep kneading until the dough is smooth (save for the bits of cheese) and no longer sticky. Shape into a ball and place back in the mixing bowl. Cover with a clean dishcloth and set in a warm, draft-free place until the dough has doubled in size. This can take 1 to 1½ hours.

4 When the dough has doubled, preheat the oven to 400°F/200°C. Place a metal cake or roasting pan at the bottom of the oven. Line a baking sheet with parchment paper.

5 Gently pull the dough out of the bowl and onto your work surface and knead it once or twice. Divide it into 16 equal pieces. Roll the pieces of dough into plump oval shapes and place them on the baking sheet, evenly spaced. Cover with the dishcloth and let sit for 10 minutes.

6 Beat the egg yolk and water in a small bowl and brush the rolls with the egg wash. Sprinkle the rolls with poppy seeds, caraway seeds, or sesame seeds. Then slash the rolls once lengthwise with a very sharp knife.

7 Place the baking sheet in the oven and then quickly dump the ice cubes in the hot pan on the bottom. Close the oven door immediately and bake for 25 minutes, or until the rolls are a rich golden brown and sound hollow when tapped.

8 Place the hot baking sheet on a rack until the rolls are cool enough to handle, and then transfer them from the baking sheet to the rack. Serve warm or at room temperature. The rolls are best the day they are made, but will keep for 1 additional day in a bread box or plastic bag. They can be crisped up in a 325°F/165°C oven. Freshly baked, fully cooled rolls can be frozen, packaged in plastic freezer bags, for up to 3 months. To defrost and serve warm, place the frozen rolls on a baking sheet and bake at 350°F/180°C for 5 to 8 minutes.

QUARKBRÖTCHEN
Sweet Quark Rolls

MAKES 8 ROLLS

When used in dough, *Quark* contributes both tenderness to the crumb and a gently sour flavor. There may be no better showcase for *Quark*'s usefulness in baking than these lightly sweetened, rich and tender rolls. I confess to literally dancing with joy in my kitchen the day I first made them—they were that good. I found the recipe on Stefanie Herberth's excellent and exhaustive bread-baking blog, *Hefe und Mehr* (hefe-und-mehr.de/en).

The method for making them is a little unusual because you start by making a milk roux, cooking the milk with a little flour until you get a thick, smooth mixture. Stefanie explains that this process causes the starch in the flour to swell and gelatinize, which creates not only a fluffier crumb but a longer-lasting one, too. The cooled milk roux is then mixed into the rest of the ingredients. The soft and floppy dough is formed into balls and snipped into clover shapes with sharp scissors. I add a pan of ice cubes to the oven when I bake the rolls because the steam helps the rolls develop a beautifully glossy crust.

These rolls would be a luxurious addition to a weekend breakfast spread and are best paired with a bit of jam or honey (a thin layer of butter underneath makes them particularly decadent).

½ cup plus 2 tablespoons/150ml whole milk

2¼ cups, scooped and leveled/280g all-purpose flour, plus more for kneading

¾ cup plus 1 tablespoon/200g *Quark* (page 264), drained if necessary (see page 8)

1 teaspoon instant yeast

½ teaspoon salt

¼ cup/50g granulated sugar

3½ tablespoons/50g unsalted high-fat, European-style butter, at room temperature

1 tablespoon heavy cream

2 large handfuls of ice cubes, for baking

1 Line a baking sheet with parchment paper.

2 Place the milk and ¼ cup/30g of the flour in a small pot; whisk together until no clumps remain. Cook over medium heat, stirring constantly, until the mixture has thickened to the consistency of pudding, about 3 minutes. Set aside to cool.

3 Place the cooled milk roux, the remaining 2 cups/250g of flour, and the *Quark*, yeast, salt, sugar, and butter in a bowl and stir together by hand until shaggy. Scrape the dough out onto a lightly floured work surface and knead until smooth and no longer sticky. Try to resist adding flour as you knead; you want the dough to remain as soft as possible. Form into a ball and place back in the bowl. Cover with a clean dishcloth and set in a warm, draft-free spot to rise for 1 hour.

4 Gently tug the dough and out of the bowl onto your work surface and divide into 8 equal pieces. Form each piece into a ball and place on the prepared baking sheet, evenly spaced. Cover the baking sheet with the dishcloth and set in a warm, draft-free spot for 1 hour.

5 Preheat the oven to 400°F/200°C. Place a metal cake or roasting pan on the bottom of the oven. Remove the dishcloth and brush the rolls evenly all over with the cream. Using very sharp kitchen shears, cut each roll into a clover shape by snipping into the rolls three times from the sides. The cuts should almost meet in the middle.

6 Place the baking sheet of rolls in the oven and immediately dump the ice cubes into the hot pan on the bottom of the oven. Close the oven door as quickly as you can. Bake the rolls for 20 to 25 minutes, or until they are golden brown. They will be quite soft to the touch.

7 Let cool on a rack until the rolls are cool enough to handle. Serve them warm or at room temperature. The rolls are best the day they are made but will keep for 2 additional days in a plastic bag or airtight container.

QUARK-OSTERHASEN
Soft Quark Bunny Rolls

MAKES 12 TO 14 ROLLS

This all-purpose, lemon-scented yeasted dough, made with copious amounts of butter, milk, and *Quark*, is incredibly rich and tends not to rise as much in the proofing stage. But it shoots outward in the heat of the oven, making for wonderfully plump rolls. I like to use it for Easter morning treats, shaping it into small oval rolls and then snipping them into bunnies, mice, or hedgehogs with a pair of sharp kitchen shears and adding some judiciously placed raisins or currants for their little faces. Alternatively, you can roll the dough out to ½ inch/12mm thickness and stamp out bunny or other animal shapes if you have a large cookie cutter. The dough can also be turned into small braided nests for dyed Easter eggs. Simply divide the dough into 8 equal portions, and then cut each of those in half. Roll out 2 strands of dough and twist them together to create a twisted rope, which you press together in a circle shape, repeating to make 8 nests. Let the twisted circles rise, and then place a food-safe dyed Easter egg in the center and bake until golden brown (the egg should be hard-boiled prior to using).

For regular weekend breakfasts or celebration brunches, the dough can also be turned into what in Germany are called *Flachswickel*, or "flax twists," referring to the sheaves of flax that used to decorate the landscape after harvest. Traditional Swabian *Flachswickel* are made with a regular yeasted dough—with no *Quark* or lemon peel—so another way to make them is to use the dough for the *Rosinenzopf* on page 213, leaving out the raisins. But I like to use this dough. You roll out a long piece of dough, fold it in half, and twist the strands around each other. Before baking, the rolls are brushed with egg wash for a gorgeous burnishing and sprinkled with pearl sugar for a delectable crunch.

For an alternative, "fuzzy" finish to either the animal rolls or the *Flachswickel*, leave off the egg wash and the pearl sugar. Instead, while the rolls are baking, melt 8 tablespoons/115g of unsalted butter and place 1 cup/200g of granulated sugar in a bowl. As soon as the rolls come out of the oven, brush them all over with the melted butter and roll them in the sugar. Set on a rack to cool.

¾ ounce/20g fresh yeast, or 1 teaspoon instant yeast

4 cups, scooped and leveled/500g all-purpose flour, plus more for kneading

½ cup plus 2 tablespoons/125g granulated sugar

½ cup minus 1½ tablespoons/100ml whole milk, lukewarm

½ teaspoon salt

Grated peel of 1 organic lemon

8½ tablespoons/120g unsalted high-fat, European-style butter, at room temperature

½ cup/120g *Quark* (page 264), drained if necessary (see page 8)

2 whole eggs, at room temperature

1 egg yolk

1 teaspoon water

2 tablespoons pearl sugar (see page 7; optional)

Currants or raisins (optional)

1 If using fresh yeast, place the flour in a large bowl and make a well in the middle. Crumble the yeast into the well. Add a pinch of the sugar. Pour a couple of spoonsful of the milk over the yeast, stirring carefully with a fork to dissolve the yeast and mix it with a bit of the flour. Cover the bowl with a clean dishcloth and set aside for 15 minutes. (If using instant yeast, stir the flour, yeast, sugar, salt, and grated lemon peel together in a large bowl.

In a separate bowl, beat together the milk and whole eggs. Make a well in the flour and pour the milk mixture into the well, stirring as you go. Add the butter and *Quark*, stir briefly, then knead the dough by hand in the bowl until it starts to come together. Proceed to the kneading phase of Step 2.)

2 Remove the dishcloth and sprinkle the remaining sugar and the salt around the edges of the bowl. Pour the remaining milk into the bowl and stir. Add the grated lemon peel, butter, *Quark*, and whole eggs. Knead together by hand until the dough starts to come together. Then scrape out onto a well-floured work surface and knead until smooth and no longer sticky, about 5 minutes, adding more flour only if absolutely necessary. Form the dough into a ball and place back in the bowl. Cover with the dishcloth and set in a warm, draft-free spot for 1 hour. The dough will not double in size, but don't worry.

3 Line a baking sheet with parchment paper.

4 Gently pull the dough out onto a lightly floured surface and knead together once. Then divide into 12 to 14 equal pieces (if possible, use a scale to weigh them evenly). Cover them with the dishcloth to keep them from drying out. Form the pieces into ovals to turn into bunny, mouse, or hedgehog buns. Alternatively, for *Flachswickel*, take out one piece and roll out to a 12-inch-/30cm-long roll. Fold the roll in half and twist the 2 strands together several times. Place the twisted roll on the prepared baking sheet and repeat with the next piece. When all the dough has been formed and placed on the baking sheet, cover with the dishcloth and set aside in a warm, draft-free spot for 30 minutes.

5 Preheat the oven to 350°F/180°C.

6 Beat the egg yolk with the water. When the rolls have fully proofed, remove the dishcloth and brush the rolls thinly all over with the egg wash. If making animal buns, hold a pair of sharp kitchen sheers at a 45-degree angle to the dough and snip in ears, tails, or quills. Push raisins or currants into the dough to create a face (eyes and nose). If making *Flachswickel*, sprinkle the rolls evenly with the pearl sugar.

7 Place the pan in the oven and bake for 15 minutes. The dough will expand quite a bit in the oven. Remove from the oven and place on a rack to cool. The rolls are best eaten warm the day they are made. Leftovers can be kept for 1 additional day in a plastic bag.

SCHWARZWÄLDER KARTOFFELBRÖTCHEN
Potato Rolls with Bacon and Caraway

MAKES 12 ROLLS OR 24 MINI ROLLS

My assistant, Maja, is married to a man from Baden-Württemberg, which is a region known throughout Germany for its excellent food and wine—and elsewhere, too. The famed Black Forest (*Schwarzwald*) is in Baden-Württemberg, and it is the birthplace of *Schwarzwälder Kirschtorte* (page 123) and innumerable other delicacies.

Several years ago, Maja's sister-in-law gave her a tiny, 5 by 5-inch/12 by 12cm cookbook with recipes from the region. As usual for older German cookbooks, it had no helpful photos, nor did it offer much background information for any of the recipes, but it ended up being an absolute treasure trove of inspiration for us. Among other things, it helped us develop this recipe for delectably soft potato rolls seasoned with caraway and bacon.

The dough for the rolls is made with mashed potatoes in addition to flour, as well as quite a bit of milk and butter. This makes the rolls moist and very tender, almost floppy. Because of their texture, they're not the kind of rolls you would split for sandwiches. Instead, I like to serve them alongside a large spread of vegetable salads or with soup, though I warn you: they might end up overshadowing everything else on the dinner table.

We made several versions of this recipe until we were happy with the results. In the process, we found that we liked the rolls best of all when topped with tiny cubes of *Schinkenspeck*, big pinches of flaky sea salt, and whole caraway seeds. *Schinkenspeck* is a very lean, cured German bacon (see page 270 for sources), but you could substitute cubes of slab bacon, as long as it's relatively lean. The soft, mild crumb of the bread works really well with the big, punchy flavors of cured pork and caraway.

If you are not a bacon fan, you can absolutely leave it out. Just be sure to use at least 2 teaspoons of flaky salt to top the rolls.

1 pound/455g russet potatoes

3²/₃ cups, scooped and leveled, minus 1 tablespoon/ 450g all-purpose flour, plus more for kneading

2 teaspoons instant yeast

Pinch of sugar

½ cup/120ml whole milk

1 whole egg

5 tablespoons plus 1 teaspoon/75g unsalted butter, melted

¾ teaspoon fine salt

1 egg yolk, at room temperature

1 tablespoon water

2 teaspoons caraway seeds, or more to taste

²/₃ cup/100g diced *Schinkenspeck* or lean bacon

Flaky salt, for sprinkling (optional)

1 Place the potatoes in a pot and add enough cold water to cover. Cover the pot and bring to a boil over high heat; reduce to a simmer and let the potatoes cook until tender, 20 to 25 minutes. Drain the potatoes and let cool. This step can be done up to 1 day in advance.

2 Place the flour in a large bowl and make a well in the middle. Pour in the yeast and add the sugar. Slowly pour the milk over the yeast, stirring continuously and drawing in just a little bit of the surrounding flour. Cover the bowl with a clean dishcloth and let sit for 10 minutes.

3 Peel the potatoes and push them through a ricer or a food mill. Add them to the flour mixture, along with the whole egg, melted butter, and fine salt and mix together until you have a kneadable dough. It will be quite sticky and floppy.

4 Knead the dough in the bowl a few times, and then dump out onto a liberally floured work surface. Knead until relatively smooth, adding a few sprinkles of flour to the dough if you must. This dough is by nature sticky, so try to resist adding too much extra flour, as this will result in stiff rolls. Knead until you can form a relatively smooth ball (dotted with little bits of potato), and then place back in the bowl and cover with the dishcloth. Place somewhere warm and draft-free for 30 minutes.

5 Preheat the oven to 350°F/180°C. Line a baking sheet with parchment paper.

6 Flour your work surface and gently scrape the dough onto the surface. Using a sharp knife or bench scraper, divide the dough into 12 equal pieces for larger (5½-inch-/14cm-long) rolls. You can also make smaller rolls by dividing the dough into 24 equal pieces. Keeping a light hand on the rolling pin, gently roll out each piece into an oval roll. Place on the prepared baking sheet. They should all fit on one sheet.

7 Beat the egg yolk with the water and brush the rolls evenly with the egg wash. Then sprinkle with the caraway seeds and the *Schinkenspeck*. Sprinkle on a few pinches of flaky salt. Press the *Schinkenspeck* very lightly into the egg wash to make sure it sticks.

8 Bake for 35 minutes, rotating halfway through, or until the rolls are golden brown and puffed and sound hollow when tapped on the underside. Place the baking sheet on a rack to cool for 20 minutes. Serve the rolls while still warm. They will keep for 1 day and can be reheated in a warm oven.

BREZELN
Soft Pretzels

MAKES 10 PRETZELS

The humble pretzel is a hugely important thing in the German baking world. It is the traditional symbol of the national bakers guild and was one of the first devotional breads created many centuries ago. While to many outsiders, pretzels are to Germany what apple pie is to the United States, pretzels are actually a southern German tradition. In fact, in 2014 the state of Bavaria successfully registered the protected status of the Bavarian pretzel with the European Union. In Bavaria, pretzels are uniformly plump, with a wonderfully crunchy "skin," a chewy and yielding interior, and a torn "belly." In Swabia, the "arms" and "shoulders" of the pretzel are thin, making them crisp and crunchy, while the belly is plump and soft. Instead of letting the belly tear during baking, on a Swabian pretzel the belly is slashed crosswise with a very sharp knife after proofing.

One thing both pretzels have in common is that they are dipped in a lye solution before baking, which not only gives the pretzels their inimitable flavor, but also imparts the dark mahogany gloss that every good pretzel should have. Food-grade lye, which must be diluted with water, can be purchased online. It usually comes in granule form. Care must be taken when using it. Wear rubber gloves when preparing the solution and remember always to add lye to water, rather than water to lye. Keep small children away when you prepare the solution and dip the pretzels.

Pretzels are traditionally sprinkled with coarse salt before baking, but in recent years I've also seen them sprinkled with sesame seeds, pumpkin seeds, and even coarsely shredded cheese. Instead of shaping the dough into pretzels, you can also use it to make little round or oval rolls, also dipped in lye before baking. These are called *Laugengebäck* and make

wonderful sandwiches. I like them best split in half, spread with unsalted butter, and topped with a slice of smoked salmon or savory ham.

Once you've made your pretzels, you can indulge in the glorious tradition of *bayerisches Frühstück* (Bavarian breakfast), which consists of a freshly baked pretzel, a pair of *Weisswurst* (boiled pork and veal sausages), sweet mustard, and a tall glass of wheat beer. Or you can slice the pretzel in half horizontally and spread it liberally with unsalted butter. Put the pretzel back together again and you have yourself an excellent little snack, the classic *Butterbrezel*.

Fresh yeast gives the pretzels great flavor and a nicely puffy texture, so I think it's worth seeking out here. But instant yeast can be used instead.

DOUGH

4 cups, scooped and leveled/500g all-purpose flour, plus more for kneading

½ ounce/15g fresh yeast, or ¾ teaspoon instant yeast

1 teaspoon granulated sugar

1 cup plus 3 tablespoons/280ml water, lukewarm

2 teaspoons fine salt

1½ tablespoons/20g unsalted butter, at room temperature

LYE BATH

10 cups warm water

½ cup food-grade lye

Coarse sea salt (not kosher salt), for sprinkling

continued

1 To make the dough: If using fresh yeast, place the flour in a large bowl and make a well in the middle. Crumble the fresh yeast into the well. Sprinkle the sugar over the yeast. Pour in 3 tablespoons/40ml of the lukewarm water and stir gently just to dissolve the yeast without pulling in too much flour. Cover with a clean dishcloth and set aside for 5 minutes. (If using instant yeast, stir the flour, yeast, and sugar together in a large bowl. Proceed immediately with Step 2.)

2 Pour in the remaining 1 cup/240ml lukewarm water (if using instant yeast, add the full 1 cup plus 3 tablespoons/280ml). Add the salt and butter and stir together by hand. Knead the dough in the bowl until it comes together shaggily, and then dump out onto a floured surface and knead for 8 to 10 minutes (set a timer). You will have to keep flouring the surface at first as you knead, but as the minutes pass, you won't need to keep flouring. The dough will get very smooth and will be relatively firm. When the kneading time is up, let the dough rest, covered with the dishcloth, for 15 minutes. Then divide the dough into 10 equal portions and let the portions rest, covered with the dishcloth, for 5 minutes.

3 To form Swabian pretzels, take a ball of dough and roll out on the counter (do not flour the counter—you need the tackiness of the work surface to help propel the dough back and forth), putting more pressure on the ends of the dough to form long, thin strands and a fat middle, which will become the pretzel's "belly." The strand of dough should be about 24 inches/60cm in length. Lay the strand in an upside-down horseshoe shape. Take each end in one hand, cross them once, and press the ends into the top of the belly. Transfer the pretzel to the baking sheet and repeat with the remaining portions. To form Bavarian pretzels, roll the pieces of dough out to more uniformly thick rolls and then form as directed above. Place the pretzels on an ungreased, unlined baking sheet and repeat with the remaining dough, filling two baking sheets. Let the pretzels rest at room temperature, uncovered, for 30 minutes. Then place the pretzels in the freezer for 1 hour. If your freezer is too small, place in the refrigerator.

4 Preheat the oven to 425°F/220°C. Take the pretzels out of the freezer.

5 To make the lye bath: In a deep bowl, wearing rubber or latex gloves, pour the warm water into the bowl and then carefully add the lye to the water. Stir gently to dissolve the lye completely. Avoid splashes. Loosen each pretzel from the baking sheet and dip into the water, turning it over, for 10 to 15 seconds. If you haven't frozen the pretzels, they might stretch a bit during this process, but don't worry; the dough is forgiving. Just handle them as gently as you can, and when you place them back on the baking sheet, adjust their shape if they have gotten wonky.

6 Sprinkle the belly of the pretzels lightly with the sea salt. Using a very sharp knife and working quickly, slash the belly of each pretzel horizontally. If making Bavarian pretzels, skip the slashing. Place one baking sheet in the oven and bake for 15 to 20 minutes, or until the pretzels are a deep mahogany brown. Remove from the oven and let cool on a rack while you slide the second batch in to bake. The pretzels should be served warm or just cooled. They are best the day they are made.

FRANZBRÖTCHEN
Cinnamon-Sugar Buns

MAKES 12 BUNS

Franzbrötchen, a flaky, buttery cross between croissants and squashed cinnamon rolls, are native to Hamburg. And for many decades, Hamburg was the only place you could find them. People there were rightly passionate about their beloved cinnamon pastries, and they held strong opinions about which bakeries had the best ones and which recipe made the best at home. But around the turn of this century, *Franzbrötchen* started migrating out of Hamburg, and nowadays you can find *Franzbrötchen*, mostly mediocre ones, in bakeries all over the country.

Everyone I knew from Hamburg was evangelical about them. But the ones I'd tried in Berlin or at train stations across Germany were always a little greasy and leaden. What was the big deal about *Franzbrötchen*? Why were they always so disappointing?

Well, I got my answer when I tried making them at home. Freshly baked, using real butter instead of industrial margarine, fragrant with cinnamon, and caramelized at the edges, *Franzbrötchen* are a revelation. The signature roll-and-squash technique makes for a pastry that is both rich and satisfying *and* light and flaky. You prepare what are essentially cinnamon rolls, albeit with multilayered laminated dough, and then employ the trademark move: pressing the handle of a wooden spoon into each roll crosswise, flattening the roll and making two Princess-Leia-ish buns on either side of the depression, after which you squash the whole thing with the palms of your hands. What this produces, once the rolls proof again and go into the oven, is a roll with three different textures—the sort of squashed and chewy middle section; the lighter, flakier outer sections; and

the crisp and caramelized bottom. Alternating among the three as you work through your *Franzbrötchen* is a big part of its appeal.

The yeasted puff pastry used in the recipe, which you may recognize as Danish dough, is called *Plunderteig* in German. Meanwhile, in Denmark it is called *Wienerbrød*, or "Viennese bread." (To further confuse the matter, in Denmark turnovers made with *Wienerbrød* are called *Spandauer*, like the neighborhood in western Berlin.) *Plunderteig* seems like the kind of thing that would be intimidating to a home baker, but it really is quite simple. You prepare a simple yeasted dough and encase a slab of cold butter in the middle. The yeasted dough is folded over the cold butter, rolled out, folded again, and refrigerated. The refrigeration is really important because it keeps the butter firm throughout the rolling process. This process is repeated two more times, ultimately producing a gorgeous batch of *Plunderteig*—cold, slightly puffy, and velvety soft. *Plunderteig* can then be used to make turnovers filled with cooked apples or sweetened *Quark*, or *Rosinenschnecken* (raisin-filled spiral buns; page 202), or even a batch of decadent breakfast crescent croissants (simply roll out the dough, cut it into equal-size squares and then triangles, and then roll the triangles up into crescent shapes before baking). Make *Franzbrötchen* once, though, and you may decide that the best thing you could ever do with *Plunderteig* is bake another batch of *Franzbrötchen*.

continued

Fresh yeast gives these rolls a bit of added moisture, oven spring, and flavor, so I prefer to use it here, but instant yeast can also be substituted. One more thing to note: The larger amount of butter, folded and rolled together with the yeasted dough to create all those flaky layers, must be in one block before using. If you can find that amount of butter in one block, you're good to go. If your butter consists of several pieces, let them soften, knead them together until cohesive, and chill until cold and firm.

DOUGH

4⅔ cups, scooped and leveled/580g all-purpose flour, plus more for kneading and dusting

¾ cup plus 2 tablespoons/200ml whole milk, lukewarm

¾ ounce/20g fresh yeast, or 1 teaspoon instant yeast

3 tablespoons granulated sugar

¾ teaspoon salt

2 eggs, at room temperature

4 tablespoons plus 2 teaspoons/65g unsalted high-fat, European-style butter, at room temperature

18 tablespoons/250g unsalted high-fat, European-style butter, cold

FILLING

¾ cup/150g granulated sugar

2 teaspoons ground cinnamon

1 First, make the dough: If using fresh yeast, place the flour in a large mixing bowl. Place the milk in a small bowl and crumble the yeast into the milk; add a pinch of the sugar. Stir to dissolve the yeast. Add ¼ cup/30g of the flour and stir to combine. Cover the bowl with a clean dishcloth and set aside in a warm, draft-free spot for 30 minutes. (If using instant yeast, place the flour, yeast, sugar, and salt in a bowl and whisk. Make a well in the middle. In a separate bowl, whisk together the milk and eggs. Pour the milk mixture into the well, stirring as you pour, and then cut the 4 tablespoons plus 2 teaspoons/65g of room-temperature butter into rough chunks and add to the bowl. Stir until a shaggy dough comes together, and then knead by hand in the bowl. Dump out onto a work surface [you probably won't need to flour it] and knead by hand until the dough is smooth and no longer sticky, about 5 minutes. Resist adding any flour unless absolutely necessary. Proceed to Step 3.)

2 Whisk the remaining sugar and the salt into the bowl of flour. Make a well in the middle. Crack the eggs into the well. Add the 4 tablespoons plus 2 teaspoons/65g of room-temperature butter to the bowl. Scrape the yeast mixture, which should be thick and creamy, into the bowl. Stir together briefly, and then begin kneading with your hands. Knead in the bowl until a relatively cohesive dough forms, and then dump out onto a lightly floured work surface and knead vigorously until you have a smooth ball that is no longer sticky, about 5 minutes.

3 Place the ball of dough back in the bowl and cover with the dishcloth. Set in a warm, draft-free spot to rise for 2 hours.

4 Meanwhile, make the filling: Mix the sugar and cinnamon together in a small bowl.

5 When the dough has doubled in size, gently punch it down and scrape it out of the bowl and onto the work surface. Knead it a few times, and then roll it out into a 13-inch/33cm square. Take the cold butter out of the refrigerator and dust it liberally with flour. Roll out the butter to a 9-inch/23cm square, adding flour as needed to keep the rolling

continued

pin from sticking. Place the butter diagonally on top of the dough and fold the corners of the dough square over the butter, encasing it completely. Roll out the dough to an 8 by 12-inch/20 by 30cm rectangle. Fold up the rectangle in thirds like a business letter and place in the refrigerator to chill for 20 minutes.

6 Remove the dough from the refrigerator and roll out to an 8 by 12-inch/20 by 30cm rectangle again. Fold up the rectangle in thirds, like a business letter, and place in the refrigerator to cool for another 20 minutes. Repeat this entire step a third time.

7 Preheat the oven to 400°F/200°C. Line a baking sheet with parchment paper. After the third cooling, remove the dough from the refrigerator and cut in half. Place one half back in the refrigerator. Place the other half on a lightly floured surface and roll out to a 13-inch/33cm square. Sprinkle the dough evenly with half of the cinnamon-sugar mixture, leaving no border. (This will seem like a lot, but don't worry.) Roll up the dough and slice crosswise into 6 equal pieces.

8 Take one piece and place it on the counter with one of the cut ends facing you. Place the handle of a wooden spoon crosswise (parallel to the cut ends)

in the middle of the roll and press down firmly. The spoon will sink all the way down through the roll, making the cut ends furl out and up. Stop before the spoon severs the roll in half. Press the palms of your hands down on both of the fanned-out sides to flatten the roll. Don't pancake it completely, but don't be too timid either, or you'll end up with rolls that look like croissants rather than squashed *Franzbrötchen*. Transfer the squashed roll to the prepared baking sheet. Repeat with the remaining pieces of dough, arranging them evenly on the baking sheet. When all the rolls have been pressed and squashed, cover them with the dishcloth and let rise for 20 minutes.

9 Place the baking sheet of risen rolls in the oven and bake for 20 to 25 minutes, or until golden brown, puffed, and flaky, with caramelizing bottoms. Transfer the hot rolls to a rack to cool and repeat the whole process with the second batch of chilled dough.

10 The *Franzbrötchen* are best eaten the day they are made, but they will keep for a day or two. To refresh them, they should be reheated in a 350°F/°180°C oven for 5 minutes. Freshly baked *Franzbrötchen*, fully cooled and placed in a resealable bag, can be frozen for up to 2 months.

ROSINENSCHNECKEN
Raisin-Frangipane Spiral Buns

MAKES 8 BUNS

Saucer-size spiraled buns studded with raisins are
a fixture in German bakeries. Along with the raisins,
they're usually filled with a creamy vanilla pudding or
an almond cream and then glazed with apricot jam.
Unlike their French brethren, *pain aux raisins*, which
are made with puff pastry, *Rosinenschnecken* ("raisin
snails," a name that refers to their spiral shape) are
made with Danish dough, the same silky *Plunderteig*
as used in the *Franzbrötchen* (page 197). This makes
Rosinenschnecken both light and flaky on the outside,
and moist and toothsome on the inside. They are
sticky delights and an excellent afternoon pick-me-up.

I found that the winey complexity of a frangipane
filling—and its pleasing graininess—was better suited to
the *Rosinenschnecken* than a vanilla cream or pudding,
but this is a matter of taste. If you prefer, you can
leave off the frangipane mixture and spread the dough
with about ½ cup/120ml prepared vanilla pudding
instead (along with the plumped raisins). When you
roll up the dough and slice it, handle it carefully to
avoid squeezing out too much pudding. The apricot
glaze is optional if using the pudding filling.

DOUGH

2⅓ cups, scooped and leveled/290g all-purpose flour,
plus more for kneading and dusting

½ cup minus 1½ tablespoons/100ml whole milk,
lukewarm

⅓ ounce/10g fresh yeast, or ½ teaspoon instant yeast

1½ tablespoons granulated sugar

½ teaspoon salt

1 egg, at room temperature

2 tablespoons/30g unsalted high-fat,
European-style butter, at room temperature

9 tablespoons plus 1 teaspoon/130g unsalted high-fat,
European-style butter, cold

FILLING

⅔ cup/110g raisins

½ cup hot water

3½ ounces/100g almond paste

2 tablespoons/30g unsalted butter, softened

2 teaspoons whole milk

Pinch of salt

GLAZE

½ cup/150g smooth apricot jam

1 To make the dough: If using fresh yeast, place
the flour in a large mixing bowl. Place the milk
in a small bowl and crumble the yeast into the
milk, adding a pinch of the sugar. Stir to dissolve
the yeast. Add ¼ cup/30g of the flour and stir to
combine. Cover the bowl with a clean dishcloth and
set aside in a warm, draft-free spot for 30 minutes.
(If using instant yeast, stir the flour, yeast, sugar,
and salt together in a bowl. In a separate bowl,
whisk together the milk and egg. Make a well in
the flour and pour in the milk mixture, stirring
as you go. Roughly cube the 2 tablespoons/30g of
room temperature butter and add to the bowl. Stir
together briefly and then knead the dough by hand
in the bowl until somewhat cohesive. Proceed to the
kneading phase of Step 2.)

2 Whisk the remaining sugar and the salt into
the bowl of flour. Make a well in the middle.
Crack the egg into the well. Roughly cube the
2 tablespoons/30g room temperature butter and
add to the bowl. Scrape the yeast mixture, which
should be thick and creamy, into the bowl. Stir
together briefly, and then begin kneading with your
hands. Knead in the bowl until relatively cohesive,
and then dump the dough out onto a lightly floured

work surface and knead vigorously until you have a smooth ball that is no longer sticky. Add flour only if absolutely necessary.

3 Place the ball of dough back in the bowl and cover with the dishcloth. Set in a warm, draft-free spot to rise until doubled, 1 to 2 hours.

4 When the dough has doubled in size, gently punch it down and scrape it out of the bowl and onto the work surface. Knead it a few times. Then roll out the dough to a 13-inch/33cm square. Take the cold butter out of the refrigerator and dust it liberally with flour. Roll out the butter to a 9-inch/23cm square, adding flour as needed to keep the rolling pin from sticking. Place the butter diagonally on top of the dough and fold the corners of the dough square over the butter, encasing it completely. Roll out the dough to an 8 by 12-inch/ 20 by 30cm rectangle. Fold up the rectangle in thirds, like a business letter, and place in the refrigerator to cool for 20 minutes.

5 Remove the dough from the refrigerator and roll out again to an 8 by 12-inch/20 by 30cm rectangle. Fold up the rectangle in thirds, like a business letter, and place in the refrigerator to cool for another 20 minutes. Repeat this entire step a third time.

6 While the dough cools for the last time, make the filling: Place the raisins in a bowl and cover with the water. Set aside. Place the almond paste in a bowl and, using your fingers, knead in the softened butter, milk, and salt until you have a smooth, creamy mixture. Drain the raisins. Line a baking sheet with parchment paper.

7 After the third cooling, remove the dough from the refrigerator and place on a lightly floured surface. Roll out to an 8 by 22-inch/20 by 55cm rectangle. Spread the dough evenly with the almond cream, leaving no border. Sprinkle evenly with the plumped raisins. Roll up the dough from a short end and then slice the roll crosswise into 8 equal pieces. Place the pieces on the prepared baking sheet and cover with the dishcloth. Set aside for 20 minutes.

8 Preheat the oven to 400°F/200°C.

9 Remove the dishcloth and place the baking sheet of risen buns in the oven. Bake for 18 to 20 minutes, or until golden brown.

10 While the buns are baking, make the glaze: Warm the apricot jam in a small pot over medium heat until loose. Transfer the hot buns to a rack to cool and immediately brush them all over with the hot apricot jam. Let cool before serving.

11 The buns are best eaten the day they are made but will keep for an extra day or two in a plastic bag. To refresh them, the buns should be reheated in a 350°F/180°C oven for 5 to 8 minutes.

BREMER KÜRBISBROT
Roasted Squash Bread

MAKES 1 (17-INCH/43CM) ROUND LOAF

This glowingly orange loaf, which looks like it's made with turmeric or food coloring, is native to the Hanseatic town of Bremen, near the North Sea. The bread is made with roasted pureed squash, which gives the loaf its otherworldly color and distinctive squash flavor, as well as a pleasant amount of moistness. Most yeasted breads are really best the day they are made, but *Kürbisbrot* stays moist and tasty for a couple of days at least.

In Bremen, *Kürbisbrot* is traditionally made in autumn, when the temperature falls and winter squash appear regularly in the markets again. Lightly sweetened but not rich, the bread is good sliced and spread with unsalted butter for a simple breakfast, but people in Bremen eat it topped with slices of salami or ham as well, or even spread with liverwurst, for a sweet-salty contrast.

The recipe here makes a simple round loaf that keeps well for a few days. If you would like to make a slightly more special loaf of *Kürbisbrot*, however, for a celebration or a weekend breakfast table, add 2 egg yolks and 2 tablespoons of whole milk to the dough in the Step 2. Follow the Step 3, and then divide the risen dough into 2 equal pieces. Roll out the pieces of dough until they are both about 27 inches/68cm long, and then follow the weaving instructions for the *Schweizer Zopf* on page 209 or the *Rosinenzopf* on page 213. Place the woven loaf on the prepared pan, cover it with a clean cloth, let it rise for 45 minutes while you preheat the oven, and then bake until golden brown and hollow when tapped, 40 to 45 minutes. The bread will be richer and softer than the original recipe, sort of like a squash-flavored brioche. It is lovely sliced and spread with butter and jam, either at breakfast or as a quick and thrifty substitute for cake in the afternoon.

1 butternut squash, or 1 cup/250g canned pureed squash

4 cups, scooped and leveled/500g all-purpose flour, plus more for kneading

1 teaspoon instant yeast

½ teaspoon salt

¼ cup plus 1 tablespoon/60g granulated sugar

5 tablespoons plus 1 teaspoon/75g unsalted high-fat, European-style butter, at room temperature

Milk, for the dough and for brushing

1 To prepare the squash puree, preheat the oven to 375°F/190°C. Line a baking sheet with aluminum foil. Cut the squash in half lengthwise. Scoop out the seeds and strings and discard. Place the squash halves, cut-side down, on the baking sheet. Roast in the oven for 35 to 45 minutes, or until the squash skin is browned and blistering and the flesh is soft to the touch. Remove the pan from the oven and let the squash cool until you can handle it. Peel off and discard the squash skin. Place the roasted squash flesh in the bowl of a food processor and process until it is a creamy puree with no lumps. Alternatively, place the flesh in a large bowl and use an immersion blender to puree the squash. Measure 1 cup/250g of squash puree. Refrigerate or freeze the remaining puree for another use.

2 Place the flour, yeast, salt, sugar, butter, and squash in a large bowl and stir together until a shaggy dough comes together. Depending on how moist or dry the pureed squash is, you may need to add a spoonful or two of milk or a spoonful or two of flour to the dough.

3 Dump the dough out onto a lightly floured work surface and knead until the dough is soft, smooth, and no longer sticky. Wash and dry the mixing bowl; form the dough to a ball and place in the bowl. Cover with plastic wrap and place in a warm, draft-free spot for 2 hours. Alternatively, you can refrigerate it overnight.

4 Two hours later or the next morning, line a baking sheet with parchment paper. If the dough was refrigerated, let it come to room temperature for 30 minutes. Gently deflate the dough. Dump it out onto the counter and knead it for a few moments until the dough is smooth. Form the dough into a smooth, round ball and place on the prepared baking sheet. Cover with a clean dishcloth and place in a warm, draft-free spot for 1 hour.

5 Preheat the oven to 350°F/180°C. Brush the dough evenly with a bit of milk. Place the pan in the oven and bake for 1 hour, until the loaf is golden brown and sounds hollow when tapped. Remove the pan from the oven and place on a rack to cool. Wait until the bread has almost fully cooled before slicing and serving. The bread will keep, wrapped in plastic wrap, for a few days.

AACHENER POSCHWECK
Easter Bread with Raisins and Sugar Cubes

MAKES 1 (13-INCH/33CM) LOAF

This gorgeously burnished sweet bread has been an Easter tradition in Aachen, Germany's westernmost city, since medieval times. It was the enriched celebration bread, studded with expensive (and high-calorie) ingredients like raisins and almonds, served after the strict Lenten fast. In fact, Aachen's bakers distributed the bread to the city's residents free of charge for centuries (for much of that time against their will, as it was a most expensive bread to produce). Its name is derived from the local dialect's word for Easter (*Posch*) combined with *Weck*, a regional term for white bread rolls. *Poschweck* therefore simply means "Easter bread."

What's unusual about *Poschweck* is that whole sugar cubes are kneaded into the dough in addition to dried fruit and nuts. This makes for slightly unwieldy kneading, but when the loaf bakes in the oven, the sugar cubes partially melt, leaving behind sugar-crusted holes in the crumb, like tiny little geodes. Some sugar cubes stay intact, for an occasional pleasurable crunch as you eat. The interplay of rich yeasted dough and crunchy sugar is reminiscent of Liège waffles. Not surprisingly, the two cities are less than 37 miles/60km apart.

I call for fresh yeast in the recipe because I find that it makes for a particularly flavorful and fluffy crumb. However, if you cannot find fresh yeast where you live, instant yeast can be substituted. The bread will not be quite as exuberantly risen, but it will still taste very good.

Brushed with an egg wash and slashed three times diagonally, the dough bakes up into an impressive loaf. I like to present it as the centerpiece on my Easter Sunday breakfast table, sliced thickly, along with boiled eggs, homemade jams, and sweet butter though the bread is delicious all on its own. It is best the day it is made, but leftovers can be toasted for a decadent Easter Monday breakfast.

LOAF

¾ cup/100g chopped blanched almonds

1½ ounces/42g fresh yeast, or 2 teaspoons instant yeast

2 tablespoons granulated sugar

1 cup/240ml whole milk, lukewarm

4 cups, scooped and leveled/500g all-purpose flour, plus more for kneading

10½ tablespoons/150g unsalted high-fat, European-style butter, at room temperature

1 teaspoon vanilla extract

2 egg yolks

¾ teaspoon salt

1 cup/150g raisins

1 cup/125g sugar cubes

EGG WASH

1 egg

2 tablespoons granulated sugar

1 To make the loaf: Place the chopped almonds in a dry skillet and toast over medium-high heat, stirring constantly, until pale golden and fragrant, 5 to 7 minutes. Remove from the heat and set aside to cool.

2 If using fresh yeast, crumble the yeast into a medium bowl and add the sugar. Whisk in the milk until the yeast dissolves. Cover the bowl with a clean dishcloth and set aside for 15 minutes. (If using instant yeast, skip this step and simply add the yeast, sugar, and milk to the flour and other ingredients in Step 3.)

3 Place the flour in a large mixing bowl and make a well in the middle. Cube the butter and place in the well. Add the vanilla extract to the yeast mixture and pour and scrape it all into the well. Before mixing, add the egg yolks and the salt. Using your hands, mix everything together and knead in the bowl for about 5 minutes, until smooth and elastic. You want the dough to remain as light and floppy as possible, so resist the urge to add additional flour unless absolutely necessary (for example, if the dough still is sticky after several minutes of kneading). The more you knead, the less sticky the dough should become. At the end of kneading, the dough should be smooth and silky to the touch. Form it into a ball and let it rest on the work surface for a few minutes to relax.

4 Gently roll out the dough until it is about 1 inch/2.5cm thick. Place the raisins, toasted almonds, and sugar cubes on the surface of the dough. Gather the dough up and around the fillings and knead them in until well distributed throughout the dough. The add-ins won't incorporate right away, but be gently persistent as you knead and eventually the dough will come together again. Form the dough into a ball and put it back into the mixing bowl. Cover with the dishcloth and place in a warm, draft-free spot for 1 hour.

5 After 1 hour, preheat the oven to 350°F/180°C. Line a baking sheet with parchment paper. Gently push down the dough to knead once, and then shape into a 9-inch-/23cm-long loaf. Place on the baking sheet.

6 To make the egg wash: Whisk the egg with the sugar in a small bowl. Brush the loaf evenly all over with the egg wash. Using a very sharp (ideally serrated) knife, slice the top of the loaf three times diagonally. Set aside in a warm, draft-free spot for 15 minutes.

7 Bake for 45 minutes, or until the *Poschweck* is a rich, deep golden brown and sounds hollow when tapped. Place the baking sheet on a rack and let the loaf cool completely before serving in thick slices. The bread is best eaten the day it is made, but leftovers can be lightly toasted the next day.

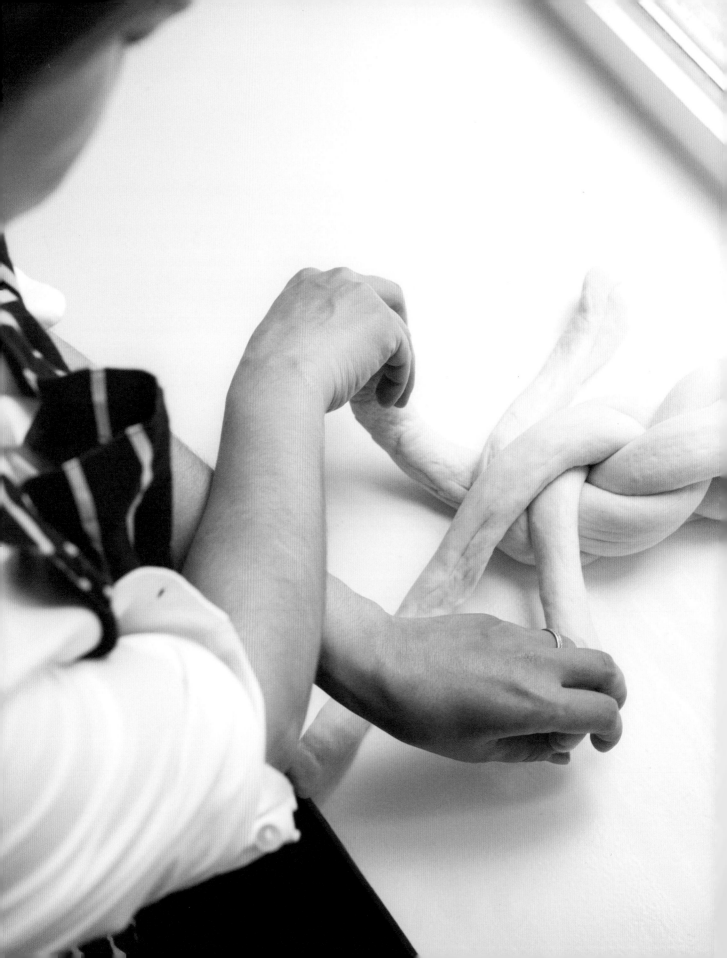

SCHWEIZER ZOPF
Swiss Braid

MAKES 2 (12-INCH/30CM) LOAVES

Many years ago, when food blogs were still a new and rare phenomenon, I was a devoted reader of the blog *In the Red Kitchen*, written by a woman from New Zealand who lived in a small Swiss town with her Swiss husband and their two children. Her posts were funny and touching, mostly about adjusting to life so far away from home and trying to figure out Swiss food and culture. I couldn't get enough and checked in as often as I could.

It was on her blog that I first read about classic Swiss-style *Zopf*, a thick, plaited white bread that she made once a week for her family. (Literally translated, *Zopf* means "braid.") She got the recipe from a Swiss farmer friend who vouched for its authenticity. That was all fine and good by me, but mostly I was bewitched by the idea that there was such a thing as a national bread in Switzerland and that it was easy enough to make at home for your family once a week. Okay, yes, it looked pretty amazing too—gorgeously bronzed on the outside and fine-crumbed snowy-white on the inside.

This recipe yields a very firm dough that must be kneaded by hand for at least 15 minutes. This time goes by faster than you would think, especially if you treat it as a kind of meditative escape. The recipe makes enough for 2 large loaves. The classic Swiss braiding technique is a little different from the German one, and it results in a loaf that is larger at one end than at the other. Instead of braiding 3 long rolled pieces as you would hair, you roll out 2 equal pieces of dough until they are the same length, place them in a plus-sign arrangement, and form the loaf by crossing the strands of dough back and forth over each other in the middle. Sara Hindrichs's YouTube channel

is a great resource for this particular technique, along with many other kinds of yeasted dough art (braids of all kinds, knots, lizards, hearts, and more).

The lovely thing about braiding the loaves (besides how pretty they look and how insanely accomplished they will make you feel) is that later, when the breads have baked and cooled and you slice into them, you can actually see the braided strands in the tight, sturdy crumb, like ocean currents. You can, however, also form the dough into smaller buns if you prefer (just be sure to reduce the baking time). I like to roll out 10-inch/25cm strands, tie them into knots, and then tuck the ends under.

Unlike German yeasted breads like *Rosinenzopf* (page 213), which have a higher fat-to-flour ratio, Swiss *Zopf* is relatively lean. It's also unsweetened, which makes it quite versatile. You don't have to wait for a special occasion to make it, and it pairs just as well with a slice of savory ham as it does with a smear of Nutella.

I recommend using fresh yeast in this recipe.

1½ ounces/42g fresh yeast, or 2 teaspoons instant yeast

Pinch of granulated sugar

2½ cups/600ml whole milk, lukewarm

8 cups, scooped and leveled/1kg all-purpose flour, plus more for kneading

7 tablespoons/100g unsalted high-fat, European-style butter, melted and cooled

1 tablespoon salt

1 egg yolk

1 teaspoon water or milk

continued

1 If using fresh yeast, crumble the yeast into a small bowl, add the sugar and a few spoonsful of the warm milk, and then whisk to dissolve. Cover and set aside for a few minutes. (If using instant yeast, stir the yeast, sugar, flour, and salt together in a large bowl. In a separate bowl, whisk together the milk and melted butter. Make a well in the flour and slowly pour in the milk mixture, stirring as you go. When you can no longer manageably stir the flour, proceed to the kneading phase of Step 2.)

2 Place the flour in a very large bowl and make a well in the middle. Pour the yeast mixture into the well. Start stirring in very small circles with a wooden spoon or fork, drawing only a little bit of flour into the yeast mixture as you stir. Then, as you continue to stir, slowly pour in the remaining milk and the melted butter, and then add the salt. When you can no longer manageably stir the dough, dump it out onto a lightly floured work surface and begin to knead. Do not add any additional flour as you knead.

3 Knead the dough for 15 to 20 minutes (set a timer if you must; the long kneading time is integral to creating the tight yet fluffy crumb). If you find yourself getting tired, step away from the dough for a minute to rest, and then continue kneading. At the end, the dough should be heavy and smooth. Wash out the mixing bowl, form the dough into a ball, and place it in the bowl. Cover it with a clean dishcloth and place it somewhere warm and draft-free for 1 hour, or until it has doubled in bulk.

4 Preheat the oven to 350°F/180°C. Line a baking sheet with parchment paper.

5 Gently tug the risen dough out of the bowl and onto your work surface. To make 2 braided loaves, cut the dough in half, place one half back in the bowl, and cover. Then cut the remaining piece of dough into 2 equal pieces. Roll out each piece until it is approximately 30 inches/75cm long. Place one roll horizontally on your work surface. Place the other roll vertically across the first roll. You will have a large plus sign in front of you. Now cross your right hand over your left hand. With your right hand pick up the left end of the horizontal roll, and with your left hand pick up the right end of the horizontal roll. Uncross your wrists and lay the pieces of dough back down. Now deal with the second roll in a similar way: take the top end of the vertical piece of dough in your right hand and the bottom end in your left hand, and then bring the top piece down and the bottom piece up. Your plus shape will now be shorter, with a quasi-knot in the middle. Repeat the process, starting by crossing your right wrist over your left wrist again, and continue until the dough strands have been completely woven together. Tuck the ends under the loaf and transfer the loaf to the prepared baking sheet. Repeat with the second piece of dough.

6 Beat the egg yolk with the water and brush each loaf with the egg wash. Place in the oven and bake for 40 minutes, or until the loaves are bronzed and sound hollow when tapped.

7 Remove the baking sheet from the oven and transfer the loaves to a rack to cool completely. This bread is best eaten the day it is made, but it will keep for a few days in a plastic bag, at which point it will taste best if toasted.

ROSINENZOPF
Sweet Raisin Braid

MAKES 1 (13-INCH/33 CM) LOAF

A lightly sweetened braided loaf of bread is a cultural touchstone all over Germany (as well as Austria and Switzerland) and has been so for many centuries. In ancient times, women would cut their braided hair off after their husbands died and put the plait in the grave along with the corpse. As in many cultures all over the world, a woman's hair had great emotional value and was a symbol of her strength and devotion. Later, braided loaves of bread replaced the actual hair and became the food that the dead would take along with them on their journey to the afterlife. The richer the family was, the more additions could be added to the loaf, such as raisins or nuts or candied fruit.

Nowadays, sweet braided loaves of bread studded with raisins have become more commonplace throughout the German-speaking world. In some regions, they are baked every weekend and eaten for breakfast or teatime, spread with butter, jam, or honey. In others, like Baden-Württemberg, they are given as gifts on New Year's Day. And in Austria and Switzerland, homemade braided loaves are still considered a traditional offering to be brought to friends who are mourning a deceased loved one on All Saints' Day, as well as to celebrate Easter. In Germany, it is also traditional to bring a sweet raisin braid to parents in honor of their new baby.

When my son was a few weeks old, my friend Joanie brought us an enormous raisin loaf that she had braided and sculpted into the shape of a swaddled newborn child, complete with a plump and peaceful little face and a quilted (!) coverlet. As if that weren't enough, she even studded the nooks and crannies of the loaf with little balls of almond paste. The loaf was almost the size of my newborn! It was also amazingly delicious, though I almost wanted to dip it in wax and keep it forever instead of eating it.

This recipe is for a great all-purpose loaf that can be tweaked depending on your taste. A little grated lemon peel gives the finished loaf a lovely floral flavor, but you can leave it out if you want a plainer loaf. You can bake the loaf with nothing but an egg wash, to help turn it a rich bronze color in the oven, or you can top it with either pearl sugar, which will stay crunchy and white during baking, or sliced almonds, which will give the finished loaf a gorgeous look and a nice added crunch—or you can use both pearl sugar and almonds.

You can also leave out the raisins completely for a plain yet still festive braided loaf. In that case, consider adding another tablespoon or two of sugar to the dough. A plain dough can be divided into 12 to 14 equal portions and shaped into individual loaves in the shape of bunnies, mice, or hedgehogs. Each roll should be rolled into a 3-inch-/8cm-long oval and brushed thinly with egg wash. Then, holding a pair of sharp kitchen shears at a 45-degree angle to the roll, snip little ears, tails, or quills into the dough. Push raisins into the dough for eyes and noses. Bake for 20 minutes, or until golden brown and puffed. These are traditionally made for Easter breakfast.

A word on the braiding, for those who feel intimidated: It's easier than it looks, but of course practice and a little bit of confidence help. The good thing is that yeasted dough is very forgiving and patient. If you feel like you've messed up your braid in some way, just undo it and start over. If you've ever braided someone's hair, you already know what you're doing. And if all else fails, knead the dough strands into a single loaf again, place in a loaf pan, and bake as a regular loaf—you'll have made something called *Rosinenstuten*, which is just as beloved and just as delicious as *Rosinenzopf*.

continued

DOUGH

1 cup/240ml whole milk

4 cups, scooped and leveled/500g all-purpose flour, plus more for kneading

¼ cup/50g granulated sugar

2 teaspoons instant yeast

1 teaspoon salt

Grated peel of ½ organic lemon (optional)

5 tablespoons plus 1 teaspoon/75g unsalted high-fat, European-style butter, at room temperature

1 egg, at room temperature

½ cup/75g raisins

TOPPING

1 egg yolk

1 teaspoon whole milk

1½ tablespoons pearl sugar (see page 7; optional)

2 tablespoons blanched sliced almonds (optional)

1 Line a baking sheet with parchment paper.

2 To make the dough: First warm the milk slightly. Place the flour, sugar, instant yeast, salt, and grated lemon peel (if desired) in a large bowl. Add the milk, butter, and egg and stir to combine. As soon as you have a slightly cohesive dough, dump it out onto a lightly floured work surface and start to knead. Knead for 10 to 15 minutes (set a timer), or until the dough is smooth and elastic. Form into a ball. Place in the mixing bowl, cover with a clean dishcloth, and place in a warm, draft-free spot to rise for 1 hour, or until doubled in size.

3 When the dough has doubled in size, gently tug it out of the bowl and onto a work surface. Knead the raisins gently into the dough, and then divide the dough into 3 equal pieces. Roll out each piece to a 16-inch/40cm strand. Braid the strands together,

tuck the ends under the loaf, and place on the prepared baking sheet. Poke any exposed raisins back into the dough or remove and tuck into the bottom of the loaf (this is to keep the raisins from burning in the oven). Cover with the dishcloth and let rise for 20 minutes.

4 Meanwhile, preheat the oven to 350°F/180°C. After 20 minutes, remove the dishcloth and check for any additional protruding raisins. Remove them or poke them farther into the dough.

5 To make the topping: Beat together the egg yolk and milk, and brush the egg wash evenly over the loaf. Sprinkle the loaf evenly with the pearl sugar, the sliced almonds, or both. Place the baking sheet in the oven and bake for 30 minutes. The loaf will turn a rich bronze. If your oven runs hot and you are worried about the loaf burning, you may cover it with a piece of aluminum foil after 25 minutes of baking.

6 Remove the baking sheet from the oven and let cool slightly on a rack. Transfer the loaf to the rack to cool further. Serve slightly warm or at room temperature, in thick slices. The bread is best the day it is made, but it will keep, wrapped tightly in plastic wrap, for 1 additional day at room temperature.

CHRISTMAS FAVORITES

The subject of German Christmas baking is so vast that, much like German bread, it deserves its own book. For the sake of conciseness in this book, I restricted myself to sharing only those recipes I truly adore and those I think are emblematic of the beautiful traditions that are still essential to Christmastime in Germany. And yet I could have easily doubled the number of recipes in this chapter.

The pomp and circumstance that surround the Advent season and Christmas not just in Germany, but in Austria and Switzerland too, are still alive and well, even in this age of materialism and store-bought cookie dough. Almost every single person I know here in Berlin, young or old, heads to the kitchen to bake Christmas cookies in early December—even those who spend the rest of the year firmly on the other side of the house from the oven.

The weeks before Advent—which starts on the fourth Sunday before Christmas—are the official start of the German baking season. Advent Sundays are when friends and family come over in the afternoon for cookies and tea or coffee, instead of the usual cakes or tortes. A generous assortment of holiday cookies, sweet breads, and marzipan confections arrayed on a big platter are enjoyed by candlelight, since at that time of year, daylight is usually gone by midafternoon. The combination of Christmas music playing, flickering candles, hot drinks, and one cookie after another shared with those who are dear to me is what I consider the epitome of coziness. This is a modern convention; in earlier times, Advent was a time of fasting, like Lent.

That groaning platter filled with homemade treats is called a *bunter Teller*, or "colorful plate." Bakers can, of course, fill the plate with whatever cookies they like, but particularly successful examples of *bunter Teller* are the ones that manage to showcase a wide variety of textures, flavors, and ingredients. My assistant, Maja, makes a magazine-worthy *bunter Teller* each year, with no less than ten different kinds of cookies, all baked in slightly smaller shapes to allow people to try more than they usually would. My friend Christa always has several thin slices of buttered *Stollen* on her *bunter Teller*, in addition to chocolate-covered gingerbread and *Baumkuchen* and sandy *Spekulatius* cookies. Christine, my Viennese friend, makes sure that hers includes chocolate-rum balls, marzipan-stuffed dates, and dark, aromatic Austrian fruitcake (page 250).

Beyond always having enough treats around to feed a group on weekends, it is also traditional to present gifts of homemade cookies packaged in little cellophane bags to colleagues, friends, and family. Luckily, there are so many Christmas cookies to choose from that a baker need never get bored. If you're doing the math, yes, this means that late November and early December require a lot of time set aside for baking. Maja, for example, makes at least one hundred cookies per recipe to fill all those bags and have enough left over for snacking at home. One year, after having baked seventeen different recipes, she had close to two thousand cookies stored in tins around her apartment!

For bakers accustomed to thinking of cookies as quick treats dropped from a spoon and finished in an hour or two, this chapter will be a bit of an education. German Christmas baking can be hard work. There are a lot of stiff batters and fussy steps, some long ripening times, and, for more than a few, some artfulness required. Traditional *Lebkuchen* doughs (page 218) are prepared as early as October so they can ripen in time for holiday baking. And *Springerle* (page 231) and *Zimtsterne* (page 241), for example,

require overnight rests. But the payoff is worth it; German Christmas baking produces some of the most flavorful and beautiful cookies around. I also include recipes for cakes associated with Christmas, like *Baumkuchen* (page 259) and *Stollenkonfekt* (page 257).

A note on texture and taste: Many of the cookies in this chapter are made with honey-based dough because, historically, honey, not sugar, was Europe's sweetener; and often the dough has no added fat other than eggs. As a result, the cookies are both chewier and drier than the cookies you might be used to. Keep in mind that the goal with many of these cookies is for them to stay fresh for a long time in an airtight container and to be eaten with hot drinks like tea or coffee, into which the cookies can be dunked to moisten them. A trick often used in Germany to keep cookies soft and moist is to place a slice of fresh bread or a wedge of apple in a tin of *Lebkuchen* or *Springerle*. (Macaroon-type cookies, which have enough moisture on their own, should be stored in airtight containers by themselves.)

LEBKUCHEN
Old-Fashioned German Gingerbread

MAKES 55 TO 65 COOKIES

There seem to be as many *Lebkuchen* recipes as there are German families. These simple *Lebkuchen*, made with a honeyed, cocoa-tinged dough, are the ones for everyone. I found this recipe on *Chefkoch.de*, Europe's largest recipe website, and was intrigued by the method for making them. You make the dough quickly enough, but instead of rolling it out, stamping out cookies, and baking them right away, you let the dough rest for at least 2 months before using it. Yes, 2 whole months! The *Lebkuchen* are leavened with potassium carbonate, also known as potash, which requires a long rest period for it to develop its leavening power. The long wait also allows the flavors of the dough to ripen fully. When we tested this recipe, we tried baking a batch of *Lebkuchen* after just a couple of weeks. They were fine, but not nearly as good as the rich and complexly flavored *Lebkuchen* made after the full 2-month resting process.

Freshly baked, the *Lebkuchen* feel improbably light and are crisp, a hallmark of potassium carbonate. If you break one apart, you'll find that the crumb looks almost honeycombed. But as the *Lebkuchen* age, they get softer and chewier. (Because they store so well, they are exceptionally well suited to shipping.) You can leave the cookies plain and unadorned; decorate them prettily with blanched and split almonds, glacé cherries, or both; or—my favorite—enrobe them in a thin coating of dark chocolate. I love the interplay of the spicy, chewy flavors of the cookie with the winey-rich chocolate coating. If you would like to coat the cookies with a sugar glaze, you must do so while the baked *Lebkuchen* are still hot, so prepare the glaze while cookies are baking. Place 1 cup/100g confectioners' sugar and ¼ cup/60ml water in a small pan over medium-high heat. Bring to a boil and cook until the water has mostly evaporated and the glaze is thick with big bubbles. Remove from the heat, timing

it to coincide with taking the cookies out of the oven. Immediately brush the *Lebkuchen* with a thin layer of the hot glaze. Double or halve the glaze quantities as needed.

To have these *Lebkuchen* ready in early December, mark your calendar in early October. Find a nice big bowl to mix the dough in and a quiet spot for storage. (I like to store mine in our pantry, which has a fairly steady low temperature.) Don't worry about the eggs spoiling during the rest time—the large amounts of sugar and honey in the dough act as preservatives and keep the eggs from growing bacteria. You'll need to buy or make some *Lebkuchengewürz* (*Lebkuchen* spice mix) for this recipe.

¾ cup/250g honey

1⅓ cup plus 1 tablespoon, firmly packed/250g light brown sugar

7 tablespoons/100g unsalted high-fat, European-style butter

4 cups, scooped and leveled/500g all-purpose flour

¼ cup/25g *Lebkuchengewürz* (page 265)

2 teaspoons ground cinnamon

Grated peel of 1 organic lemon

2 tablespoons cocoa powder

1 scant tablespoon potassium carbonate (potash; see page 8)

1 tablespoon kirsch or water

2 eggs

Blanched whole almonds (see page 7), split lengthwise (optional)

Glacé cherries (optional)

Candied citrus peel (optional)

7 ounces/200g bittersweet chocolate (55% to 70% cacao; optional)

1 Place the honey and brown sugar in a small pot and warm gently over low heat; do not bring to a boil. As soon as the sugar has melted, remove from the heat and add the butter. Let the butter melt completely. Set aside.

2 In the bowl of a stand mixer, stir together the flour, *Lebkuchengewürz*, cinnamon, grated lemon peel, and cocoa powder.

3 Stir the potassium carbonate into the kirsch to dissolve.

4 Make a well in the middle of the flour mixture and crack the eggs into the well. Attach the bowl to the stand mixer and fit it with the whisk attachment. Mix on low speed, and then continue mixing as you slowly pour the honey mixture into the bowl. With the mixer still running, pour the potassium carbonate mixture into the bowl. The potassium carbonate smells a little unpleasant, but the odor will dissipate during the storage period. Continue mixing for 5 minutes. The dough will glisten faintly.

5 Scrape the dough into a ceramic bowl and cover with a plate. The covering should not be airtight; the dough needs to be able to breathe. Place it in a cool, dark place for a minimum of 1 day. Optimally, the dough should rest for 2 months; its flavor will become more developed and nuanced, and it will be faintly tacky to the touch.

6 A couple of hours before you plan to bake, line two baking sheets with parchment paper. Assemble an assortment of cookie cutters. In Germany, hearts, bells, animals, boots, and stars are all traditional shapes for *Lebkuchen*. Scrape the dough out onto a lightly floured work surface. Knead once or twice, and then cut the dough into quarters. Working with one quarter at a time, roll out the dough to ¼ inch/6mm thickness. Cut out cookies and lay them close together on the first prepared baking sheet. Once all of the cookies are cut out and laid on the baking sheet, set them aside to rest for 1 to 2 hours at room temperature. Decorate the cookies with nuts or candied fruits, if desired, gently pressing them into the cookies.

7 Heat the oven to 325°F/165°C and position a rack in the center of the oven. Bake the cookies for 15 to 20 minutes, or until they are puffed. They should be firm and dry to the touch. Don't let the tops brown or bottoms burn. Remove the baking sheet from the oven and place on a rack to cool. Repeat with the remaining dough.

8 To coat the *Lebkuchen* with chocolate, they should be undercooked and fully cooled. Coarsely chop the chocolate, place in a metal bowl over a pot of simmering water, and melt, stirring, until smooth and glossy. Turn the fully cooled *Lebkuchen* upside down and dip them evenly into the melted chocolate. Let them cool right-side up on a rack until set.

9 When the glazed and chocolate-coated *Lebkuchen* are set, store them in an airtight container, where they will keep for at least 2 months and up to 6 months.

ELISENLEBKUCHEN
Glazed Flourless Nuremberg Lebkuchen

MAKES ABOUT 120 (2-INCH/5CM) OR 15 (3½-INCH/9CM) LEBKUCHEN

Lebkuchen, a blanket term for German gingerbread, must be one of the world's oldest cookies. Historical texts show that they have been in production since at least the thirteenth century. There is no real consensus on where the word *leb* comes from—but the most likely etymological explanation is that it is derived from the Latin *libum*, which means "pancake."

These *Elisenlebkuchen*, the archetypal German gingerbread, hail from the Bavarian city of Nuremberg and are soft and chewy round cookies baked on thin wafers called *Oblaten*. *Elisenlebkuchen* can run anywhere from saucer-size (most traditional) to bite-size, depending on the size of the wafer used as the base. Often covered in a thin glaze, either sugar or chocolate, *Elisenlebkuchen* are considered the finest of all German *Lebkuchen* varieties, of which there are dozens (also called *Honigkuchen*, "honey cake," or *Pfefferkuchen*, "pepper cake," depending on their region).

They are flourless, studded with tiny pieces of candied citrus peel, and rich in ground nuts and almond paste, which help keep them moist and chewy. The lack of flour makes not only a delightfully textured cookie, but also one that keeps incredibly well—always an important characteristic of German holiday baking in general. Like most other Christmas cookies, *Elisenlebkuchen* are supposed to be made in late November or early December and then eaten throughout the Advent run-up to Christmas.

Compared to some of the other *Lebkuchen* recipes in this book, *Elisenlebkuchen* are quite simple to make—there is no ripening time required (though the cookies taste best a few days after being baked, and their texture improves, too, becoming almost juicy). The work of spreading the batter on the wafers

and coating the *Elisenlebkuchen* with a glaze after baking is a little fussy, but the payoff is worth it. I like making them on the smaller side so that they can be eaten in one or two bites. Their chewy texture is addictive. They even ship well. For a particularly lovely homemade Christmas gift, I suggest looking online for vintage *Lebkuchen* tins and filling them with an assortment of *Elisenlebkuchen*.

To make the *Elisenlebkuchen*, you need prepared *Lebkuchengewürz* (a spice blend, page 265), candied citron and orange peel (see page 6), and the thin baking wafers called *Oblaten* (see page 270).

COOKIES

5 eggs

1¾ cups/350g granulated sugar

7 ounces/200g almond paste

3 tablespoons *Lebkuchengewürz* (page 265)

¼ teaspoon salt

Grated peel of 1 organic lemon

⅔ cup/100g candied citron peel, finely chopped (see page 6)

⅔ cup/100g candied orange peel, finely chopped (see page 6)

2 lightly packed cups/200g toasted, skinned, and ground hazelnuts, plus more if needed

2 lightly packed cups/200g ground almonds, plus more if needed

⅔ cup/100g blanched whole almonds, finely chopped

60 2-inch/5cm, or 10 2¾-inch/7cm baking wafers (see page 270)

DECORATIONS

Blanched almonds (see page 7), split lengthwise (optional)

13 tablespoons/100g confectioners' sugar (optional)

¼ cup/60ml water (optional)

7 ounces/200g bittersweet chocolate
(55% to 70% cacao; optional)

1 Preheat the oven to 300°F/150°C. Line two baking sheets with parchment paper.

2 To make the cookies: Place the eggs and sugar in the bowl of a stand mixer fitted with the whisk attachment. Grate the almond paste using the large holes of a box grater and add it to the eggs. Turn the mixer on and beat for several minutes, until well combined and frothy. With the motor still running, add the *Lebkuchengewürz*, salt, grated lemon peel, candied citron peel, candied orange peel, and all of the ground and chopped nuts. Mix until well combined.

3 Using a paring knife, split the baking wafers in half. The inside surface will be gritty. Lay the wafers, smooth side down, on the prepared baking sheets. Using a small spoon or a palette knife, mound some of the batter neatly on each wafer. The batter should be very moist and spreadable, but it should also be able to hold its shape. If it's too liquid, add a few more spoonsful of ground nuts to the batter and mix well. For the 2-inch/5cm wafers, you'll need about 2 teaspoons of batter apiece; for the 2¾-inch/7cm wafers, about 3 tablespoons. Alternatively, you can fill a pastry bag fitted with a large round tip with the batter and pipe out rounds of the batter onto the prepared baking sheet, skipping the wafers. Leave about ½ inch/12mm of space between the rounds of batter. For a traditional look, you can decorate half of the *Elisenlebkuchen* with blanched and split almonds, pressing 1 almond half lightly into the middle of each of the 2-inch/5cm rounds

of batter, or pressing 3 lightly into the middle of each of the 2¾-inch/7cm rounds of batter. (These almond-topped *Elisenlebkuchen* should be left plain after baking or glazed with the sugar glaze. The unadorned *Elisenlebkuchen* can be coated with melted chocolate.)

4 Place one baking sheet in the oven and bake until the *Elisenlebkuchen* are golden and slightly puffed, about 20 minutes for the 2-inch/5cm size and 25 to 27 minutes for the 2¾-inch/7cm size. Repeat the assembly with the remaining wafers and batter while the first batch bakes. Remove the first batch from the oven and cool on a rack. Bake the second batch.

5 To make the decorations: If you wish to coat the cookies with a sugar glaze, they must still be hot, so while cookies you want to glaze are baking in the oven, place the confectioners' sugar and water in a small pan over medium-high heat. Bring to a boil and cook until the water has mostly evaporated and the glaze is thick with big bubbles. Remove from the heat, timing this to coincide with taking the cookies out of the oven. Immediately brush each *Elisenlebkuchen* with a thin layer of the hot glaze. Double or halve the glaze quantities as needed.

6 If you wish to coat the cookies with chocolate, the *Elisenlebkuchen* should be fully cooled. Coarsely chop the chocolate, place in a metal bowl over a pot of simmering water, and melt, stirring, until smooth and glossy. Turn the undecorated cookies upside down and dip them evenly into the melted chocolate; let cool right-side up on a rack until set.

7 When the glazed and chocolate-coated *Elisenlebkuchen* are set, store them in an airtight container, where they will keep for at least 2 months and up to 4 months.

HONIGLEBKUCHEN
Honeyed Lebkuchen Squares with Caramelized Almonds

MAKES ABOUT 70 COOKIES

This recipe for cakey *Honiglebkuchen* squares studded with toasty bits of caramelized almonds has been in my assistant Maja's family for at least three generations. Instead of cutting out or shaping individual cookies as with the other *Lebkuchen* recipes, you make an entire sheet of dough that is scored before baking and broken into pieces afterward. Caramelizing the almonds takes a little time but adds great crunch and a rich toffee flavor to the cookies.

Like all *Lebkuchen*, these improve with age, so don't plan on eating them when they're freshly made. A few days of rest will do them a world of good. Another thing to note is that these *Honiglebkuchen*, much like the *Basler Leckerli* on page 229 and other honey-based doughs, are by nature on the drier side. There is no butter to keep them moist and rich, like American drop cookies, for example. Their texture, though unusual if it's new to you, is part of their appeal. It makes them particularly well suited to pairing with a hot drink.

TOPPING
36 blanched whole almonds (see page 7)

CARAMELIZED ALMONDS
½ cup/60g raw almonds

¼ cup plus 2 tablespoons/75g granulated sugar

DOUGH
¾ cup/250g honey

4 cups, scooped and leveled/500g all-purpose flour

2 eggs

½ cup minus 1 tablespoon/90g granulated sugar

¼ teaspoon salt

Grated peel of ½ organic lemon

1 tablespoon ground cinnamon

1 tablespoon ground cloves

1½ teaspoons baking soda

⅓ cup/50g candied citron peel, minced

⅓ cup/50g candied orange peel, minced

1 Line two baking sheets with parchment paper. To make the topping: Split the blanched almonds in half lengthwise and set aside.

2 To make the caramelized almonds: Coarsely chop the raw almonds. Place the almonds and the sugar in a pot over medium-high heat and let the sugar melt. Don't stir the mixture as the sugar melts. If necessary, you can swirl the contents of the pot. When the sugar has melted and is starting to caramelize, stir the mixture carefully so that all the nuts are coated with caramel. The process should take no more than 7 minutes. Then dump out the mixture onto one of the prepared baking sheets and press flat with a wooden spoon or a spatula. Let cool completely, and then coarsely chop the caramelized almonds.

3 To make the dough: Place the honey in a small saucepan over medium-high heat. When the honey is almost boiling (you will see little bubbles snaking upward to the surface from the bottom of the pot), take the pot off the heat and quickly stir in 2 cups/250g of the flour. Set aside and let cool.

4 Place the eggs, sugar, salt, grated lemon peel, cinnamon, and cloves in the bowl of a stand mixer fitted with the flat beater attachment and beat until frothy, about 3 minutes. Beat in the cooled honey mixture. In a separate bowl, whisk together the remaining 2 cups/250g of flour and the baking soda, and then knead the flour mixture into the batter by hand. Add the caramelized almonds and the candied peels; knead until well combined. The

chopped caramelized nuts are quite sharp—be careful as you handle the dough. If you have close-fitting silicone gloves, this would be a good time to use them.

5 Scrape the dough out onto the second prepared baking sheet and spread it out to a 13-inch/33cm square. This is easiest if you lay a second piece of parchment paper or a silicone baking mat on top of the sticky dough and press it out with your hands or a rolling pin.

6 Using a sharp knife, cut the dough into 1½ by 2-inch/4 by 5cm rectangles, but do not separate. Press a halved blanched almond in the middle of each rectangle. Cover the dough with plastic wrap and place the baking sheet in the refrigerator overnight or for at least 8 hours.

7 The next day, preheat the oven to 400°F/200°C. While the oven heats up, take the baking sheet out of the refrigerator and let rest at room temperature.

8 Bake the cookies for 15 minutes, or until golden brown. Place the pan on a rack to cool for 10 minutes, and then cut through the scored lines with a sharp knife. Let cool completely before separating into pieces and storing in an airtight container. The *Honiglebkuchen* will keep for at least 2 weeks and up to 1 month.

LEBKUCHEN-POWIDLTATSCHKERLN
Plum-Filled Gingerbread Pockets

MAKES ABOUT 50 COOKIES

Last fall, my husband and I went on a weekend getaway (and cake-eating research trip) to Vienna. It's just an hour from Berlin by plane and it's where my parents met and fell in love, but I had never been there before. While we were there, we met up with friends and drove out to Burgenland, a narrow Austrian state near the Hungarian border, to visit a friend's winery. We tasted all of his delicious wines, as well as a whole line of fruit vinegars, well into the night. But what really got me going was the magazine I found on the breakfast table in our little *Pension* the next morning. It featured an elaborately decorated, cherry- and almond-topped *Lebkuchen* cookie on the cover, linked to a story on regional Christmas baking from none other than Austria's Burgenland.

I'd been a little disappointed by the cakes we'd sampled in Vienna's famous coffeehouses the day before. They'd been mostly soggy and dull. But finding these family recipes from a handful of Burgenland women, who'd been baking them for decades, felt like total kismet. Back home in Berlin, I baked them all and fell head over heels for these soft little gingerbread pockets filled with *Powidl* (which is what Austrians call *Pflaumenmus*, roasted plum jam). The cookie dough is made with rye flour instead of wheat flour, which makes the cookies amazingly tender. The cookies require a bit of time: first, the dough must rest for at least 12 hours, and then the baked cookies need some days to ripen. But it's worth the wait, which gives the spices time to unfold their flavors. You'll need to make or buy the *Pflaumenmus* and the *Lebkuchengewürz* (*Lebkuchen* spice mix) beforehand (see page 270 for sources).

The cookies keep well for at least a month, which make them ideal at Christmastime in Austria, Germany, and Switzerland when cookies need to be ready by the time the first Advent rolls around at the beginning of December (sometimes it's even at the end of November). They're also ideal for shipping, if you are the Christmas cookie–mailing type. Just remember that when shipping or storing the cookies, they must be kept separate from crisp cookies because of their moisture content.

⅓ cup/70g granulated sugar

1 whole egg

2 tablespoons *Lebkuchengewürz* (page 265)

½ teaspoon baking soda

2 tablespoons water

⅓ cup plus 1 tablespoon/130g honey

2½ tablespoons/35g unsalted high-fat, European-style butter, melted

3 cups, scooped and leveled/300g rye flour

⅛ teaspoon salt

All-purpose flour, for kneading

1 cup/300g *Pflaumenmus* (page 265)

1 egg white, lightly beaten

Whole milk, for brushing

1 Place the sugar, whole egg, and *Lebkuchengewürz* in the bowl of a stand mixer fitted with the flat beater attachment and beat until frothy and creamy.

2 In a small bowl, dissolve the baking soda in the water. Add the baking soda solution, honey, melted butter, rye flour, and salt to the sugar mixture and beat to combine. The dough will be dull and not sticky. Gather the dough together and wrap in plastic wrap. Refrigerate for at least 12 hours and up to 24 hours.

3 When ready to bake, line two baking sheets with parchment paper and remove the dough from the refrigerator. Lightly dust your work surface with flour. Divide the dough in half and, reserving one half, wrapped in plastic and placed back in the refrigerator, roll out the piece of dough to ⅛ inch/3mm thick. Using a round or oval cookie cutter that is 3 inches/8cm in diameter, cut out as many cookies as you can from the dough. Knead the scraps together and roll out again to cut more cookies, repeating as necessary. You will have about 25 cookies.

4 Take one of the cut-out cookies and spoon a heaping ½ teaspoon of *Pflaumenmus* in the middle of it. Using a small pastry brush, brush egg white around the perimeter of the cookie and then gently fold the cookie, encasing the filling and pressing the edges together lightly to seal. Place the cookie

on the first prepared baking sheet and repeat with the remaining pieces of dough. Let the cookies sit at room temperature for 30 minutes.

5 Preheat the oven to 350°F/180°C.

6 Brush the top of the cookies with whole milk. Place the baking sheet in the oven and bake for 18 to 20 minutes, or until the cookies are just faintly browned at the edges.

7 Remove the pan from the oven and let cool on a rack. Repeat with the second baking sheet and the remaining dough and *Pflaumenmus*. The cookies will keep for at least 1 month in an airtight container.

BIBERLE
Gingerbread Almond Nuggets

MAKES ABOUT 96 NUGGETS

My assistant, Maja, introduced me to these wondrous little confections from Switzerland. To make them, thin gingerbread dough is wrapped around a log of almond paste, and the log is cut into nuggets and baked. The almond paste keeps the cookie soft and yielding, and the marriage of warm, wintery spices and the sharp almond flavor is inspired. At first bite, I was hooked.

As with the *Bethmännchen* (page 236), *Biberle* are a great addition to a mixed cookie plate. They are a little fussy to make, but just one batch will leave you with enough cookies for the entire Christmas season. After doing some research, I've found that Maja's method is the easiest, so I've used it in this recipe. First, you make the spiced honey dough and let it chill, which helps with the consistency later when it's time to roll it out. When you're ready to roll, you divide the almond paste into 8 portions and the chilled dough into 8 portions. You roll out one piece of dough until it's quite thin and wrap an almond-paste log tightly in the dough. You cut the log into chunks, transfer them to a baking sheet, and repeat with the rest of the dough and almond paste.

Biberle improve with age as the spices ripen. The honey in the dough, as well as the almond paste inside, keeps the cookies soft and chewy. Be sure to prepare or buy your *Lebkuchengewürz* (*Lebkuchen* spice mix) beforehand.

6 tablespoons/125g honey

7 tablespoons, firmly packed/75g light brown sugar

4 tablespoons plus 2 teaspoons/65g unsalted high-fat, European-style butter

2 cups, scooped and leveled, plus 2 tablespoons/265g all-purpose flour

1 teaspoon baking powder

1 teaspoon ground cinnamon

1 teaspoon *Lebkuchengewürz* (page 265)

⅛ teaspoon salt

10½ ounces/300g almond paste

1 Place the honey, sugar, and butter in a large saucepan and melt together over medium heat, stirring occasionally. Scrape into a mixing bowl and let cool completely.

2 In a separate bowl, whisk together the flour, baking powder, cinnamon, *Lebkuchengewürz*, and salt. Stir into the cooled honey mixture and knead together until well combined. Wrap tightly in plastic wrap and refrigerate for at least 1 hour and up to 24 hours.

3 Preheat the oven to 400°F/200°C. Line two baking sheets with parchment paper.

4 Divide the almond paste into 8 equal portions. Roll each portion out to a 9-inch-/23cm-long roll that is about ½ inch/1cm in diameter.

5 Remove the dough from the refrigerator and divide into 8 equal portions. Roll out a portion of dough between two pieces of plastic wrap to a 4½ by 9½-inch/11 by 24 cm rectangle. Remove the top piece of plastic wrap. Brush the dough very thinly with cold water. Place one of the almond logs lengthwise along the edge of the dough and

press it down lightly. Using the remaining plastic wrap as a sling, tightly roll the dough up around the almond-paste log. Make sure the seam is on the bottom. Discard the plastic wrap and roll the log back and forth a few times on the counter to get rid of any air pockets and make the seam disappear. Using a sharp knife, trim off one end of the roll at a 45-degree angle and discard. You want to cut the remaining roll into trapezoidal slices. I do this by alternating diagonal slices to the left and right. When you get to the end of the roll, discard the raggedy end piece.

6 Place the nuggets on one prepared baking sheet, leaving ½ inch/12mm between them. Repeat with more almond paste and dough until the baking sheet is filled.

7 Bake for 12 to 14 minutes, or until the nuggets are lightly browned and still soft to the touch.

8 Remove the pan from the oven and let cool on a rack for a few minutes before transferring the nuggets to the rack. They will firm up as they cool. Repeat with the second baking sheet and the remaining almond paste and dough. The nuggets will keep in an airtight container for at least 2 weeks and up to 6 weeks. They improve with age.

PFEFFERNÜSSE
Iced Spice Cookies

MAKES ABOUT 48 COOKIES

Pfeffernüsse, which translates to "pepper nuts," are little domed cookies made with the same *Lebkuchen* spice mixture as *Elisenlebkuchen* and regular *Lebkuchen*, as well as a hint of white pepper for a pleasing warmth, and a little cocoa powder for color. *Pfeffernüsse* differ slightly from region to region, but this recipe is for my favorite kind, the *Offenbacher Pfeffernuss*, which has the most wonderful texture—soft yet chewy, with a thin sugar glaze offering only the faintest bit of resistance. The baker's ammonia is crucial for achieving the delectably light texture.

The cookies come out of the oven plump and crisp, but that crispness is not long-lived. After they ripen in an airtight container for a few days, they transform into chewy specimens, becoming more complex and rich in flavor, too. As with all other *Lebkuchen*-type cookies made with hardly any fat, these cookies keep for ages in a tin and are well suited for shipping.

½ cup/160g honey

¼ cup plus 2 tablespoons/75g granulated sugar

2 teaspoons *Lebkuchengewürz* (page 265)

⅛ teaspoon white pepper

1 teaspoon baker's ammonia (see page 8)

1 tablespoon rum, slightly warmed

2½ cups, scooped and leveled/310g all-purpose flour, plus more if needed

1 teaspoon cocoa powder

¼ teaspoon salt

1 egg

13 tablespoons/100g confectioners' sugar

1 tablespoon freshly squeezed lemon juice

1 tablespoon water

1 Preheat the oven to 375°F/190°C. Line two baking sheets with parchment paper.

2 Place the honey and granulated sugar in a small saucepan over medium-high heat and warm, stirring, until the sugar is completely melted. Remove from the heat and stir in the *Lebkuchengewürz* and pepper. Set aside.

3 Dissolve the baker's ammonia in the rum. Stir into the honey mixture.

4 In a separate bowl, stir together the flour, cocoa powder, and salt. Stir this mixture into the honey mixture and add the egg. Stir or knead until well combined. The dough will be quite sticky. You may have to add a little flour as you knead, but don't add much flour or the cookies will be stiff and dry. You should be able to pluck off a piece of the dough and roll it into a ball that holds its shape.

5 Roll the dough into 1-inch/2.5cm balls. Arrange on the baking sheets, leaving ½ inch/12mm between them. Place one sheet in the oven and bake for 10 minutes—the cookies will be domed and dry to the touch but shouldn't brown.

6 While the first batch of cookies is baking, prepare the glaze. Place the confectioners' sugar in a bowl and whisk in the lemon juice and water.

7 Remove the cookies from the oven and let cool on a rack. While the cookies are still hot, paint the tops and edges thinly with the glaze. As you work, the glaze may stiffen slightly—you can whisk in a few drops of water or lemon juice to loosen it. Repeat with the second baking sheet of cookies and the glaze.

8 Let the cookies cool completely before storing in a tin, and then wait 2 to 3 days before eating. The cookies will keep, in the tin at room temperature, for several weeks.

BASLER LECKERLI
Swiss Spice Squares

MAKES ABOUT 40 COOKIES

My beloved friend Joanie, who instilled in me a love of baking and who has been my guiding light in the kitchen for many decades, is the source of these spicy little squares. *Basler Leckerli* are traditional Swiss Christmas cookies that are, as with the *Honiglebkuchen* (page 222), baked as one mass and then cut into pieces afterward and brushed with a boiled sugar glaze that crackles as it cools. *Leckerli* (which translates to "little treats") are an essential part of Joanie's annual Advent baking schedule, and even though I adore every single cookie that she makes, these are one of my two very favorites (the others are the snow-white *Springerle* on page 231).

The candied peel in the dough is crucial; you need those little pockets of bittersweet citrus flavor to counterbalance the honeyed dough and to underline the freshly grated peel. The honey makes the dough quite stiff, so you might find stirring it on the strenuous side. In fact, I like to make *Basler Leckerli* when I have stronger people than me around to help me stir and knead. But if you're alone, be patient and keep kneading. Eventually it will all come together. And just think of the workout you're getting!

The only other thing to note is that you must watch your timing toward the end of the baking time: the sugar syrup for the glaze needs to be freshly made right when the scored cookies come out of the oven, so that both are hot when you glaze the *Leckerli*. Start the glaze cooking while the cookies are finishing up in the oven and keep your eye on both the pan and the oven timer to get the timing just right.

The cookies are best if allowed to rest for a 2 to 3 days before eating; they improve with time.

¾ cup/250g honey

¼ cup plus 2 tablespoons/75g granulated sugar

¼ teaspoon salt

2⅔ cups, scooped and leveled, minus 1 tablespoon/325g all-purpose flour

2 teaspoons baking powder

1 egg, beaten

Grated peel of 1 organic orange

Grated peel of 1 organic lemon

1½ teaspoons ground cinnamon

⅛ teaspoon freshly grated nutmeg

⅛ teaspoon ground cloves

⅓ cup/50g blanched whole almonds (see page 7), finely chopped

⅓ cup/50g toasted, skinned hazelnuts (see page 7), finely chopped

½ cup/75g candied orange peel, minced

½ cup/75g candied citron peel, minced

Butter, for handling the dough

½ cup/50g confectioners' sugar

2 tablespoons water

1 Heat the oven to 400°F/200°C. Melt the honey, granulated sugar, and salt together in a small saucepan and pour into a mixing bowl. Let the mixture cool to lukewarm.

2 Sift the flour and baking powder together. Stir the egg, grated orange and lemon peels, cinnamon, nutmeg, cloves, and two-thirds of the flour into the honey mixture. Beat in the almonds, hazelnuts, and candied orange and citron peel. Add the remaining flour and stir to combine.

continued

3 Line a baking sheet with parchment paper. Butter your hands and press out the dough on the parchment paper until it's ¼ inch/6mm thick.

4 Put the baking sheet in the oven and bake for 15 minutes; turn the heat down to 350°F/180°C and bake for 10 minutes longer.

5 While the *Leckerli* are still in the oven, make a glaze by combining the confectioners' sugar and water in a small saucepan over medium-high heat. Bring to a boil and cook until the water has mostly evaporated and the glaze is thick with big bubbles. Try to time it so that the glaze is ready as soon as the cookies are taken from the oven.

6 Remove the pan of glaze from the heat. Remove the pan from the oven and place on a rack. Brush the glaze thinly and evenly all over the hot *Leckerli*. Using a sharp knife, cut into 1-inch/2.5cm squares immediately, but leave the *Leckerli* in the pan to cool to room temperature.

7 When the *Leckerli* are completely cool, break them into squares and put them in airtight containers. Wait a few days before eating. The *Leckerli* will keep for at least 2 months. A slice of apple in the cookie tin (replaced with a fresh slice every couple of days) will keep the *Leckerli* soft and chewy.

SPRINGERLE
Swabian Anise Cookies

MAKES ABOUT 20 (5-INCH/12CM) COOKIES

If you were to ask me what my very favorite Christmas cookie is, despite my abiding love for all kinds of *Lebkuchen* and chewy, jam-filled nut meringues and little almond-paste nuggets, it would have to be this one: my beloved snow-white, anise-flavored, hard-as-rock *Springerle*. *Springerle*, which come from Swabia in southwestern Germany, are molded cookies flavored simply, with lemon peel and aniseed, and leavened with baker's ammonia, which gives the cookies an incredible honeycombed crumb.

Every year, in the early days of December, Joanie, our mutual friend Ann, and I get together in one evening to make *Springerle*. Joanie and Ann, who between them have collected enough *Springerle* molds to open a small museum, spread out their molds all over the table. Joanie will have made a triple batch of this dough. She sprinkles several baking sheets with aniseed and sets them out next to us. Then we each get a spot at the table with a sharp knife, a pastry brush, and a pile of flour. It's time to get to work.

First, we select a mold we want to use. Next, we pull off a lump of dough and pat it into the approximate shape of the mold. We brush both the mold and the dough liberally with flour—you do not want any dough sticking in the intricate carving or you'll have to start over. We place the floured piece of dough on the floured table and press the mold firmly onto the dough. Then we remove the mold, use the sharp knife to trim the edges of the molded dough, and transfer the cookie to a prepared baking sheet. And then we look for the next mold. The next several hours progress in this manner, until all the dough has been used up and all the baking sheets are filled.

The cookies rest at room temperature for 24 hours to dry out. The drier the cookies get, the more detailed the image will be. There's just one more thing to do before the cookies bake: dampen a dishcloth and set every single cookie on it for a few minutes before transferring them back to the baking sheets and putting them straight into the oven. This dampening of the cookies' bottoms helps them rise and grow little "feet," which is the term for the frilly layer that develops around the cookies' edges as they rise and bake in the oven.

Once fully cooled, *Springerle* must be stored in airtight containers, where they will keep for months. Do not eat them right away; they need time to develop their flavor and, more important, their texture. When they are freshly made, in the first few weeks or so, they will be crunchy on the outside but, when pressed, their crust will shatter slightly, giving way to a soft interior. As time goes on, they will get harder and harder, eventually getting so hard that you'll be able to eat them only after dunking them in hot tea. I prefer *Springerle* when they get this hard, but others prefer to keep them soft. To do so, store the cookies with a piece of bread or a chunk of apple, which will supply them with moisture and keep them soft (replace the bread or apple every few days) .

I urge you to find molds online (see page 270) to make these. Keep in mind that wooden molds are better than ones made from other materials—they make a more precise and lovely image on the cookie. You can, if you absolutely must, roll out the cookie dough and simply stamp out shapes (keep them simple and geometric—squares, circles, rectangles) instead of using molds before baking. And yes, I grudgingly admit they will taste the same as the molded ones, but they just won't have the same appeal.

continued

2½ cups/500g granulated sugar

4 eggs

Grated peel of 1 organic lemon

4 cups, scooped and leveled/500g all-purpose flour, plus more as needed for dough and molds

⅛ teaspoon baker's ammonia (see page 8)

¼ teaspoon salt

2 tablespoons whole aniseed

1 Place the sugar in a food processor and pulse once or twice to make it finer.

2 Place the eggs in the bowl of a stand mixer fitted with the whisk attachment and add the sugar. Begin whisking at medium speed until the sugar is well incorporated, and then raise the speed. Whip for 8 to 10 minutes, until the mixture is light and fluffy. Whip in the grated lemon peel.

3 In a separate bowl, whisk together 3¼ cups minus 1 tablespoon/400g of the flour with the baker's ammonia and salt. With the mixer at medium speed, beat in the flour mixture. Then, with the motor running, add the remaining ¾ cup plus 1 tablespoon of flour by spoonsful, beating after each addition, until the dough is no longer runny but has not become dry. Scrape down the sides of the bowl, cover the bowl with plastic wrap, and refrigerate for 1 hour.

4 Line two baking sheets with parchment paper. Scatter each one with 1 tablespoon of aniseed. Set aside.

5 If you are using wooden molds, set up your work space: you will need your molds, a dry pastry brush, a little pile of flour, and a sharp paring knife. Remove the dough from the refrigerator and pull off a small lump. Cover the rest of the dough and place back in the refrigerator. Pat the dough out to be a bit larger than the mold you're using. Dust the mold liberally with flour, making sure it gets into all the nooks and crannies. Then dust the flattened dough liberally with flour. Place the floured dough on the floured mold and press it gently into the mold; turn it over, and with the dough facing the work surface, press down firmly on the mold. Remove the mold and trim the edges of the dough neatly with the knife. Then transfer the molded cookie to one of the prepared baking sheets. Repeat with the remaining dough. Alternatively, if you do not have wooden *Springerle* molds, you can simply roll out the dough on a well-floured surface until it's ¼- inch/6mm thick. Cut out cookies and place them on the prepared baking sheets.

6 When all the cookies have been formed, set the baking sheets out, uncovered, at room temperature to dry. The room should be comfortable—not cold and not humid. Leave the cookies out for 24 hours, until they are completely dry to the touch.

7 When you're ready to bake, preheat the oven to 300°F/150°C. Wet a clean dishcloth and wring it out so it's just damp. Stretch it out on the counter. Remove all the cookies from the baking sheet and place them on the damp dishcloth for 5 minutes. Then return them all to the baking sheets.

8 Bake the cookies, one batch at a time, for 20 to 25 minutes. The *Springerle* should remain white and not brown, and they should develop little "feet" as French *macarons* do. The *Springerle* will be firm to the touch but still a little soft if poked. Remove from the oven, put the baking sheet on a rack, and let the cookies cool completely. Store the *Springerle* in an airtight container for 2 to 3 months.

SPEKULATIUS
Almond Spice Cookies

MAKES ABOUT 48 COOKIES

You may be more familiar with the cookies known as *speculoos* in Belgium and *speculaas* in the Netherlands, which are more buttery and toffee-flavored than the German version. In Germany, they are called *Spekulatius* (shpeh-koo-lah-tsee-oos) and are nuttier, crisper, and lighter than their sandier western brethren. Originally, *Spekulatius* were most known in the Rhineland region of Germany, which borders Belgium. Over the centuries, however, they have become a favorite everywhere in the country.

Spekulatius belong to the category of molded cookies that depict woodcut images, like *Springerle* (page 231), certain types of *Lebkuchen*, and the Swiss *Tirggel* cookie. The ancient tradition of stamping or molding cookies came to Germany sometime in the late Middle Ages. In earlier centuries, the scenes would have paid homage to pagan deities. Those gave way to religious depictions and, later, to symbolic images and portraiture. Molded *Spekulatius* often depict individual men and women, animals, or windmills.

Since you are probably not in possession of any *Spekulatius* molds, you'll be happy to know that this recipe works just as well without them. Simply roll out the dough thinly and cut it into squares, rectangles, or diamonds before baking. Traditionally, the dough was molded into the forms and sliced almonds were scattered on the backside. After baking, the almonds were embedded in the bottom of the cookie. You can approximate this by scattering almonds on the baking sheet before laying the cookies on top of them, but bear in mind that this will cause the top of your cookies to become slightly bumpy and lumpy. An alternative is to brush the cookies with egg white and scatter the almonds on top before baking. This keeps the cookie tops smoother, but would of course not work with a molded cookie.

There are many different recipes for *Spekulatius*, but I found the basis for this recipe in a stained and shredded handmade booklet that my dear friend Joanie starting keeping when she first moved to Germany in the 1950s. I bumped up the spices and added the almonds for decoration and extra crunch.

2¼ cups, scooped and leveled/280g all-purpose flour, plus more for kneading

¾ cup/150g granulated sugar

¼ cup plus 1 tablespoon/30g ground almonds

¼ cup/25g ground hazelnuts

Grated peel of ½ organic lemon

Grated peel of ½ organic orange

2 teaspoons ground cinnamon

¾ teaspoon ground cloves

¾ teaspoon ground nutmeg

¼ teaspoon ground aniseed

¼ teaspoon ground ginger

¼ teaspoon salt

¼ teaspoon baking soda

5 tablespoons/70g unsalted high-fat, European-style butter

½ cup minus 1 tablespoon/105ml heavy cream

2 teaspoons whole milk

1 egg white, beaten

¾ cup/60g blanched sliced almonds

1 Preheat the oven to 375°F/190°C. Line two baking sheets with parchment paper.

2 In a large bowl, mix together the flour, sugar, ground almonds and hazelnuts, grated lemon and orange peels, cinnamon, cloves, nutmeg, aniseed, ginger, salt, and baking soda.

3 Melt the butter in a small saucepan over medium heat. Remove from the heat and stir in the cream and milk. The mixture should be lukewarm. Stir into the flour mixture and knead until well combined.

4 Roll the dough out on a lightly floured work surface to a 16-inch/40cm square that is ⅛ inch/3mm thick, trimming the edges if desired. Using a sharp knife, cut the dough crosswise into 8 equal strips and then lengthwise into 6 equal strips, yielding 48 cookies. Brush the cookies thinly with the egg white. Either sprinkle them evenly with the sliced almonds and transfer to the prepared baking sheets, or scatter half of the almonds evenly over each baking sheet and place the cookies on top of the almonds. In either case, leave ½ inch/12mm between the cookies. Bake the first batch for 10 minutes, or until the cookies are golden brown and firm.

5 Remove from the oven and let the baking sheet cool on a rack, where the cookies will crisp up as they cool. Repeat with the second baking sheet. Fully cooled, the cookies can be stored in an airtight container for at least 10 days and up to 1 month.

BETHMÄNNCHEN
Almond Domes

MAKES 30 COOKIES

Less of a cookie and more of a confection, *Bethmännchen* are chunky little domes of almond-paste dough that are decorated with 3 split almonds, glazed with egg wash for color and shine, and baked until chewy. A specialty of Frankfurt, they were developed in the nineteenth century by a pastry chef for the well-to-do Bethmann family.

Almond paste (*Marzipanrohmasse*) is one of the holy trinity of flavors of Christmastime in Germany. It's often paired with chocolate, but here its rich, almost alcoholic flavor shines purely. You can make your own *Marzipanrohmasse* (page 264), or you can buy it.

Bethmännchen are often considered an integral element of a well-balanced *bunter Teller* because of their small size (you can pop a whole one in your mouth at once) and pleasingly plump shape. If you combine them with the more austere-looking *Springerle*, chocolate-covered *Lebkuchen*, and perhaps some sandy batons of hazelnut cookies, you're well on your way to a *bunter Teller* to be proud of. *Bethmännchen* are gluten-free.

7 ounces/200g almond paste (page 264)

½ cup/50g confectioners' sugar

½ to ¾ cup/50 to 80g almond meal (see page 7)

Pinch of salt

1 tablespoon cornstarch or potato starch

1 egg white, beaten

45 blanched whole almonds (see page 7), split lengthwise

1 Preheat the oven to 400°F/200°C. Line a baking sheet with parchment paper.

2 Place the almond paste, the sugar, ½ cup/50g of the almond meal, the salt, and the cornstarch in a mixing bowl. Add half of the egg white to the bowl and knead together by hand. The dough will be quite moist but should not be very sticky; if necessary, add the reserved almond meal a few spoonsful at a time. You want to be able to roll the dough without too much trouble.

3 Roll out the dough on a piece of plastic wrap or parchment paper to form a cylinder 15 inches/38cm long. Cut into 30 equal pieces. Wet your hands with cold water and roll each piece into a ball, placing it on the prepared baking sheet.

4 Press 3 almond halves into the sides of each ball, with the split side against the cookie. (I like to have the pointy end of the almond pointing up.) By doing so, you will press the balls into a slightly triangular dome shape.

5 Brush all the *Bethmännchen* evenly with the remaining egg white and place one baking sheet in the oven for 8 minutes, or until the domes are lightly golden.

6 Remove from the oven and let cool completely before storing in an airtight container. Repeat with the second baking sheet. The *Bethmännchen* will keep for 2 weeks.

ZEDERNBROT
Lemon-Almond Crescent Cookies

MAKES ABOUT 65 COOKIES

I like to think of these simple, chewy, crescent-shaped cookies made with ground almonds, egg whites, and lemons as the far-less complicated cousin of the fussier *Zimtsterne* (page 241). Between the lemon peel in the cookie and the lemon juice in the glaze, they pack a powerful citrus punch that is softened by the rich, nutty flavor of the ground almonds.

Zedernbrot translates as "citron bread," and indeed, some recipes include candied citron in the cookie dough while others rely solely on the peel and juice of fresh lemons. The cookies look nicest, finer and lighter in color, if you use almond flour, the finely ground cousin of almond meal. If you grind the almonds yourself in a food processor, the cookies will be slightly more textured. I even tested these with ground unblanched almonds. The cookies were darker and coarser but no less delicious—just different.

Because the size of egg whites varies minutely from egg to egg, I had to give a range for the amount of almond flour used. Start out with 1½ cups/150g, and have more on hand in case the dough is too moist to roll out. Keep adding almond flour by spoonful until the dough is firm enough to be rolled out and stamped with a cookie cutter. *Zedernbrot* are gluten-free.

2 organic lemons

2 egg whites

1¼ cups/250g granulated sugar

¼ teaspoon salt

3 to 4 cups/300 to 400g almond flour, almond meal, or blanched finely ground almonds

1¼ cups/125g confectioners' sugar

1 Using a Microplane grater, grate the peel of the lemons into a mixing bowl. Squeeze the lemons and add 2 tablespoons of the juice to the peel, reserving the rest for a glaze. Whisk in the egg whites, granulated sugar, and salt. Add 1½ cups/300g of the almond flour and knead together until well combined. The dough should be firm enough to roll out; you may need to knead in some of the remaining almond meal. Cover the bowl with plastic wrap and refrigerate for at least 1 hour and up to 2 days.

2 Preheat the oven to 325°F/165°C. Line two baking sheets with parchment paper.

3 Remove the dough from the refrigerator and roll out between two sheets of plastic wrap until the dough is ¼ inch/6mm thick. Using a 2-inch/5cm crescent-shaped cutter, cut out cookies and transfer to the prepared baking sheets, leaving 1 inch/2.5cm between them. Periodically dip the cookie cutter in cold water to keep it from sticking to the dough.

4 Place one baking sheet in the oven and bake for 10 minutes, or until the edges of the cookies are turning golden brown but not the centers. They should still be a little soft to the touch.

5 While the first batch of cookies is baking, sift the confectioners' sugar into a bowl and whisk in 2 to 3 tablespoons of the remaining lemon juice. Set aside.

6 Remove the baking sheet from the oven and place on a rack. Wait for a few minutes and then brush the top of each cookie evenly with some of the lemon glaze. Let the cookies cool and set completely while you bake the second sheet.

7 Store the cookies in an airtight container with the layers separated by a piece of parchment paper. The cookies will keep for 2 weeks.

NUSSSTANGEN
Hazelnut-Almond Batons

MAKES 48 COOKIES

To balance out all the chewy, spicy *Lebkuchen* and nutty, crunchy macaroons at Christmastime, it is a relief to come across a nice sandy, buttery cookie that melts in your mouth. This recipe for hazelnut-flavored shortbread studded with pearl sugar and chopped nuts comes from my assistant Maja's Swabian mother-in-law, who has been making it for decades. With six children in the house, she favored recipes that could be made easily with the assistance of young helpers. In this recipe, brushing the dough with egg wash, sprinkling it with chopped nuts and sugar, and transferring the cookies to the baking sheet are all jobs that can be outsourced to small and eager hands.

Maja's husband remembers that on cookie-baking days, he and his siblings would secretly eat so much cookie dough that they wouldn't be hungry for dinner. Lest they arouse suspicion, they'd force themselves to choke down a piece of bread with ham, so that their older sisters and parents wouldn't crack down on their dough consumption next time around.

The dough is made by kneading ground hazelnuts into a short-crust dough made with confectioners' sugar instead of granulated sugar for maximum sandiness. The ground nuts add friability and a rich, toasty flavor to the dough. When the dough has been kneaded and is smooth and rolled out, it is brushed with egg yolks and sprinkled liberally with pearl sugar and a mixture of chopped almonds and hazelnuts. The nuts toast and crisp in the oven, and combined with the pearl sugar, which doesn't dissolve, they give a terrific crunch to each cookie baton.

These cookies are relatively delicate and should be kept as dry as possible, so avoid storing them with other cookies and take care when packaging.

2¾ cups, scooped and leveled, plus 1 tablespoon/350g all-purpose flour

⅛ teaspoon salt

Scant ½ cup/50g ground unskinned toasted hazelnuts

⅔ cup plus 2 tablespoons/100g confectioners' sugar

14 tablespoons/200g unsalted high-fat, European-style butter, softened

2 egg yolks

1 teaspoon water

2 tablespoons pearl sugar (see page 7)

2 tablespoons finely chopped unskinned hazelnuts

2 tablespoons finely chopped blanched whole almonds (see page 7)

1 Combine the flour, salt, ground hazelnuts, and confectioners' sugar in a large bowl. Cut the butter into cubes and add to the flour mixture. Work the butter into the flour, adding one of the egg yolks as you go, until you have a workable dough (it will be on the dry side). Wrap the dough tightly in plastic wrap and refrigerate for 1 hour.

2 Remove the dough from the refrigerator and knead again briefly. The dough will feel a little crumbly and dry. Knead until the dough is smooth and quite firm.

3 Heat the oven to 350°F/180°C. Line a baking sheet with parchment paper.

4 Using a rolling pin, roll out the dough to a 7 by 9-inch/17 by 23cm rectangle. Trim the edges. Using a sharp knife, cut the rectangle lengthwise into 12 even strips. Quarter the rectangle crosswise. Do not separate the pieces yet.

5 Beat the second yolk with the water to make an egg wash. Brush the dough evenly with the egg wash. Sprinkle the pearl sugar and finely chopped nuts evenly all over the dough and, using the palms of your hands, press the toppings very lightly into the dough to anchor them.

6 Using a bench scraper or spatula, transfer the individual batons onto the prepared baking sheet. The cookies won't spread in the oven, so you can place them close together. Place the baking sheet in the oven and bake for 15 to 18 minutes, or until the dough is biscuit colored and the nuts are toasted.

7 Remove the pan and let it cool on a rack. The completely cooled cookies will keep in an airtight container for at least 1 week and up to 3 weeks.

ZIMTSTERNE
Cinnamon-Almond Meringue Stars

MAKES ABOUT 55 COOKIES

Among my German friends, there may be no Christmas cookie more popular than the beautiful *Zimtsterne*: thick and chewy star-shaped cookies topped with a drift of white meringue that shatters under your teeth. Just the mention of them never fails to elicit deep longing sighs and a faraway look in people's eyes.

Flavored only with cinnamon and the naturally toasty flavor of roasted almonds, *Zimtsterne* are a study in what is possible with simple ingredients and a little elbow grease. Making *Zimtsterne* requires some stamina. The dough is sticky, fine motor skills are required for painting on the meringue, and you need lots of counter space to let them dry overnight before baking them. But the effort is all worthwhile.

There is much debate about how to bake *Zimtsterne* so that the cookie stays soft and chewy and the meringue as white as possible. I've tried every method out there, but find that drying the cookies overnight and then baking them briefly is the best way.

3 egg whites

⅛ teaspoon salt

1½ cups plus 2 tablespoons/200g confectioners' sugar

2¼ to 3 cups/225 to 300g finely ground raw almonds

2 teaspoons ground cinnamon

1 Place the egg whites and salt in the bowl of a stand mixer fitted with the whisk attachment. With the motor running on medium-high speed, begin whisking the egg whites. Pour in the sugar slowly and whip for 7 minutes, or until the mixture is glossy and stiff. Measure out ¾ cup and set aside.

2 Fold 2¼ cups/225g of the ground almonds and the cinnamon into the remaining egg whites mixture. Add more of the ground almonds, up to 3 cups/300g total, until you have a firm, only slightly sticky dough. Depending on the precise size of your egg whites and the grind of your almonds, you may not need the full amount of almonds. Wrap the dough in plastic wrap and refrigerate for 30 minutes.

3 Line two baking sheets with parchment paper. Unwrap the dough, leaving the plastic wrap underneath it. Place a second piece of plastic wrap on top of the dough and roll it out to ¼-inch/6mm thickness. Discard the top piece of plastic wrap. Using a 1½-inch/4cm cookie cutter in the shape of a star, cut out the cookies, dipping the cutter in cold water every so often to keep the dough from sticking. Place the cookies on the prepared baking sheets.

4 Using a pastry brush and a spoon or a toothpick, spread the reserved meringue evenly over each star, taking care to drag it out to the points of the stars. Then let the cookies sit at a cool room temperature for 12 to 24 hours. The meringue will be dry to the touch.

5 Heat the oven to 350°F/180°C and position a rack in the bottom of the oven. One baking sheet at a time, bake the cookies for 3 to 4 minutes, or until the meringue is set but still snowy white.

6 Remove the baking sheet from the oven and place on a rack. Let the cookies cool completely on the baking sheet. Repeat with the second baking sheet. Stored in an airtight container, *Zimtsterne* will keep for up to 1 month.

MAKRONENSCHNITTEN
Walnut Macaroon Slices with Jam

MAKES ABOUT 25 COOKIES

Makronen, or macaroons, are chewy cookies made from a base of sweetened egg whites and ground nuts. In the United States, coconut macaroons are the most familiar of this type of cookie, but macaroons made with ground almonds or walnuts or hazelnuts are much beloved across the spectrum here in Germany. Historical cookbooks show that they've been part of the cookie landscape for at least three centuries here, after having most likely been imported from Italy. They're typically seen as drop or formed cookies, and almost always made only around Christmastime. And often they're topped with a dollop of tart jam, which offsets the tooth-aching sweetness of the macaroon dough.

Makronen, which are gluten-free, can be made with almost any nut, though the most typical would be almonds or hazelnuts. In this recipe, which I discovered in an old Time-Life cookbook, earthy ground walnuts are paired with apricot jam. The combination works beautifully together, the tart jam cutting the richness of the nuts quite ably. And a bonus is the unfussy preparation. You make a long loaf of macaroon dough with a trough down the middle. Once the log is baked, you fill the trough with hot jam. When the jam and log have both cooled completely, you slice the log into pieces.

2 cups/175g walnut halves

½ cup/100g granulated sugar

¼ teaspoon salt

1 to 2 egg whites

⅔ cup/200g apricot jam

1 Heat the oven to 350°F/180°C. Line a baking sheet with parchment paper. Put the walnuts in the bowl of a food processor and pulse until very finely ground.

2 Put the ground walnuts in a mixing bowl and add the sugar and salt. Pour in one of the egg whites and stir until incorporated. If the mixture seems too dry and doesn't hold together, beat the remaining egg white briefly with a fork and add just enough of it to bind the dough.

3 Form the dough into 2 rolls 10 inches/25cm long and 1 inch/2.5cm in diameter. Dip your index finger or the handle of a wooden spoon in cold water and make a channel down the center of each roll, tamping down the dough as you go. Leave a ¼-inch/6mm border at each end. Place both rolls on the prepared baking sheet.

4 Bake the rolls for 15 minutes, or until lightly browned. While they are baking, heat the jam in a small saucepan. When it starts bubbling, cook for 2 to 3 minutes, stirring constantly, before removing it from the stove. Remove the rolls from the oven and tamp down the channels again (they will have risen slightly in the oven). Fill the channels with the hot jam and let cool completely before cutting the rolls into ¾-inch/2cm slices. If you have any jam left over, let it cool and then spoon it back into the jar.

5 Alternatively, you can form little balls with the dough, place them on the baking sheet about 1 inch/2.5cm apart, and then tamp a well in the center of each one. Bake the cookies for about 10 minutes and fill as directed above.

BASLER BRUNSLI
Swiss Almond-Chocolate Cookies

MAKES ABOUT 32 COOKIES

If you, like me, are an unabashed fan of the combination of chocolate and gingerbread, then *Basler Brunsli* are the Christmas cookies for you. They come from the town of Basel in Switzerland and are made by grinding almonds and chocolate to a fine rubble and then kneading them together into a dough with egg whites for chew, and kirsch (or dark rum) for a plummy aroma.

After mixing, the dark, textured dough is chilled for a bit and then rolled thickly and cut out. Hearts are the most traditional shape for *Basler Brunsli,* though you could cut out any shape as long as it is relatively simple, such as a square or a circle. The dough is too coarse for more fiddly shapes like stars or animals. The cookies are briefly baked at a relatively low temperature, mostly just to dry them out a touch. As they cool, they go from soft to chewy. Don't worry; the alcohol in the kirsch burns off in the oven, making these absolutely fine for children. Some cinnamon and cloves give the mixture a wintry flair. *Basler Brunsli* are gluten-free.

I am pleased to report that I have made *Brunsli* with everything from fancy dark chocolate to the no-name baking chocolate I can buy at the corner store, and they don't seem to suffer from the lower-quality chocolate at all. So use what you like. As with other chewy macaroon-type cookies, these should be stored on their own and not with crisper cookies, which will draw out their moisture.

1²⁄₃ cups/250g raw almonds

9 ounces/250g bittersweet chocolate (60% to 70% cacao)

1½ cups/180g confectioners' sugar

¼ teaspoon salt

¼ teaspoon ground cinnamon

⅛ teaspoon ground cloves

3 egg whites

2 tablespoons kirsch or dark rum

Granulated sugar, for rolling

1 Place the almonds in a food processor and grind until very fine, but do not let them turn to a paste. Transfer to a large bowl. Break the chocolate into pieces and place in the food processor. Pulse until finely ground but not melted. If your kitchen is warm, refrigerate the chocolate before pulsing. Transfer to the bowl with the almonds.

2 Add the confectioners' sugar, salt, cinnamon, and cloves to the bowl and mix until combined. Stir in the egg whites, one at a time, and then stir in the kirsch. Stir or knead until well combined. Cover the bowl with plastic wrap and place in the refrigerator for 12 to 24 hours.

3 When you are ready to bake, preheat the oven to 300°F/150°C. Line two baking sheets with parchment paper.

4 Remove the bowl from the refrigerator. Scatter granulated sugar on your work surface. Place the dough on the sugar and cover with the plastic wrap. Roll out to ⅓ inch/8mm thickness. Using a heart-shaped or round cookie cutter, cut out 2-inch/5cm cookies and transfer to the prepared baking sheets, leaving ½ inch/12mm between them. Place one baking sheet in the oven and bake for 18 minutes. The cookies will be dry to the touch but soft. Place the baking sheet on a rack to cool. Repeat with the remaining baking sheet.

5 When the cookies have cooled completely, store them in a tin. They'll keep for at least 1 month.

HASELNUSS-HIMBEER MAKRONEN
Hazelnut-Raspberry Macaroons

MAKES ABOUT 30 COOKIES

Hazelnuts and raspberries go together like, well, cabbage and caraway. The combination of the two is hard to beat. Unlike the walnut macaroons on page 242, this recipe is made by beating egg whites until stiff and then folding in roasted, ground hazelnuts. Pieces of the dough are then pinched off, rolled into balls, and baked. While they're still soft, you press a well in the middle of each cookie and fill it with hot raspberry jam. It's important that the raspberry jam be brought to boiling once before you use it as a cookie filler; this way it sets quickly and won't run.

Because of the ubiquity of nut macaroons at Christmastime in Germany, I put this recipe in the Christmas chapter. But the reality is that these cookies are wonderful all year long. Better still, they keep well, so feel free to make a double batch. They are, of course, gluten-free.

Buy your hazelnuts at a store with high turnover and store them in the freezer, as they go rancid quickly. Toasting them before grinding is important, because it truly transforms the flavor of the hazelnut into something rich, sweet, and deep.

1¾ to 2¼ cups/230 to 290g whole unskinned hazelnuts

2 egg whites

¼ teaspoon salt

¾ cup/150g granulated sugar

½ cup/150g raspberry jam

1 Preheat oven to 400°F/200°C.

2 Place the hazelnuts on a baking sheet in a single layer and toast in the oven for 15 minutes, or until fragrant. Lay a clean linen dishcloth flat on a work surface and dump the hot hazelnuts onto the dishcloth. Gather the dishcloth around the hazelnuts

and rub them together, massaging them until they are mostly skinned (don't worry about removing the skins entirely). Let the nuts cool completely.

3 Line two baking sheets with parchment paper. Place the nuts in a food processor and pulse until finely ground, but not so long that they turn into a paste.

4 Place the egg whites and salt in a spotlessly clean mixing bowl and whip until frothy. Slowly add the sugar and continue beating until the egg whites have formed soft peaks. The sugar will not be completely dissolved. Fold in all but ¼ cup/25g of the ground hazelnuts until well combined. The mixture should be thick but should hold its shape when dropped from a spoon. Add some of the remaining hazelnuts if needed, folding in until well combined.

5 Using two small spoons, scoop out heaping teaspoonsful of batter and mound on the prepared baking sheets, leaving about 1 inch/2.5cm between them. Place one baking sheet in the oven and bake for 10 minutes, or until golden brown. Remove from the oven and, using the back of a teaspoon, immediately press a well into the center of each cookie. Transfer the cookies to a rack and repeat with the remaining batch.

6 When all the cookies are on the rack and are still warm, heat the raspberry jam in a small pot over medium heat until liquefied and let it bubble for 30 seconds. Spoon a little bit of the hot jam into the well of each cookie. Let the jam set and the cookies cool completely.

7 Store in an airtight container with parchment paper between the layers. The cookies will keep for at least 1 week and up to 3 weeks.

WEIHNACHTSPLÄTZCHEN
Simple Christmas Cookies

MAKES ABOUT 55 COOKIES

Every German baker has a recipe for simple Christmas cookies in his or her archive—the kind of endlessly riffable, easy-to-make dough that comes together in no time, is good for baking with children, and produces crisp, delicious cookies that can be decorated for both young (lemon glaze with sprinkles) and old (rum glaze with glacé cherries). The combination of grated lemon peel and vanilla extract in the dough is essential for giving the cookies a lovely and delicate floral flavor, while the confectioners' sugar and egg yolk make the cookies deliciously friable.

I've made this recipe using all white flour, half white and half whole wheat flour, and even four parts whole wheat to one part white flour, and the cookies always turn out wonderfully. The whole wheat flour gives the cookies a nutty, wholesome flavor. You can also try subbing in a ground nut flour for some of the flour to make a sandier, richer cookie. You can use this dough to make *Spitzbuben*, jam sandwich cookies. Cut out an equal amount of round cookies and rings and bake. Cover each round cookie with a spoonful of hot raspberry jam, and then sandwich a ring-shaped cookie on top. Once the cookies have fully cooled, dust with confectioners' sugar, if desired. Another alternative is *Terrassenplätzchen*, which are three circular cookies of varying sizes stacked in a pyramid with hot raspberry jam between the layers, and then dusted with confectioners' sugar when cool.

This is my favorite dough to make with my three-year-old on a dark December afternoon. He pushes his stool up to the kitchen counter and helps cut out cookies with his favorite cookie cutters; afterward he decorates the finished cookies with his favorite candies when I've spread on a thin layer of glaze. When he has gone to bed, I usually make another batch that I use for jam sandwich cookies and for

tins of backup cookies in the Advent season. When friends come over for tea, a whole batch of these cookies can easily disappear in a single afternoon.

One thing to keep in mind for storage: The glazed, decorated cookies will soften sooner than the unglazed cookies.

COOKIES

2 cups, scooped and leveled/250g all-purpose flour

7 tablespoons/100g unsalted high-fat, European-style butter, softened

½ cup/100g confectioners' sugar

½ teaspoon baking powder

Grated peel of ½ organic lemon

⅛ teaspoon salt

1 egg yolk

2 tablespoons whole milk

1 teaspoon vanilla extract

1 whole egg, beaten (optional)

Heavy cream (optional)

DECORATIONS

13 tablespoons/100g confectioners' sugar (optional)

2 to 3 tablespoons freshly squeezed lemon juice, kirsch, or rum (optional)

Sprinkles, silver dragées, or candy lozenges (optional)

Glacé cherries (optional)

Raspberry jam (optional)

1 To make the cookies: Place the flour and butter in a large bowl and work together by hand until clumpy, as for streusel. In a separate bowl, whisk together the confectioners' sugar, baking powder, grated lemon peel, and salt. In a third bowl, whisk together the egg yolk, milk, and vanilla extract.

2 Dump the sugar mixture into the bowl with the flour mixture and start working together with one hand while you pour the egg mixture in with the other. Knead the dough together until well combined and smooth. Cover and refrigerate for 1 hour.

3 Preheat the oven to 350°F/180°C. Line two baking sheets with parchment paper. Remove the dough from the fridge.

4 Break off half of the dough and place on a lightly floured surface. Roll out until very thin (just a few millimeters) and cut out cookies using cookie cutters. Arrange the cookies on the prepared baking sheets, leaving ½ inch/12mm between them. If you like, brush the cookies thinly with beaten egg or heavy cream, which will give the cookies some color and shine after baking. If you plan on glazing the cookies, skip this step.

5 Bake one sheet of cookies for 10 minutes, or until pale golden brown. Remove from the oven and put the baking sheet on a rack to cool. Bake the second sheet of cookies, and then repeat with the remaining dough.

6 To decorate the cookies: When the cookies have fully cooled, you can glaze them if you wish. Whisk together the confectioners' sugar and lemon juice to make a very thick glaze. (To make these cookies slightly more adult, substitute kirsch or rum for the lemon juice.) Using a butter knife or palette knife, spread a thin layer of glaze on each cookie. Arrange the sprinkles or other decorations on the still-wet glaze, and then return the cookies to the rack to set. Alternatively, you can heat raspberry jam in a small pot until loose and bubbling and use teaspoonsful to sandwich 2 cookies together. Return to the rack to set. Stored in an airtight container, the cookies will keep for at least 1 week and up to 2 weeks.

VANILLEKIPFERL
Melting Vanilla-Almond Crescents

MAKES ABOUT 50 COOKIES

If Austria has a more famous cookie than the powdery, sandy, meltingly tender *Vanillekipferl*, I have yet to meet it. A buttery vanilla-scented dough is made with ground almonds and confectioners' sugar for an exceptionally tender texture. Shaped into little crescents and baked until just set, the cookies are incredibly delicate—even just picking them up with anything less than a gentle touch will break them.

While still hot from the oven, the crescents are dredged in confectioners' sugar mixed with ample amounts of *Vanillezucker* (vanilla sugar). Making your own vanilla sugar (see page 267) will give the *Kipferl* an even more luxurious fragrance. *Vanillekipferl* will stay fresh for several weeks and are, in their stark simplicity, a welcome change from all the spiced honey-based cookies and chewy macaroons.

The classic recipe is made with ground almonds, but regional differences abound, so feel free to swap in ground hazelnuts or ground walnuts for the almonds. Using ground walnuts purportedly makes the most moist *Kipferl*. If you can buy almond meal, that will give you the sandiest, finest cookies. If you grind your own nuts for this recipe, take care to grind them very finely, without turning them into butter.

1⅔ cups, scooped and leveled, plus 1 tablespoon/175g all-purpose flour

8½ tablespoons/120g unsalted high-fat, European-style butter, at room temperature

2 cups plus 1 tablespoon/250g confectioners' sugar

2 tablespoons *Vanillezucker* (page 267)

1 cup/100g very finely ground blanched almonds (see page 7) or almond meal

1 egg yolk

Pinch of salt

1 Put the flour, butter, ¼ cup/50g of the confectioners' sugar, 1 tablespoon of the *Vanillezucker*, and the ground almonds, egg yolk, and salt in the bowl of a stand mixer fitted with the flat beater attachment. Beat together, starting off slowly so the flour doesn't fly everywhere, until a smooth dough develops.

2 Divide the dough into 3 equal portions and roll each portion into a 1-inch-/2.5cm-thick cylinder. Wrap the rolls individually in plastic wrap and refrigerate for at least 1 hour and up to 24 hours.

3 When you're ready to bake, heat the oven to 325°F/165°C and line two baking sheets with parchment paper.

4 Remove one roll from the refrigerator and cut it into ½-inch/12mm slices. Roll out each slice until it's about 2 inches/5cm long and the ends are tapered but not pointy. Form each into a crescent and place on one of the prepared baking sheets. Repeat with the remaining dough until the baking sheet is filled. The cookies should have about 1 inch/2.5cm of space between them on all sides.

5 Bake for 10 to 15 minutes, or until the cookies are just lightly browned. Repeat with the remaining dough.

6 Mix together the remaining 1¼ cups/125g confectioners' sugar and the remaining tablespoon of *Vanillezucker* in a wide, shallow bowl. Remove the cookies from the oven, let cool for only a minute or two, and then—very carefully as the cookies are quite delicate—dredge them completely in the sugar. Place on a rack to finish cooling. The cooled cookies can be stored in an airtight container for up to 3 weeks.

GEFÜLLTE ORANGENTALER
Candied Orange Sandwich Cookies

MAKES ABOUT 33 SANDWICH COOKIES

These flourless (and thus, gluten-free) almond macaroons are studded with candied orange peel for a pleasingly bitter note, and sandwiched together with a thin film of melted chocolate. The batter is simple to prepare, but it is essential that the almond paste (*Marzipanrohmasse*) you use be fresh and soft—you need it to break down with the sugar and egg whites when you beat them together. The batter is spooned or piped out in rounds, which are baked until they are pale gold, chewy, and light.

My son has loved bitter orange marmalade since he was a baby; we used to sit at the breakfast table together, him with his bowl of oatmeal looking pleadingly at me with my buttered toast spread with homemade Seville orange marmalade, until I offered him a piece of candied orange peel, and then another, and another. He can make light work of these cookies plain, but I like to make them Christmas-worthy by sandwiching the rounds together with a little bit of melted chocolate. If the texture of candied orange peel is problematic for you, you can work around it by pureeing the orange peel with the egg white and then adding this mixture to the grated almond paste and sugar.

If you don't want to make sandwich cookies, you can simply drizzle the top of each cookie with some melted chocolate. Just remember not to overdo it; you really want the bittersweet orange and winey almond flavor to shine here.

10½ ounces/300g almond paste

1½ cups/180g confectioners' sugar

⅛ teaspoon salt

⅓ cup/50g finely diced candied orange peel

2 egg whites

2⅔ ounces/75g chopped bittersweet chocolate (50% to 70% cacao)

1 Preheat the oven to 375°F/190°C. Line two baking sheets with parchment paper.

2 Grate the almond paste into a mixing bowl and add the sugar, salt, orange peel, and egg whites. Using an electric mixer fitted with the flat beater attachment, mix together until well combined. Scoop out heaping teaspoonsful of the batter and place on the prepared baking sheets, leaving 1 inch/2.5cm between them. Alternatively, you can scrape the mixture into a pastry bag fitted with a round tip and pipe out round cookies.

3 Bake one sheet of cookies for 10 minutes, or until the cookies are puffed and golden brown. Remove from the oven and gently tug the parchment paper, with the cookies attached, onto a rack. Repeat with the second baking sheet of cookies.

4 When all of the cookies have fully cooled, melt the chocolate in a microwave in short bursts or in the top of a double boiler set over simmering water. Using a pastry brush, paint a thin layer of chocolate on the bottom of one cookie, and then press the bottom of a second cookie against the chocolate to sandwich them together. Place on a baking sheet to let the chocolate set. Repeat with the remaining cookies. Alternatively, if you don't want to make sandwich cookies, you can drizzle a little bit of melted chocolate in a zigzag over the tops of the cookies.

5 Let the chocolate set for at least 2 hours before transferring the cookies to an airtight container. The cookies will keep for 2 weeks.

FRÜCHTEBROT
Austrian Fruit Bread

MAKES 4 (8-INCH/20CM) LOAVES

Our family friend Christine's platters of Christmas confections, which she passes out as gifts each year, are veritable works of art. Each platter holds an assortment of tiny, perfectly crafted morsels, from exquisitely light meringues to rich chocolate-brandy balls, and from marzipan-stuffed dates to the sandiest *Vanillekipferl*. But my favorite thing on her platter each year is her dark and aromatic fruit bread, cut into sticky slices.

Dark and heavy loaves made with dried fruit are an integral part of the Advent baking tradition in Germany and Austria. The traditional dried fruit used for *Früchtebrot* is a type of pear called *Kletze* or *Hutze*, depending on the region. Long before more exotic fruits, such as dates, raisins, and figs, were available in northern and central Europe, these shriveled pears were a reliable local product. While *Kletzenbrot* or *Hutzelbrot* is still quite popular regionally, fruit breads in Germany have evolved today to include all kinds of dried fruits, spices, and nuts. Some are leavened with yeast or baking powder; others have a sourdough base.

The "batter" for Christine's wonderful *Früchtebrot* is quite simple and consists largely of chopped dried dates, figs, and raisins, plus blanched almonds, all soaked in an abundant quantity of dark rum. (Rum is traditional, but I have made this with bourbon, too.) Eggs, confectioners' sugar, and flour help to produce sturdy, sliceable loaves, which make excellent gifts. The *Früchtebrot* stores well for a couple of weeks and improves with age. The rum aroma in the finished loaves is mild, not biting. In other words, unlike some fruit breads from other parts of Europe, it won't leave you tipsy.

Feel free to play with the types and quantities of dried fruit you use here. Golden raisins and dried pears would be excellent swap-ins.

1 pound 1 ounce/500g pitted dried dates

8¾ ounces/250g dried figs

7 ounces/200g prunes

½ cup/75g raisins

1 cup/150g blanched whole almonds (see page 7)

1½ cups plus 2 tablespoons/200g confectioners' sugar

½ cup/120ml dark rum

2¼ cups, scooped and leveled/280 grams all-purpose flour

4 eggs

1 Chop the dried dates, figs, and prunes into ¼-inch/6mm pieces, put them in a large bowl, and mix in the raisins. Coarsely chop the almonds by hand or in a food processor until pebbly. Add the almonds to the fruit and stir in the sugar. Pour the rum into the bowl and mix until well combined, with no streaks of sugar. Cover with a clean dishcloth and let sit at room temperature for 8 hours or overnight.

2 When ready to bake, preheat the oven to 350°F/180°C. Line a baking sheet with parchment paper.

3 Remove the dishcloth from the bowl and add one-quarter of the flour. Mix well and add an egg. Mix well. Repeat with the next one-quarter of the flour and egg, mixing well after each addition. Repeat with the remaining flour and eggs. The dough will become increasingly stiff and difficult to mix, but do your best. After you've added all the flour and eggs, use your hands to knead the dough, which will

be quite sticky, making sure that all the flour and eggs have been well mixed into the dough.

4 Divide the dough into quarters. Wet your hands with cold water and form each quarter into an 8-inch/20cm long loaf. Place them on the baking sheet.

5 Put the baking sheet in the oven and bake for 35 minutes, or until the loaves are golden brown and dry to the touch. Place the pan on a rack and let the loaves cool completely. To store, wrap the loaves in plastic wrap and then aluminum foil. The *Früchtebrot* will keep for 2 weeks. Before serving, slice very thinly (⅛ inch/3mm) with a sharp or serrated knife.

CHRISTBROT

Sweet Christmas Bread

MAKES 2 LOAVES

I tried, I really did, to find an excellent, reliable recipe for homemade *Stollen*, that heavy, raisin-studded holiday sweet bread with its distinctive folded shape and thick coating of confectioners' sugar. But every *Stollen* I tried failed to live up to my expectations. With each successive loaf, I felt more and more like Goldilocks, except without the eventual appearance of Baby Bear's perfect bowl of porridge. My *Stollen* turned out too hard, too flat, or too insipid, and none were anywhere near as delicious as the ones you can buy at the bakery.

I was starting to despair. What kind of German baking book would this be without *Dresdner Christstollen*, after all? And then I came across a recipe for *Christbrot*, which has the same gorgeous flavoring as *Stollen*—rum-soaked candied peels and raisins, thick drifts of vanilla-scented sugar on top—but with far less butter than in *Stollen*, which allows the dough to rise higher and develop a fluffier, lighter crumb.

Unlike *Stollen*, which must rest for at least 2 weeks after being baked before it can be eaten, *Christbrot* requires no storage period and can be eaten right away. It also freezes very well (wrap a cooled loaf well in aluminum foil before freezing). Once defrosted, it requires nothing more than a dusting of more confectioners' sugar to prettify it before it is served.

If possible, use fresh yeast here.

DOUGH

¾ cup/110g raisins

⅔ cup/100g chopped candied orange peel

⅔ cup/100g chopped candied citron peel

¼ cup/60ml dark rum

4¾ cups, scooped and leveled/600g all-purpose flour, plus more for kneading

1¼ ounces/35g fresh yeast, or 1½ teaspoons instant yeast

½ cup/120ml whole milk, lukewarm

8½ tablespoons/120g unsalted high-fat, European-style butter, melted and slightly cooled

2 eggs

⅓ cup/70g granulated sugar

¼ teaspoon salt

Grated peel of 1 organic lemon

¾ cup/110g blanched whole almonds (see page 7), chopped

TOPPING

½ vanilla bean

½ cup/100g granulated sugar

9 tablespoons plus 1 teaspoon/130g unsalted butter, melted

13 tablespoons to ¼ cups/100 to 150g confectioners' sugar

1 To make the dough: Two days before baking, place the raisins and candied citrus peels in a bowl and add the rum. Cover and set aside, stirring occasionally.

continued

2 The day you plan to bake, finish making the dough: If using fresh yeast, place the flour in a large bowl and make a well in the middle. Crumble in the fresh yeast. Pour one-third of the milk over the yeast, stirring carefully with a fork to dissolve the yeast and mix in a little bit of the surrounding flour. Cover the bowl with a clean dishcloth and set aside for 5 minutes in a warm, draft-free spot. (If using instant yeast, stir the flour, yeast, sugar, salt, and grated lemon peel together in a large bowl. In a separate bowl, whisk together the milk, melted butter, and eggs. Make a well in the flour and pour the milk mixture into the well, stirring as you go. Knead briefly by hand in the bowl until a shaggy dough forms, then proceed to the kneading phase in Step 3.)

3 In a separate bowl, whisk together the butter, eggs, sugar, salt, and grated lemon peel. Pour this mixture into the bowl with the flour and stir together until shaggy. Dump the dough out onto a lightly floured work surface and knead by hand until smooth, 5 to 7 minutes. Add flour only if absolutely necessary. Form the dough into a ball and place back in the large bowl. Cover with a clean dishcloth and set aside in a warm, draft-free spot for 30 minutes.

4 Gently pull the dough onto your work surface and pat out until about 1 inch/2.5cm thick. Distribute the chopped almonds and rum-soaked fruit (including any dregs of rum that may still be in the bowl) over the dough, and then gather the sides up around the fruit and almonds. Knead together until the fruit and nuts are well distributed throughout the dough. Form the dough into a ball, place back in the bowl, and cover with the dishcloth. Set aside for another 30 minutes.

5 Line a baking sheet with parchment paper.

6 Divide the dough in half and form each half into a round loaf. Place the loaves on the prepared baking sheet, cover with the dishcloth, and set aside for 30 minutes.

7 Meanwhile, preheat the oven to 400°F/200°C. Place the baking sheet in the oven and bake for 40 minutes, or until the loaves are a deep golden brown.

8 While the loaves are baking, make the topping: Place the vanilla bean in a small food processor with 2 tablespoons of the granulated sugar and process at high speed until the vanilla bean is pulverized and the sugar is turning to powder. Combine with the remaining ¼ cup plus 2 tablespoons/75g granulated sugar and set aside.

9 Remove the baking sheet from the oven. Let the loaves cool on a rack for 5 minutes. Then brush the loaves evenly with all of the melted butter. You will need to do this in several coats. When all of the butter has been brushed onto the loaves, sprinkle the vanilla sugar evenly all over the buttered loaves, lifting up the loaves to coat the sides evenly as well. Then sift the confectioners' sugar evenly all over the loaves, making sure you coat the sides as well. Let the loaves cool completely.

10 When the loaves are completely cool, wrap them in aluminum foil. The loaves can be frozen at this point for up to 1 month (defrost at room temperature) or served in slices.

QUARKSTOLLEN
Quark-Almond Sweet Bread

MAKES 1 (12-INCH-/30CM-LONG) LOAF

For those who hate raisins—and I know there are many of you out there—German baking can be challenging. From *Rosinenzopf* (page 213) to *Käsekuchen ohne Boden* (page 50), from *Gedeckter Apfelkuchen* (page 46) to *Aachener Poschweck* (page 206), raisins abound. And let's not even get started with *Stollen*, whose raison d'être (or, as the case may be, raisin d'être) is basically a raisin delivery system suspended in a few delicious shreds of yeasted dough.

Luckily, Germany has a work-around for this problem. It's called *Quarkstollen*. Unlike a traditional *Stollen*, it's not made with yeasted dough, but is a baking powder–leavened dough made with a healthy scoop of *Quark* for moisture and tenderness. Ground almonds and toasted slivered almonds give the loaf heft and flavor, while lemon peel scents it. It's a supremely easy thing to make—a relief in the crazy baking time that is December—and it requires no monthlong ripening process, as a traditional *Stollen* would.

But now, the brief story of a convert: When my assistant, Maja, started working with me on this book, she confessed an aversion to raisins. I didn't dwell on it—we had too many recipes to test and many of them called for raisins. Maja baked, tasted, and endured those raisin-studded loaves and cakes so professionally that I forgot all about her aversion. The funny thing is that she did, too. By the time the recipe testing was drawing to a close, Maja was actually reaching for things with raisins in them, *on purpose*. Sometimes she even suggested they go in a recipe that needed a little extra oomph. I'm not sure who was more surprised!

However, Maja's husband, Bertram, who was kind enough to give us this recipe, still thinks raisins are the devil's work.

1 cup plus 2 tablespoons/150g slivered almonds

1 cup/100g ground blanched almonds (see page 7)

3¼ cups, scooped and leveled, minus 1 tablespoon/400g all-purpose flour

1 tablespoon baking powder

¾ cup/150g granulated sugar

¼ teaspoon salt

Grated peel of 1 organic lemon

8½ tablespoons/120g unsalted high-fat, European-style butter, at room temperature

1 cup/250g *Quark* (page 264), drained if necessary (see page 8)

2 eggs

Confectioners' sugar, for dusting

1 Preheat the oven to 350°F/180°C. Place the slivered almonds on a baking sheet and toast until golden brown and fragrant, 7 to 10 minutes. Remove from the oven and let cool. Line a second baking sheet with a piece of parchment paper.

2 Place the toasted slivered almonds, ground almonds, flour, baking powder, granulated sugar, salt, grated lemon peel, butter, *Quark*, and eggs in a bowl. Stir together to start with, and then knead together until well combined. The dough will be quite sticky. Form into a 6 by 12-inch/15 by 30cm rectangle and place on the prepared baking sheet.

3 Bake for 60 to 65 minutes, or until golden brown. Place on a rack to cool completely. Dust with confectioners' sugar before serving. The *Stollen* can be eaten the day it is made, but it will also keep, wrapped in plastic wrap, at room temperature for 3 to 4 days. The stale *Stollen* can be sliced and toasted for breakfast.

STOLLENKONFEKT
Bite-Size Stollen

MAKES ABOUT 36 PIECES

As I mentioned on page 252, making *Stollen* is not for the faint of heart. Avoiding it altogether because excellent store-bought *Stollen* abounds is further abetted by the invention of *Stollenkonfekt,* bite-size chunks of spiced, tender *Quark* dough studded with almonds and raisins and thickly cloaked in vanilla-scented confectioners' sugar. They may be a relatively recent development in the world of *Christstollen,* which dates back to the Middle Ages, but they more than make up for their youth. In other words, want the rich, buttery, spicy flavor of *Stollen* without the work of a yeasted dough and the weeks of impatiently waiting for the loaves to be ready? If so, *Stollenkonfekt* is the thing for you.

Instead of being leavened with yeast, the basis of *Stollenkonfekt* is a *Quark*-enriched dough made with baking powder. You cram more raisins and almonds than you would think possible into the dough, which is flavored with the trio of *Stollen* spices: cinnamon, cloves, and cardamom. Then you pinch off little lumps of dough and bake them until they're just turning a light golden brown. After a quick dip in a molten butter bath and a roll in a bowl of powdery *Vanillezucker* (vanilla sugar), the *Konfekt* only have to cool off before they're ready to eat. That said, I find that *Stollenkonfekt* that have had a few days to rest taste even better than when fresh from the oven. The spices ripen and the texture settles.

An added bonus which is admittedly more about vanity than anything else, is that *Stollenkonfekt* are easier to arrange on a platter with other Christmas cookies than slices of *Stollen* loaf. And while *Stollenkonfekt* don't have the shelf life of regular *Stollen,* they'll keep for at least 10 days in an airtight container. They are surprisingly sturdy for such tender little things.

DOUGH

7 tablespoons/100g unsalted high-fat, European-style butter, at room temperature

⅓ cup plus 1 tablespoon/80g granulated sugar

1 cup/250g *Quark* (page 264), drained if necessary (see page 8)

Grated peel of 1 organic lemon

½ teaspoon vanilla extract

1 tablespoon dark rum

2⅓ cups, scooped and leveled, plus 1 tablespoon/300g all-purpose flour

¼ teaspoon salt

¾ teaspoon ground cinnamon

½ teaspoon ground cloves

⅛ teaspoon ground cardamom

1½ teaspoons baking powder

½ cup/75g blanched whole almonds (see page 7), chopped

1 cup/150g raisins

TOPPING

7 tablespoons/100g unsalted butter

13 tablespoons/100g confectioners' sugar

3 tablespoons *Vanillezucker* (page 267)

1 Preheat the oven to 350°F/180°C. Line two baking sheets with parchment paper.

2 To make the dough: Place the butter and sugar in the bowl of a stand mixer fitted with the whisk attachment and cream together until fluffy. Add the *Quark,* grated lemon peel, vanilla extract, and rum; beat until well combined.

continued

3 In a separate bowl, whisk together the flour, salt, cinnamon, cloves, cardamom, and baking powder. Add to the *Quark* mixture and beat together until just combined. Briefly beat in the almonds and raisins.

4 Using your hands, pinch off golf ball–size pieces of dough and, without overhandling them, form them into 2-inch/5cm ovals or blocks. Place them on the prepared baking sheets, leaving 1 inch/2.5 cm between them. Place one baking sheet in the oven and bake for 30 minutes, or until the *Stollen* bites are a pale golden brown.

5 Meanwhile, make the topping: Melt the butter in a small saucepan. Place the confectioners' sugar and *Vanillezucker* in a small bowl and whisk to combine.

6 Remove the *Stollen* bites from the oven and slide in the second batch. Let the finished bites cool briefly, just until you can handle them. Dip each bite into the melted butter, and then toss in the confectioners' sugar mixture and place back on the baking sheet to set. Repeat with the second batch when they have baked.

7 When the *Stollen* bites are completely cool, store in airtight containers, separated by pieces of waxed or parchment paper, for at least 1 day. They are best if allowed to rest for 3 to 4 days before serving. Just before serving, dust the bites again with a fresh layer of sifted confectioners' sugar. The bites will keep in an airtight container for at least 10 days and up to 3 weeks.

BAUMKUCHEN
Chocolate-Glazed Tree Cake

MAKES 1 (9-INCH/23CM) CAKE

Every Christmas without fail, my dear family friends Muck and Jürgen leave a little paper bag under our Christmas tree. Inside the bag is a white paper doily and a hefty, chocolate-covered log of *Baumkuchen* from one of Berlin's finest *Konditoreien* (confectioners), Café Buchwald in Moabit. *Baumkuchen*, which means literally "tree cake," is made by painting layers of vanilla-flavored cake batter onto a rotating spit in an oven. (Historically, it was over an open fire.) When the cake is several inches thick, it is removed from the spit, cooled, and then glazed with jam and a thin layer of chocolate that crackles quietly when you take a bite. A slice off the top of the cake exposes the thin golden "rings" of the cake trunk. On Christmas Eve each year, we unpack our *Baumkuchen* with glee. In an attempt to make it last, we shave off tender pieces that we eat with our fingers until the last scrap is gone, which is always too soon. It may be the greatest edible gift I've ever had the pleasure of receiving.

Baumkuchen has quite an illustrious pedigree. While the pretzel is the official symbol of Germany's bakers guild, *Baumkuchen* is the traditional symbol of its *Konditoren*, or pastry makers. The practice of spit-baked cakes reaches far back to the late Middle Ages and was traditional all over Europe, but the tender, vanilla-flavored cake that is popular today was most likely developed sometime in the seventeenth century. There are a few different versions of *Baumkuchen*, depending on where they developed, but my favorite is the *Cottbusser Baumkuchen* that Café Buchwald specializes in.

Buchwald, a family-run establishment, has been making their excellent *Baumkuchen* for the past 160 years. At their old-world café in the Moabit neighborhood of Berlin, Buchwald sells *Baumkuchen* in myriad ways: sugar-glazed, chocolate-glazed, cut into rings, cut into chunks and dipped in chocolate, and cut into cake wedges and dipped in chocolate. (They also sell by mail order worldwide, just in case you were wondering. For more info, contact the bakery at baumkuchen-buchwald@web.de. And if you come to Berlin, visit the café at Bartningallee 29.)

While no home-baked *Baumkuchen* will ever come close to the tender glory that is Buchwald's, this recipe does produce a very nice cake with those trademark rings. A light and eggy batter is painted on the bottom of a springform pan and put under the broiler to cook quickly before the next layer is painted on. When the multilayered cake has fully cooled and any crisp spots have been trimmed off, hot apricot jam is poured over the top. Once that sets, melted chocolate coats the cake. The jam layer gives the cake moisture and the faintest note of fruitiness, but it is so thin that you don't really register its presence.

The protective coatings of jam and chocolate allow the cake to last for a few days at room temperature. If desired, you can serve plated wedges of it with whipped cream, or you can cut the torte into slightly larger than bite-size chunks and arrange them on your *bunter Teller*.

6 eggs

Pinch of salt

18 tablespoons/250g unsalted high-fat, European-style butter, at room temperature, plus more for the pan

1¼ cups/250g granulated sugar

1 teaspoon vanilla extract

continued

1 tablespoon dark rum

1½ cups, scooped and leveled/190g cake flour

⅓ cup plus 1 tablespoon/60g cornstarch

2 teaspoons baking powder

½ cup minus 1 tablespoon/125g apricot jam

3½ ounces/100g bittersweet chocolate
(50% to 70% cacao), coarsely chopped

½ teaspoon sunflower oil, or other neutral vegetable oil

1 Separate 3 of the eggs, putting the yolks and whites into separate bowls. Whip the egg whites until small bubbles form, and then add the salt and continue whipping until the egg whites hold stiff peaks.

2 Place the butter and sugar in the bowl of a stand mixer fitted with the flat beater attachment and beat until light and fluffy. Beat in the 3 remaining whole eggs, one at a time, and then the 3 egg yolks, one at a time. Scrape down the sides of the bowl. Beat in the vanilla extract and the rum.

3 In a separate bowl, sift together the flour, cornstarch, and baking powder. Beat this mixture into the egg mixture just until combined. Then fold in the beaten egg whites until no streaks remain.

4 Preheat the broiler. Butter a 9-inch/23cm springform pan or line the bottom of the pan with parchment paper and butter the sides of the pan.

5 Place a couple of heaping spoonsful of batter in the prepared pan and, using a pastry brush, spread the batter out evenly in the pan. Place the pan on a rack in the upper third of the oven and broil, watching constantly, until the layer is golden brown. This should take about 5 minutes but could be as little as 2½ or 3 minutes, depending on the strength of your broiler. If the top browns in less than 2½ minutes, the cake is too close to the broiler or the broiler heat is too high; lower the rack.

6 Remove the pan from the oven and immediately add a couple more spoonsful of batter, spreading them out evenly over the first layer. Return to the oven and broil until golden brown. Repeat with the remaining batter. (Toward the last layers, you will need to move your oven rack down a notch to keep the top cake layer from burning before it's done.) The cake batter should provide approximately 8 layers.

7 Remove the pan from the oven and let cool completely on a rack. Run a thin knife around the edges of the pan before removing the springform ring. Your cake may have some crunchy edges—trim these off gently with a serrated knife. Place a piece of parchment paper on the rack and set the cake on it.

8 Warm the apricot jam over medium heat until bubbling, stirring continuously. Press the hot jam through a fine-mesh sieve over the top of the cake, and then spread the jam in a thin, even layer all over the top and sides of the cake. Let the jam cool completely.

9 Melt the chopped chocolate in a microwave in short bursts or in the top of a double boiler set over simmering water, until smooth and runny. Stir in the oil until well combined. Pour the chocolate over the cake and use a spatula or bench scraper to coat the top and sides of the cake evenly. Let the chocolate cool completely.

10 Transfer the cooled cake from the rack to a serving platter, removing the parchment paper. Cut the cake into wedges and serve. The cake will keep, wrapped in plastic wrap, for 3 to 4 days at room temperature.

BASICS

Several of the required ingredients for German baking, like *Quark*, *Marzipanrohmasse*, *Pflaumenmus*, and mixed *Lebkuchen* spice are difficult to find outside of Germany and actually quite easy to make, so I've included recipes for them in this chapter. I've also included basic recipes for *Vanillezucker*, two different kinds of *Streusel*, and the ultimate accessory to any good German *Kaffeetafel* (afternoon coffee table), *Schlagsahne*: lightly sweetened whipped cream.

QUARK

Sour Fresh Cheese

MAKES 2 TO 2⅔ CUPS/500 TO 670G, DEPENDING ON HOW LONG YOU DRAIN IT

To make your own *Quark*, all you need is buttermilk, an oven, and some time. The buttermilk is warmed in the oven over a period of 8 to 12 hours, during which time the milk solids separate from the whey. You pour this mixture into a cheesecloth-lined sieve, and after several hours of draining, you'll have a big pile of sour, creamy *Quark*. Most of the recipes in this book call for either 1 or 2 cups of *Quark*, so one batch of this recipe will leave you with some leftovers, which can be refrigerated. I'm grateful to Meeta Khurana Wolff for sharing this method—from her husband's grandmother—on her blog, *What's for Lunch, Honey*.

I like spreading *Quark* on my morning slice of bread and topping it with jam, but you can also mix it with salt and herbs and dollop it next to boiled potatoes for a light meal. Using buttermilk will result in skim *Quark*, which is best for baking recipes. If you want a creamier *Quark* to eat as is, simply stir a little heavy cream into the *Quark* to loosen and enrich it. (Mixed with high-quality fruit preserves, this makes for a luxurious little snack.)

Don't throw away the whey that has drained off the *Quark*. It tastes just like buttermilk and is really high in protein. It's quite refreshing as a cooled drink. I like to salt it lightly and spice it with ground coriander, which makes it taste like a salty Indian *lassi*. You can also blend it into your morning smoothie.

8½ cups/2L buttermilk

1 Preheat the oven to 150°F/65°C. Pour the buttermilk into a baking dish and cover tightly with aluminum foil or a lid.

2 Place the baking dish in the oven and bake for 8 to 12 hours. When the buttermilk is ready to drain, the solids will have separated from the whey, either in soft clumps or in one lightly set uniform mass.

3 Place a fine-mesh sieve over a large pot and line the sieve with cheesecloth. Remove the pan from the oven and pour the contents of the pan into the sieve. Let sit for at least 2 hours and as long as 5 hours. Then gently pick up the corners of the cheesecloth and twist to squeeze out any residual moisture in the *Quark*.

4 The *Quark* can be refrigerated in an airtight container for several days or used immediately.

MARZIPANROHMASSE

Almond Paste

MAKES 1 POUND/455G

A lot of recipes in German baking depend on almond paste, which in Germany is known as *Marzipanrohmasse*. To make your own almond paste, which you can use immediately or store in the refrigerator, all you need is a good food processor. A warning: To get the paste as smooth as possible, with no hint of grittiness, you will need to process the mixture for at least 10 minutes, if not more, in total.

1½ cups/220g raw almonds

1 cup plus 2 tablespoons/225g granulated sugar

2 teaspoons almond extract

1 teaspoon rum

2 to 4 teaspoons water

1 First, blanch the almonds by placing them in a bowl and covering them with boiling water. Let the almonds sit for 5 to 10 minutes. Their skins will have loosened considerably, so that you can simply push the nut meats out of the skins. Place the skinned nuts on a clean dry dishcloth and rub to dry.

2 Place the sugar in the bowl of a food processor and process until powdery. Add the dried, peeled almonds and process until a paste starts to form. Add the almond extract and rum and continue to process. Stop the motor and stir when necessary.

3 Continue to process, adding a teaspoon of water at a time, until you have a very smooth paste. You may need anywhere from 2 to 4 teaspoons of water, depending on how moist your almonds were. When the paste is completely smooth and no longer grainy or granular, scrape it out of the processor and knead into a ball. Place in a plastic bag and refrigerate until ready to use. The almond paste will keep for several weeks in the refrigerator, wrapped tightly.

PFLAUMENMUS

Spiced Plum Butter

MAKES ABOUT 4 (8-OUNCE/225G) JARS

Pflaumenmus, also known as *lekvár* in eastern Europe and *Powidl* in Austria, is a thick, dark, sticky plum butter subtly spiced with cinnamon and cloves. It is used as a filling for doughnuts and gingerbread pockets (*Lebkuchen-Powidltatschkerln*, page 224); it's also layered in cream tortes (*Friesentorte*, page 122) and used as a topping for bread or toast. I also like stirring it into yogurt.

Unlike most recipes for preserves, this one has you cook the sugared, spiced plums in a heavy cast-iron pot in the oven until they've completely broken down and reduced to an inky blue mass. After a quick pass with an immersion blender, you have yourself a smooth, rich fruit butter.

I don't do water-bath processing of these preserves because with the amount of sugar in them, there's really no reason to cook them further. No amount of bacteria could survive in them. I simply fill sterilized jam jars with the boiling-hot plum butter and turn them upside down to cool. This process creates a vacuum seal of the lids. They will keep for at least 1 year, though I doubt you'll have them that long.

The recipe is easily doubled.

4½ pounds/2kg Italian prune plums

2 cups/400g granulated sugar

1 cinnamon stick

2 whole cloves

1 Pit and quarter the plums and put them in a 4-quart cast-iron pot. Add the sugar, cinnamon stick, and cloves. Stir well and let sit overnight or for at least 8 hours.

2 The next day, heat the oven to 350°F/180°C. Put the pot, uncovered, in the oven and cook for 2 hours, stirring the mixture occasionally. Wash four or five 8-ounce/225g glass jam jars and lids thoroughly in very hot, soapy water and let them dry completely.

3 When the plums have broken down and the liquid in the pot has reduced to a thick consistency, remove the pot from the oven and fish out the cinnamon stick (if you can find the cloves, fish them out, too).

4 Using an immersion blender, puree the *Pflaumenmus* until it's smooth, and then fill the clean, dry jars with the hot puree. Immediately screw on the tops and turn the jars upside down. (The jars will be boiling hot, so take care.)

5 Let the jars cool completely before turning them right-side up again and labeling them. The jam will keep for at least 1 year.

LEBKUCHENGEWÜRZ

Lebkuchen Spice Mix

MAKES ABOUT ½ CUP/ABOUT 50G SPICE MIX

Every autumn, German grocery stores start stocking specialty items just for the Christmas baking season. Little cardboard display cases are set out that are fully stocked with bars of baking chocolate, packets of potash and baker's ammonia, candied citron and orange peel, vials of flavor extracts, and spices like anise and cardamom, as well as spice mixtures for *Stollen* and *Lebkuchen*. When January rolls around, the picked-over stands are packed up and put away again. It's one of those cultural rituals I am very fond of.

Lebkuchen spice—a mixture of all the "usual suspects" in wintertime baking—is called for in several of the recipes in the Christmas chapter. I like to make a batch of this in early fall so that I'm ready for the baking season. The mixture below is a great all-purpose one. But you can also tinker with the amounts if you want to highlight one flavor or another.

5 tablespoons/30g ground cinnamon

1½ tablespoons ground cloves

1 teaspoon ground allspice

1 teaspoon ground cardamom

1 teaspoon ground ginger

1 teaspoon ground mace

¾ teaspoon ground aniseed

1 Combine all the ingredients in a bowl and mix well to combine. Store in a glass jar with a tight-fitting lid. Kept in a dark, cool place, the mix will stay fresh for 1 year.

STREUSEL

Basic Streusel

MAKES ENOUGH FOR 1 (9 BY 13-INCH/23 BY 33CM) PAN

A basic batch of streusel can be used to gussy up any fruit-topped cake, for example the *Rhabarberkuchen* (page 70) or the *Apfelkuchen* (page 86). *Streusel* freezes well, so if you have leftovers or would like to make a batch for future use, simply chill the *Streusel* for an hour after making, and then transfer to a plastic freezer bag. To use frozen *Streusel*, remove from the freezer an hour before baking, and then break apart and distribute over the cake.

1 cup, scooped and leveled, plus 1 tablespoon/140g all-purpose flour

½ cup/100g granulated sugar

¼ teaspoon salt

7 tablespoons/100g unsalted high-fat, European-style butter, softened

1 In a large bowl, mix together the flour, sugar, and salt. Cut the butter into cubes and add to the flour mixture. Using your fingertips, rub the butter into the flour mixture until lima bean- and pea-size pieces develop. The *Streusel* should not be entirely uniform; a good mixture of smaller and larger pieces is desirable. Cover and refrigerate the *Streusel* until ready to use. *Streusel* can also be frozen in an airtight container or resealable bag for up to 3 months.

MANDELSTREUSEL

Almond Streusel

MAKES ENOUGH FOR 1 (9 BY 13-INCH/23 BY 33CM) PAN

Adding ground almonds to basic *Streusel* gives it a richer flavor and more body. Any fruit-topped cake benefits from *Streusel*, but you could also use this *Streusel* in place of the plain one on *Streuselkuchen* (page 84) for a twist on an old classic (a layer of jam between the cake and the *Streusel* would be nice, too). Adding a pinch of cinnamon to almond *Streusel* is also a delicious alternative.

¾ cup plus 1 tablespoon/100g all-purpose flour

½ cup/50g ground almonds

½ cup/100g granulated sugar

¼ teaspoon salt

7 tablespoons/100g unsalted high-fat, European-style butter, softened

1 In a large bowl, mix together the flour, almonds, sugar, and salt. Cut the butter into cubes and add to the flour mixture. Using your fingertips, rub the butter into the flour mixture until lima bean- and pea-size pieces develop. The *Streusel* should not be entirely uniform; a good mixture of smaller and larger pieces is desirable. Cover and refrigerate the *Streusel* until ready to use. Streusel can also be frozen in an airtight container or resealable bag for up to 3 months.

VANILLEZUCKER

Vanilla Sugar

MAKES 2 CUPS/400G

Vanilla extract is unheard of in most of Europe; *Vanillezucker*, vanilla sugar, rules instead. But most commercial vanilla sugars are made with artificial vanillin flavor instead of the real thing. I've adapted almost all the recipes in this book to use pure vanilla extract instead of vanilla sugar, but there are a few times when only vanilla sugar will do (in the apple and plum *Strudels* on pages 138 and 141, for example).

While you can make a very nice vanilla sugar by simply plunging a vanilla bean into a jar of sugar and leaving it there (for a really, really long time), I actually like to make a slightly fancier version by processing vanilla and sugar together until the bean is all broken down and the sugar is speckled with countless tiny beans and specks of pod. The sugar is more intensely flavored than regular vanilla sugar. Packaged in a pretty glass jar, it also makes for a great gift.

2 cups/400g granulated sugar
1 vanilla bean

1 Cut the vanilla bean in quarters and place in the bowl of a small food processor. Add the sugar. Process until the vanilla bean is finely ground and well distributed. The sugar will be powdery.

2 Transfer the sugar to an airtight container. It will keep indefinitely.

SCHLAGSAHNE

Lightly Sweetened Whipped Cream

MAKES 4 CUPS/225G (ENOUGH TO SERVE 6 TO 8 WITH CAKE)

Lightly sweetened whipped cream is a must on every German *Kaffeetafel*, particularly when serving cakes made with fruit. This ratio of sugar to cream makes the best, not-too-sweet whipped cream. If you are serving only 3 to 4 people, you can halve the amounts here.

2 cups/480ml whipping cream
4 teaspoons *Vanillezucker* (see left), or 4 teaspoons granulated sugar plus 1½ teaspoons vanilla extract

1 Place the cream and *Vanillezucker* in a bowl. Beat with an electric mixer until the cream is stiff. Use immediately or refrigerate for up to 1 hour.

PRONUNCIATION GUIDE

Aachener Poschweck:
AHKH-enn-err POSH-vek

Amerikaner: ah-mare-ee-KAHN-err

Ammoniakaner:
ah-moan-ee-ah-KAHN-err

Anisbrot: a-NEES-broat

Apfelkuchen: AHP-fell-koo-khenn

Apfel-Marzipan-Kuchen:
AHP-fell-mar-zee-PAHN-koo-khenn

Apfelstrudel: AHP-fell-SHTREW-dell

Aprikotieren: ah-pree-co-TEE-ren

Basler Brunsli:
BAHS-lerr BROONS-lee

Basler Leckerli: BAHS-lerr LECK-ur-lee

Baumkuchen: BOWM-koo-khenn

Bethmännchen: BATE-men-shen

Biberle: BEEB-err-luh

Bienenstich: BEE-nenn-shtish

Blitzkuchen: BLITS-koo-khenn

Bremer Kürbisbrot:
BRAY-merr KERB-iss-broat

Brezeln: BRAY-tselln

Brötchen: BROAT-shen

Brot: BROAT

Brote: BROAT-uh

Bunter Teller: BOON-terr TELL-err

Butterkekse: BUHT-err KAYKS-uh

Butterkuchen: BUHT-err koo-khenn

Christbrot: KRIST-broat

Dunkler Kirschkuchen:
DOONK-lerr KEERSH-koo-khenn

Eierschecke: EYE-err-SHEH-kuh

Eisenbahnschnitten:
EYE-zen-BAHN-shnitt-enn

Elisenlebkuchen:
ell-EE-zen-LAPE-koo-khenn

Erdbeer-Sahne Biskuitrolle:
AIRD-bear ZAH-nuh bis-KWEET-roll-uh

Fein passiert: fine pah-SEERT

Fraktur: frahk-TOUR

Franzbrötchen: FRANTS-broat-shen

Friesenkekse: FREE-zen-kayks-uh

Friesentorte: FREE-zen-toart-uh

Früchtebrot: FROOSH-tuh-broat

Gasthäuser: GAHST-hoy-zerr

Gedeckter Apfelkuchen:
guh-DECK-terr AHP-fell-koo-khenn

Gefüllte Orangentaler:
guh-FOOL-tuh oh-RANZH-enn-tah-lerr

Grüner Kuchen: GROON-err KOO-khen

Gugelhupf: GOOGLE-hoopf

Hallignüsse: HALL-ig-NOOSE-uh

Hannchen-Jensen-Torte:
HAHNN-shen-YENN-zen-TOART-uh

Haselnuss-Himbeer Makronen:
HAH-zell-noose-HIM-bear MAH-
kron-enn

Heidesand: HI-deh-zahnd

Heidjertorte: HI-djair-toart-uh

Heisswecken: HICE-veck-enn

Herzhafter Käsekuchen:
HAIRTS-hahff-turr KAYZA-koo-khenn

Honiglebkuchen:
HONE-ig-LAYB-koo-khenn

Imbissbuden: IMM-biss-bood-enn

Käsekuchen: KAYZA-koo-khenn

Käsekuchen ohne Boden:
KAYZA-koo-khenn OH-na BOH-denn

Käse-Kümmel Brötchen:
KAYZA-koomell broat-shen

Kaffeezeit: KAH-fay-tsight

Kartoffel-Käse Dinnede:
kar-TOFF-ell-kayza DINN-uh-duh

Kartoffelstrudel:
kar-TOFF-ell-SHTREW-dell

Keks: KAYKS

Kekse: KAYKS-uh

Kirsch: KEERSCH

Kirschkuchen: KEERSCH-koo-khenn

Kirschstreuselkuchen:
KEERSCH-SHTROY-zell-koo-khenn

Knerken: KNAIR-kenn

Kranzkuchen: KRAHNZ-koo-khenn

Krautstrudel: KROWT-shtrew-dell

Kuchen: KOO-khenn

Lebkuchen: LAPE-koo-khenn

Lebkuchengewürz:
LAPE-koo-khenn-gah-verts

Lebkuchen-Powidltatschkerln:
LAPE-koo-khenn-POH-veedel-
tatch-kairln

Linzertorte: LINZ-err-toart-uh

Löffelbiskuit: LUH-fell-biss-kweet

Mandelstreusel: MAHN-dell-shtroy-zell

Makronenschnitten:
mah-KRONEN-shnitt-enn

Mandelhörnchen:
MAHN-dell-horn-shenn

Marillenfleck: marr-ILL-EN-fleck

Marmorierter Mohnkuchen:
marr-more-EER-terr MOAN-koo-khenn

Marmorkuchen:
MARR-MORE-koo-khenn

Marzipanrohmasse:
mar-tsee-PAHN-row-mahss-uh

Mohnhörnchen: MOAN-horn-shenn

Mohnstreuselkuchen:
MOAN-shtroyzel-koo-khenn

Mohntorte: MOAN-toart-uh

Mohnzopf: MOAN-tsohpf

Nussecken: NUHSS-eck-enn

Nusskuchen: NUHSS-koo-khenn

Nussstangen: NUHSS-shtang-enn

Nusstorte von Hammerstein:
NUHSS-toart-uh fohn HAH-murr-shtein

Nusszopf: NUHSS-tsohpf

Peterlingskuchen:
PAY-turr-lings-koo-khenn

Pfeffernüsse: FEFF-urr-noose-uh

Pflaumenmus: FLAU-men-moose

Pflaumenstreuselkuchen:
FLAU-men-stroy-zel-koo-khenn

Pflaumenstrudel:
FLAU-men-shtrew-dell

Platz: PLAHTS

Plätzchen: PLETZ-shen

Prasselkuchen mit Blätterteig:
PRAH-sell-koo-khen mitt BLEH-
terr-teyg

Preiselbeeren: PRY-zell-bairn

Pottasche: POTT-ahsh-uh

Quark: KVARK

Quarkbrötchen: KVARK-broat-shen

Quarkkuchen mit Mandarinen:
KVARK-koo-khenn mitt mahn-dar-
EEN-enn

Quark-Osterhasen:
KVARK-OHST-ERR-ha-zen

Quarkstollen:
KVARK-shtoh-lenn

Rhabarberkuchen:
rha-BARB-ah-kooh-khenn

Roggenbrötchen: RUG-EN-broat-shen

Rosenkuchen: ROSE-EN-koo-khenn

Rosinenbrötchen:
rose-EEN-en-broat-shen

Rosinenschnecken:
rose-EEN-en-shnek-en

Rosinenzopf: rose-EEN-en-tsopf

Rüblitorte: ROOB-lee-toart-uh

Russisch Brot: ROOSE-ish broat

Russischer Zupfkuchen:
ROOSE-ish-err TSUPF-koo-khenn

Sachertorte: ZAHKH-err-toart-uh

Sahnequark: ZAH-nuh-kvark

Salzekuchen: ZAHLTS-uh-kooh-khenn

Schinkenspeck: SHINK-enn-shpeck

Schlagsahne: SHLAHG-zah-neh

Schlesische Mohnrolle:
SHLAY-zish-uh MOAN-rull-uh

Schokoladen-Gugelhupf:
shoh-koh-LAH-denn-google-hoopf

Schultüte: SHOOL-toot-uh

Schwäbischer Prasselkuchen:
SHVAY-bish-err PRAH-sel-koo-khenn

Schwarzwälder Kartoffelbrötchen:
SHVARTS-vell-durr kar-TOFF-ell-
broat-shen

Schwarzwälder Kirschtorte:
SHVARTS-vell-durr KEERSH-toart-uh

Schwarz-Weiss Gebäck:
shvarts-VICE guh-BECK

Schweizer Zopf: shveyts-err TSOPF

Seelen: ZAY-lenn

Spandau: SHPAHN-dow

Speck: shpeck

Speck-Walnuss Gugelhupf:
shpeck-VAHL-noose GOOGLE-hoopf

Spekulatius: shpeck-ooh-LAT-SEE-oos

Springerle: SHPRING-err-luh

Stollen: SHTOH-lenn

Stollenkonfekt: SHTOH-lenn-kon-FEKT

Streusel: SHTROY-zel

Streuselkuchen:
SHTROY-zel-koo-khenn

Streuselschnecken:
SHTROY-zel-shneh-kenn

Süddeutsche Lauchtorte:
ZOO-doytsh-uh LAUKH-toart-uh

Teilchen: TILE-shen

Topfenstrudel:
TOP-fenn-SHTREW-dell

Träubelestorte: TROY-bless-TOART-uh

Versunkener Apfelkuchen:
fair-ZOONK-en-err AHP-fell-koo-khenn

Vanillekipferl: va-NILL-uh-kipf-url

Vanillezucker: va-NILL-uh-tsoo-kerr

Walnuss-Zwieback:
VAHL-noose-TSVEE-back

Weihnachtsplätzchen:
VINE-akhts-plets-shen

Zedernbrot: TSAY-dern-broat

Zimtbrezeln: TSIMT-bray-zelln

Zimtsterne: TSIMT-shtair-nuh

Zitronenbiskuitrolle:
TSEE-trohn-en-biss-kweet-roll-uh

Zuckerkuchen: TSOOK-err-koo-khenn

Zwiebelkuchen: TSWEE-bell-koo-khenn

SOURCES

auifinefoods.com
For candied orange and citron peel in bulk.

batesnutfarm.com
For nuts and candied citrus peel.

bavariasausage.com
For pitted sour cherries, cured meats, *Pflaumenmus*, and lingonberry preserves.

cookiemold.com
For hand-carved *Springerle* and *Spekulatius* molds.

edelweissimports.com
For potash, baker's ammonia, candied citrus peel, pearl sugar, baking wafers, *Quark*, almond paste, lingonberry preserves, and *Pflaumenmus*.

fantes.com
For *Gugelhupf* pans, *Springerle* molds, baker's ammonia, pearl sugar, almond paste, vanilla and almond extracts, poppy-seed grinders, and candied citron peel.

frontiercoop.com
For vanilla and almond extracts, poppy seeds, and vanilla beans.

germandeli.com
For baking wafers, cured meats, *Pflaumenmus*, and pitted sour cherries (labeled *Schattenmorellen*).

germangrocery.com
For almond paste, baking wafers, potash, baker's ammonia, *Pflaumenmus*, redcurrant preserves, lingonberry preserves, double-smoked slab bacon, canned sour cherries, and canned gooseberries.

germanshop24.com
For candied citron and orange peel, baking wafers, *Pflaumenmus*, redcurrant jelly, and preserves.

hungariandeli.com
For *Pflaumenmus*, smooth apricot jam, whole and ground poppy seeds, baker's ammonia, and poppy-seed grinders.

igourmet.com
For *Speck* and *Quark*.

IKEA stores
For lingonberry preserves, baking wafers, candied citrus peel, potassium carbonate (potash), and baker's ammonia.

kalustyans.com
For nuts and poppy seeds in bulk, vanilla beans, and almond extract.

kingarthurflour.com
For pearl sugar, baker's ammonia, almond extract, vanilla beans, instant yeast, rye flour, buckwheat flour, and various nut flours.

markethallfoods.com
For candied citrus peel, almond paste, vanilla beans, and almond extract.

nuts.com
For nuts and dried fruits in bulk, various nut flours, almond paste, prune *lekvár* (plum butter), preserved sour cherries, potassium carbonate (sold as potassium bicarbonate), candied orange peel, and glazed diced citron.

oldtownspices.com
For baker's ammonia, instant yeast, lingonberries, assorted nuts, and dried fruits.

spoonandwhisk.com
For *Gugelhupf* pans, *Springerle* molds, and cookie cutters.

springerlejoy.com
For baker's ammonia, almond extract, cookie cutters, and carved *Springerle* molds.

thespicehouse.com
For whole and ground poppy seeds and vanilla beans.

thetasteofgermany.com
For *Lebkuchen* spice mix, potash, baker's ammonia, and baking wafers.

INDEX

Published in the United States by Ten Speed Press, an imprint of the Crown Publishing Group,
a division of Penguin Random House LLC, New York.
www.crownpublishing.com
www.tenspeed.com

Ten Speed Press and the Ten Speed Press colophon are registered trademarks
of Penguin Random House LLC.

Library of Congress Cataloging-in-Publication Data
Names: Weiss, Luisa, author. | Pick, Aubrie, photographer.
Title: Classic German baking : the very best recipes for traditional
    favorites, from pfeffernusse to streuselkuchen / Luisa Weiss ; photographs
    by Aubrie Pick.
Description: First edition. | New York : Ten Speed Press, an imprint of the
    Crown Publishing Group, a division of Penguin Random House LLC, [2016] | Includes
    bibliographical references and index.
Identifiers: LCCN 2016015734 (print) | LCCN 2016020968 (ebook) | ISBN
    9781607748250 (hardcover : alk. paper) | ISBN 9781607748267 (Ebook) | ISBN
    9781607748267 (E-book)
Subjects: LCSH: Cooking, German. | Baking. | LCGFT: Cookbooks.
Classification: LCC TX721 .W435 2016 (print) | LCC TX721 (ebook) | DDC
    641.5943—dc23
LC record available at https://lccn.loc.gov/2016015734

Hardcover ISBN: 978-1-60774-825-0
eBook ISBN: 978-1-60774-826-7

Printed in China
Design by Ashley Lima
Food styling by Kim Laidlaw
Prop Styling by Ethel Brennan
Cover illustration by Anna Ropalo

10 9 8 7 6 5 4 3 2 1

First Edition